Shakespeare
and the Common
Understanding

NORMAN RABKIN

Shakespeare and the Common Understanding

THE UNIVERSITY OF CHICAGO PRESS
CHICAGO AND LONDON

The University of Chicago Press, Chicago 60637
The University of Chicago Press, Ltd., London

91 90 89 88 87 86 85 84   1 2 3 4 5

Library of Congress Cataloging in Publication Data
Rabkin, Norman.
  Shakespeare and the common understanding.

  Reprint. Originally published: New York: Free Press,
1967.
  Includes bibliographies and index.
  1. Shakespeare, William, 1564–1616—Criticism and
interpretation.   I. Title.
PR2965.R25   1984   822.3'3   83-18153
ISBN 0-226-70180-8 (pbk.)

To Marty
and
Sarah, Bill, and Hannah

❧ ❧

Acknowledgments

Like all critics of Shakespeare, I owe a larger debt than I could hope or manage to acknowledge to the large and vigorous community which has brought us so far in our understanding of the poet's work. I have made every effort possible to recall and cite critical studies that have influenced my thinking or posed the problems with which I deal. I cannot expect, however, to have recalled every study that has been absorbed into my own thinking, or even to have seen every important study that might be relevant to my argument, and I have tried to make my references to the rapidly growing body of scholarship representative and useful rather than exhaustive.

Some of the material in the present book has been published previously, and I should like to express my gratitude for permission to include revised versions of a number of essays to the editors of *JEGP*, *Shakespeare Studies*, and *Shakespeare Quarterly*, and to Professors Waldo McNeir and Thelma Greenfield and the University of Oregon Press. The Appendix has grown out of a paper that I read to The English Institute in 1965. All citations of Shakespeare's text are from *The Complete Works of Shakespeare*, edited by Hardin Craig, copyright 1951 by Scott, Foresman and Company. I am indebted to Simon and Schuster, Inc., for permission to reprint material from *Science and the Common Understanding*, copyright 1953, 1954 by J. Robert Oppenheimer, and to Princeton University Press and B. T. Batsford, Ltd., the American and the English publisher, respectively, to reprint material from Harley Granville-Barker, *Prefaces to Shakespeare*, Vols. I and II, copyright 1946, 1947 by Princeton University Press.

The actual writing of the book was greatly facilitated by a Humanities Research Professorship granted me by the University of California in 1965.

The hardest debt to acknowledge adequately is that I owe to those who have encouraged, supported, stimulated, and aided me in the course of writing this book. My students at Berkeley, both graduate and undergraduate, have contributed so much to my thinking about Shakespeare as virtually to deserve naming as a collective collaborator. Stephanie Antalocy and Joanna Wilcove were heroic and indispensable assistants in the research the project required. John S. Anson, Joseph E. Kramer, and Sheldon Sacks have read portions of the manuscript and criticized them valuably. Max Bluestone and Robert M. Durling have done a similar task; I owe both of them a larger and less measurable debt for more than a decade of challenging, wearying, delightful, and invaluable conversation, both about literature in general and in recent years about the particular subject of this book. Jonas A. Barish has read the entire manuscript and improved it, and has helped me in countless ways with unflagging generosity. C. L. Barber has given me both personal support, which has been more valuable to me than he knows, and a model, which has reminded me in my darkest moments of the value of a life devoted to Shakespeare scholarship. Five men from whom I have learned much of what I know about reading and about reading Renaissance literature have earned a debt of gratitude that I feel renewing itself daily: Alfred Baruth, G. B. Evans, Helmut Rehder, Douglas Bush, and Alfred Harbage. Most of all I owe a debt to my wife, without whom this book would simply not exist. She has read every word, discussed every idea, cleared away every infelicity that my obstinacy did not succeed in retaining, and created for me the kind of world in which writing a book about Shakespeare could be a joy. None of those I have named should be held responsible for such deficiencies as remain in my work.

Norman Rabkin

Berkeley, California

Contents

*Shakespeare
and the Common
Understanding*

CHAPTER ONE

Shakespeare and
the Common Understanding

THE MOST OFTEN PERFORMED, STUDIED, QUOTED, AND PARODIED OF Shakespeare's plays, *Hamlet* is for most of us the key to his work. We cannot remain satisfied for long with any reading of it or its author that writes *Hamlet* off as a failure. Exasperated though we become when we attempt to make neat formulations about it, we need recall only for a moment the power it has had over us to know that the inadequacies are in our formulations rather than in the play. And yet we have our doubts. The bulk and intensity of the controversy, the range of critical disagreement, the amount of trouble *Hamlet* has stirred up nag us. Can a great play which strikes so many of us as the archetypical work of its author create so much confusion without damning him as a maker of confusions and the act of responding to it as an irresponsibly subjective gratification?

I want to raise the problem of *Hamlet* once again. I am going to argue that what makes it a problem is precisely what makes it Shakespearean. I am going to argue furthermore that the particular nature of the utterly characteristic kind of problem that Shakespeare establishes in *Hamlet* is responsible for what makes successive generations who agree on little else continue to find him more relevant to their own problems than they do many of their contemporaries. And I hope to show that our own generation has begun to think, at its best, in terms which at last explicitly provide a philosophical approximation of that most intuitively conceived and conveyed phenomenon, the Shakespearean vision. To erect such an argument I shall have to demonstrate that what is crucially problematic in *Hamlet* is not accidental but rather lies at the center of its intention. The confusions in which the play involves us, that is to say, are under Shakespeare's control. They do not detract from our sense of *Hamlet's* vivid reality; in fact, they do much to create it.

Let us set aside extrinsic, trivial, or specious problems. Whether Hamlet said "sullied" or "solid" is a question that Shakespeare does not ask us to contemplate, and it must be answered by the textual critic. Similarly such questions as "Was Hamlet fat?" or "How old is Hamlet?" are accidents of the transmission of text. The audience who saw the play performed by its author's company could not possibly have asked, as modern critics must on occasion, whether Hamlet witnesses Ophelia's commissioning as a decoy; and other such problems—what Hamlet and Claudius are doing during the dumb show, for example—are accidents of the transmission of theatrical tradition. Still other questions that merit a certain kind of exploration in the scholar's study of the play may be agreed to arise from necessities Shakespeare encounters in the size of his cast and the exposition of his plot. I should not want to argue that there is praiseworthy significance in the discrepancies of awareness in Horatio, who seems now to know everything current in Denmark, now to know nothing because he has just arrived there; nor would I suggest that Shakespeare wants us to be concerned that the mousetrap is not what Hamlet had led us to believe. It is critical fideism—bardolatry —to assume that every "ambiguity" we can find is a mark of the poet's genius. There is one other kind of problem which can in a certain sense be explained away: We cannot answer some questions —"How much did Gertrude know about Claudius' crime?" "What was her relationship with Claudius while her husband still lived?"

—because Hamlet himself cannot answer them, and our doubts intensify our sympathies with a hero who must act on insufficient knowledge.

But here we arrive at the border of the area in which we are condemned to realize that virtually *everything* in the play is problematic. I shall be highly selective in the few problems I cite, and because they are the problems that have dominated our experience with the play, I shall treat them briefly. Many of them are excruciating for Hamlet, but they are, in another way, just as disturbing to us. They are built into the universe of the play; this is why that view of *Hamlet* is too simplistic which sees it only in terms of the hero's problems, and sees those problems resolved when he makes peace with his situation.

The problems begin with the ghost. Perhaps no one doubts by the end of the play that the ghost is the spirit of Hamlet's father; but when he first appears, we do not know who he is or why he has come. Though we learn quickly that it is justice he demands, we never fully shake the very different sense of him we acquire in the first scene: a harbinger of evil to come, a spirit that starts like a guilty thing upon a fearful summons, a member of that dread community of spirits who dare not stir abroad on wholesome nights in the Christmas season, by his own later words a denizen of that purgatory which for Shakespeare's Protestant audience has its disquieting existence only in alien and pernicious Catholic theology. And yet this horrifying spook is Hamlet's great father as he claims to be, worthy of his son's sacrifice; worse, he is the moral impetus of Hamlet's action throughout the play. Whether or not, in the immediacy of our response to stage action, we reflect on this ambiguity—and certainly Hamlet asks us to, telling us that, "prompted to my revenge by heaven and hell," he must couple hell to heaven and earth in appealing to the source of his mission—we are always aware that Hamlet is impelled to the restoration of Danish political and judicial order by a spirit we associate with night and fear, disease and violence and death.

This paradox, which has made it possible for at least one sensitive if willful critic to see Hamlet wrongly as the minister of death, the diseased corrupter of a polity which although it has its imperfections at least lacks his morbidity, has received the attention it deserves in recent years.[1] Most critics are coming to agree, *mirabile dictu*, about the ambiguity of Hamlet's motivation. We cannot afford to ignore its centrality. What does the duality we sense in the ghost tell us but that the mission he assigns to Hamlet has a dual moral status? Revenge for Hamlet as for his audience is morally demanded by the situation which Claudius has created and by an ethic accepted in the popular culture represented by a generation of revenge plays; yet it is morally condemned by the Christianity of both *Hamlet* and its audience. That is, the ambiguity of the ghost leads us early and repeatedly in our experience of the play to the question of ultimate moral sanctions: what is the good act, the good man?

What is Hamlet's own problem? Not simply to determine the reliability of ghosts, or even the ethical status of revenge, but rather to question his own nature, and therefore ours. What hurts Hamlet, as in a hundred ways he tells us and as he demonstrates even more poignantly, is that the mission with which he is afflicted necessitates a radical transformation of his character. And in the poles that mark the distance he must travel Shakespeare sets up the alternatives which pose for us the play's most disturbing problem.

It is no news that in *Hamlet* Shakespeare puts the case for reasonableness in a way that has become the classic expression of that virtue. Hamlet himself has provided a model of the contemplative man, and his admiration of Horatio defines that ideal explicitly:

> As one, in suffering all, that suffers nothing,
> A man that fortune's buffets and rewards
> Hast ta'en with equal thanks: and blest are those
> Whose blood and judgment are so well commeddled,
> That they are not a pipe for fortune's finger
> To sound what stop she please. Give me that man
> That is not passion's slave, and I will wear him
> In my heart's core, ay, in my heart of heart,
> As I do thee.
>
> (III. ii. 71–79)

That reasonableness is a supreme virtue in the play is clear, especially as we watch Claudius and Gertrude and Laertes caught up in their various passions and as we contemplate the wretched Ophelia bereft of her reason.

> Sure, he that made us with such large discourse,
> Looking before and after, gave us not
> That capability and god-like reason
> To fust in us unused.
>
> (IV. iv. 36–39)

"What a piece of work is a man! how noble in reason!" angelic, even godlike in his apprehension. And it is not new either to observe how Hamlet disappoints us by becoming, in the course of time, less like his Horatian ideal. All the cruelties and impulsive aggressions he commits in the latter half of the play strike us as painful indications of a degeneration from the announced ideal. In so doing they reinforce our admiration of that ideal.

Yet we must admit uncomfortably that the play sets us against the ideal of reasonableness which it embodies. We are likely to have our reservations about it when we see it exemplified in Polonius, the attractiveness of whose prudence is undercut both by his concomitant spiritual inadequacies and by the emptiness of the language in which he and his son project their vision. Claudius' prudential counseling against excessive passion (I.ii), though it makes excellent sense, strikes us as coldly inhumane even before we learn that it is hypocritical; paradoxically, it is the villain of the play who laments the loss of reason both in Hamlet and in Ophelia. Now it could be argued that what Shakespeare mocks in Claudius and Polonius is reason misused. But in fact the rejection of reason is much deeper, for we learn with Hamlet that both the ideals and the methods of reason are irrelevant to his existential concerns. Hamlet is right to surrender his own reasonableness. He comes to recognize that in the providentially ordered, even fatalistically determined, universe in which he lives all plans must fail; the play's enginers are consistently hoist with their own petards; only destructive and self-destructive impulsiveness can make him capable of performing his divinely sanctioned mission. Conscience, thinking too precisely on the event—the pale cast of thought—makes cowards of us all. Though in Horatio Hamlet

praised only that man in whom blood and judgment are balanced,
"Diseases desperate grown/ By desperate appliance are relieved,/
Or not at all" (IV. iii. 9–11). The redeemer of political order in
Denmark must have thoughts that are bloody, or they will be
worthless.

> And praised be rashness for it, let us know,
> Our indiscretion sometimes serves us well,
> When our deep plots do pall: and that should teach us
> There's a divinity that shapes our ends,
> Rough-hew them how we will.
>
> (V. ii. 7–11)

> I must be cruel, only to be kind.
>
> (III. iv. 178)

Only the surrender to impulse can keep Hamlet from interposing
his ego between himself and his destiny.

This is to say that the play presents an ideal, that of reason,
in such a way that we must recognize its absolute claim on our
moral allegiance, and then entirely subverts that ideal by demonstrating that its polar opposite is the only possible basis for the
action its protagonist is morally committed to perform. From the
point of view of reason seen in ideal terms, the passion to which
Hamlet succumbs is only another variety of the bestial willfulness,
the mindless impulsiveness, which we have loathed in Claudius
and regretted in Gertrude and Laertes. From the point of view of
passion as the plot forces us, with Hamlet, to see it, reason leads
either to hypocrisy or to a futile kind of civilized virtue out of
touch with existential reality and with the depths of feeling which
—as much as his intellectuality—make Hamlet so much more engaging than anyone else in the play. With a characteristic sense of
the full implications of a dominant theatrical convention, Shakespeare has built his revenge play on the dialectic between conflicting ethical systems, in which the spirit who initiates all must
lead the protagonist to reject the civilized values of his earlier
days in favor of a new code which he accepts on religious grounds
(everyone has noticed the Christian cast of Hamlet's thought and
feeling in the last scenes). Poised between irreconcilable ideals,

Hamlet finds himself in a predicament which we inevitably call tragic; but that is not my point now, for I am concerned with an aspect of the play that is more Shakespearean than generic. Our experience of *Hamlet* puts us in a situation in which no matter how much we are tempted we are not permitted—unless we reduce the play, choosing one of its values and tilting with those who choose the other—to recognize a single good. Each value, or set of values, is a total way of seeing which excludes the other. There can be no compromise; we are not allowed to believe optimistically, as Hamlet does in contemplating Horatio's mixture of blood and judgment, that the opposed goods can coexist in one value system or one universe. The play says to us: Choose one or the other, and in doing so you will see how it rules out the other. And yet each makes equally compelling claims on us; at any given moment we feel ourselves drawn irresistibly to one or the other total view of things.

Because the play presents a universe in which we must decide at every moment which way to choose, yet which tells us simultaneously that no choice is possible, we are frequently surprised to discover that what seem like thoroughly plausible and convincing statements of truth and value are undercut by the play taken as a whole. I shall point at only a few instances. The most obvious is Polonius' foursquare advice to Laertes, advocating a policy of moderation which in Hamlet's case is precisely the wrong policy and which in its comfortable assumption that one need only be true to oneself begs the play's fundamental question: What is that self? Polonius' lecture, like Claudius' similarly prudential counsel to Hamlet, is of course undercut by the formulaic quality of its rhetoric and the character of its speaker, but judgments are not so easy to make on all the speeches in the play. We are moved, for example, by Hamlet's breadth of spirit when he urges the exercise of magnanimity in dealing with men: "Use every man after his desert, and who should 'scape whipping? Use them after your own honour and dignity: the less they deserve, the more merit is in your bounty" (II. ii. 554–558); but we must be reminded like him that it is his role finally to bring about a justice in which all *are* used according to their deserts. It would be charitable to forgive Claudius the crime he so regrets; it would also be unthinkable for Hamlet to do so. We like to think that justice can be tempered with mercy, but in *Hamlet* Shakespeare presents the two principles as mutually irrelevant. Or again, we are frequently asked to remember the ideal for which Hamlet sacrifices himself, the well-ordered state, necessary guarantor of the polity's well-being. Thinking of the elder Hamlet and the good old days, or of our sense of peace and resolution at the end, we feel the state tragically worth the sacrifice of individual will. But thinking of the hard and ruthless Fortinbras, who will sacrifice the lives of thousands when he finds quarrel in a straw, or thinking of the Hamletless military order imposed on the world of the play at its end, we have our doubts. Such a state as Rosencrantz admires can be no ideal to an audience which can appreciate the sensibility of a Hamlet; majesty for the flunky of a successful regime is

> a massy wheel,
> Fix'd on the summit of the highest mount,
> To whose huge spokes ten thousand lesser things
> Are mortised and adjoin'd, which when it falls,
> Each small annexment, petty consequence,
> Attends the boisterous ruin.
>   (III. iii. 17–22)

Seen thus the state is power, the enemy rather than the protector of humanity. Here again Shakespeare forces us into a predicament: We must ask what the state is, but we cannot get an unequivocal answer.

And finally, does not *Hamlet* engage us in the same predicament about the value of life itself? For much of the play we share Hamlet's faith that beneath the appearances whose falsity he laments lies a reality whose truth is absolute. As usual Shakespeare ironically plays on that faith by parodying it in Polonius, who is confident that he "will find/ Where truth is hid, though it were hid indeed/ Within the centre" (II. ii. 157–159). But only in the graveyard scene do we come to a full sense, with Hamlet, of the question he has been asking as he turns the image of painting, earlier used to characterize feminine deceptiveness, to a description of flesh itself: "Now get you to my lady's chamber," he muses as he holds Yorick's skull, "and tell her, let her paint an inch thick, to this favour she must come." Is life the absolutely demanding principle Hamlet takes it to be during most of an action in which he epitomizes the human greatness of believing that one's actions count? Or is it the joke that the reality of death makes it in a *contemptus mundi* tradition which has lost the solacing corollary conviction of redemption in a better world? It must be one or the other: Each makes the other impossible.

The experience of *Hamlet*, then, culminates in a set of questions to which there are no answers. Made unsure whether we should praise or condemn man for his reason or his lack of it, we are finally led to doubt which is man's godlike quality, the reason with which tradition says he imitates his Creator or the surrender of reason which enables him to serve Him. As always, revenge conventions make us feel that the resolution of the plot is inevitable, and so we assent to the necessity of Hamlet's losing his life. But we cannot determine the value of what he must lose his life for. On every question the play makes us ask, we find ourselves, to use Hamlet's words on another matter, "between the pass and fell incensed points/ Of mighty opposites." I am not saying that we are left merely irresolute, or that Shakespeare throws up his hands and says that the world is simply a confusing place. Quite the contrary. No matter how much the plays make us face up to the starkness of the world we live in, our response has always been in some mode of joy, of renewed pleasure in the world. Moreover, if we consider what *Hamlet* has been saying to us, we see that it does not make us see a world in which nothing is valid. We see a world in which reason and civilization are absolute values even though they are contradicted by other values that paradoxically turn out to be equally absolute. We see a world which demands that man strive for self-knowledge and act on the profoundest principles he can discover even though the self-knowledge and the principles destroy all he holds dearest. It is not as if neither of these sets of values is based on reality— the cynical response; for better or for worse, both of them are. Thus this tragedy whose "theme" as stated in cold prose is nihilistic is strangely affirmative.

The vision of *Hamlet*, I am going to argue, is utterly typical of Shakespeare. But I do not want to convey the impression that the theme I have identified in *Hamlet* is perennial in Shakespeare, or even that it recurs anywhere else in his work. In fact it is one of the keys to his greatness that no two plays represent the same stage of human awareness. He grows and changes, and his plays change with him. In *Troilus and Cressida* and *Twelfth Night*, written at about the time of *Hamlet*, he reveals and embodies in dramatic action a similar ambivalence toward reason, though that ambivalence serves other purposes than it does in *Hamlet*. But in *King Lear*, only a few years later, the negative pole of the dialectical attitude toward reason expressed in *Hamlet* has so taken over that there is no more dialectic about it. Reason is the exclusive property of the villains, and the play consistently demands that we reject it, both because, as *Hamlet* merely suggested, it is inadequate to assess and govern human life, and because it is only a deceiving and self-deceiving cover for the dark passions that really control the evil characters. There is no parallel in *King Lear* to the rational ideal that Hamlet eulogizes in his description of Horatio. Shakespeare's concerns have so changed over a few years that he no longer sets up the problem that obsessed the earlier play, and few plays that he writes after *King Lear* indicate much interest in the problems of reason. To reduce the work of his career to a set of dramatizations of a single theme—such as that of reason against passion—or to a preoccupation with a single idea is a mistake all too familiar to readers of Shakespeare criticism.

The continuity between *Hamlet* and *King Lear* is not of theme but of vision. In *King Lear* as in *Hamlet* Shakespeare creates a universe susceptible of contradictory interpretations which are voiced by the characters in it and, more important, made equally plausible by the action. In order simply to interpret the plot, we find ourselves constantly driven to make up our minds about what kind of universe the characters live in. We want to know why Lear and Cordelia and Edgar—and we ourselves—are being made to suffer. But as the intensity of our experience with the play, especially in the theater, makes us long for a sense of closure in the perplexing world in which Shakespeare involves us, we find ourselves able at almost any point in the play to read its world as godless or divine; these are the terms implicit in the action of *King Lear* and explicit in its language. If we choose the atheistic or naturalistic interpretation, we must still interpret the nature which we see constantly operant, and we find ourselves unable to determine whether it is mechanistic or ravening or somehow ordered consistently with what we consider humane in the play's best characters and in ourselves. If we entertain the possibility that there are gods who rule the world of the play, we are given adequate evidence to support both the thesis that they are indifferent to human concerns and its antithesis, that they care about us. If we allow the play to persuade us that the gods are concerned about us, we cannot determine the nature of their concern: We find ourselves tempted at any point to agree with formulations by characters who assert that the gods are malicious or pedagogical or benevolent or retributive, that they are interested in destroying us or redeeming us. One can easily think of fictions in which the action suggests many interpretations as straw men to be disposed of by a satisfying final resolution; but in *King Lear* the ending achieves much of its power precisely because it can equally sustain any one of these readings at the expense of all the others. The tragedy is thus a profoundly skeptical exploration, though even skepticism is too univocal an attitude, too much a single kind of faith, to seem anything like an equivalent to the vision *King Lear* leads us to. Now we can detect the seeds of the kind of skeptical openness to conflicting theologies that we see fully grown here in *Hamlet,* whose hero must before he can act move away from a position the Renaissance would have considered atheistic, in which "there's nothing good or bad but thinking makes it so," but *Hamlet* simply does not make us ask the same questions as *King Lear.* To those who are interested in Shakespeare's spiritual development the evidence of continuity, of relationship between the themes of his plays, is gratifying, but the problems of one play are not the problems of the other. The true constant is the dialectical dramaturgy. It may be the most notable constant in Shakespeare's work.

From the beginning of his career to its end, Shakespeare maintains amid the obvious variety of his work a strikingly consistent approach to the world he imitates. This consistency is apparent, I have been trying to say, not in the repetition of themes,

but rather in a characteristic mode of vision, a view of the world
as problematic in ways which, though infinitely various, share a
common pattern. Shakespeare tends to structure his imitations in
terms of a pair of polar opposites—reason and passion in Hamlet,
for instance, or reason and faith, reason and love, reason and imagination; Realpolitik and the traditional political order, Realpolitik
and political idealism; hedonism and responsibility, the world and
the transcendent, life and death, justice and mercy. Generally the
opposition is rather between two complexes of related elements
than simply between two single ideals. Always the dramatic structure sets up the opposed elements as equally valid, equally desirable, and equally destructive, so that the choice that the play
forces the reader to make becomes impossible. As I suggested before, this is not a matter of genre: The technique of presenting
a pair of opposed ideals or groups of ideals and putting a double
valuation on each is the basis of Shakespeare's comedy as well as
his tragedy, and it is clearly the source of a good deal of his power.
It is a mode of vision, not an ideology, and it owes much of its
viability to the fact that it serves equally well Shakespeare's youth
and his age, the most nihilistic and the most affirmative worlds
that he can create. It is an instrument susceptible of many uses.
As much part of Shakespeare as his style, it grows and changes as
does everything in this most constantly developing of all artists.

The kind of vision I have tried to point at in Hamlet and
shall attempt to define in its various forms in a number of plays
is what puts Shakespeare's plays out of the reach of the narrow
moralist, the special pleader for a particular ideology, the intellectual historian looking for a Shakespearean version of a Renaissance orthodoxy. Indeed it is that mode of vision that puts
the plays beyond philosophy and makes them works of art. They
cannot be reduced to prose paraphrase or statements of theme
because the kind of "statement" a given play makes cannot re-
spectably be made in the logical language of prose, where it will
sound merely paradoxical. Paradox is not the kind of formulation
the rational mentality has traditionally been happy with, and for
good reason. But the kind of "statement" a play like Hamlet
makes, paradoxical only when translated into discursive prose,
represents the state of intellectual and spiritual tension which

makes art. Informing such verbal constructs as the plays of Shakespeare, this approach to experience makes them essentially non-verbal because it makes them supralogical. It enables the plays to create illusory worlds which, like the world we feel about us, make sense in ways that consistently elude our power to articulate them rationally and yet seem to represent the truth better than rational articulation. Shakespeare's habitual approach makes his plays definitive embodiments of our knowledge that we live in a world which though it makes sense to our intuitive consciousness cannot be reduced to sense, and which though palpably coherent is always more complicated than the best of our analytic descriptions can say.

⇜§ II §⇝

Thus I am not arguing that Shakespeare is essentially different from other great poets in his characteristic vision. His uniqueness is related to the degree to which he builds on and constantly transforms the basic premises of his art, but those premises he shares with a surprising number of the major writers of the western tradition, and it would be a serious mistake not to recognize how much he does share with them. I would not want to argue that the Shakespearean vision is the only type of all the great literary visions, nor would I want to define a "great tradition" in which that vision is the *sine qua non* of admission. If students of arts other than literature have been stressing in recent years the idea that the painter and the composer achieve much of their effectiveness by virtue of the tensions built into their materials and the formal structure of their works,[2] if we can all agree that "tension" of some sort is an essential element in all works of art, we must still acknowledge that the particular form of aesthetic and cognitive tension that I have been describing in Shakespeare is of a special sort, and other kinds are obviously effective and valuable. On the other hand, the particular structure of Shakespearean tension is unmistakably like what we find in other poets' work. By considering some of them as a group, we may learn something about the conditions that create such similarity among men who are otherwise in so many ways dissimilar.

We learn immediately that though the aesthetic pattern I am describing is obviously cultural, it is characteristic of the entire history of western art, not just of that of the Renaissance. We find it in the earliest of our great poets, whose name is most frequently coupled with Shakespeare's. For in the *Iliad* Homer creates a dialectical pattern much like the one we have observed in *Hamlet*. On the one hand the poem leads us to admire most Hector and Troy and the civilization, order, and peace for which they stand and to reject the consuming egotism, the morbid violence, and above all the unqualifiable *wanting* that constitute Achilles; we are led, that is, to prize family and homeland, prosperity and affection and the civilized arts against the fiery force that would destroy them. In terms of Hector, Achilles is what the plot makes him: the enemy. On the other hand, the *Iliad* makes us recognize the spiritual superiority of Achilles, whose demonic egoism may begin simply as a larger than ordinary awareness of his own merits and rights, but grows swiftly into an attitude of awareness of the meaning of life and mortality such as Hector cannot attain. If Achilles' destructive passion leads to the loss of all that he wants, it also makes possible for him the vision of Zeus's urns which so well expresses what the poem is all about. Moreover, we come to realize that in terms of Achilles' honest and violent passion, Hector's commitment to civilization is out of touch with the real nature of life. Hector wants to live in accordance with the principles of order that civilized men find most attractive, but the uncompromising Achilles wants to live the life that expresses the unrepressed self. Though he makes constant demands on our allegiances, Homer does not let us choose. As we experience the life of the poem we learn to entertain simultaneously or in close conjunction contradictory readings of life which exist in terms of each other, yet which rule each other out, each telling us that it is the only and final way of seeing. Evident in every aspect of the *Iliad*, the famous objectivity of Homer is most significantly to be seen in the shape of the whole. As in the scenes depicted on Achilles' shield, that image of the poem in little, radically opposed and equally total commitments to the meaning of life coexist in a single harmonious vision.

Tension like that of the *Iliad* occurs in other works of classi-

cal antiquity very different from it. In the *Oresteia* the unresolvable conflict between matrilinear and patrilinear codes provides
a model of the tragic demands made on all men by the predicament of living in a particular moment of time and leads Aeschylus
to a final image of the just society in which the tensions between
the conflicting terms of what man wants are presented mythically
as the basis of the very structure of the ideal state. In *Oedipus
Rex* Sophocles moves us to a double vision of human destiny in
which we see ourselves as both totally responsible and not responsible at all for what we must endure. In the *Aeneid* Vergil en-
gages us continually in his double attitude toward the value of
the *Pax Romana*. As Shakespeare moved from the ambivalence
toward reason which he dramatized in *Hamlet* to the presentation in *King Lear* of a new and equally problematic ambivalence,
so Vergil resolves Homer's dichotomy—Hector versus Achilles—by
casting his hero in the mold of Hector, only to found his work
on a new dialectic as poignant as Homer's, the struggle between
history and human will.

Clearly the kind of tension we find in classical art was not
resolved in later art by the Christian faith which historically provided answers to such questions as Vergil asked. This should not
be surprising. The Christian solution to the problems of history
is entirely paradoxical in its nature and involves in its development in time a profound and uneasy amalgamation of classical
and Hebrew values, and concomitantly a double attitude toward
the value of man and the meaning of his life in this world, in
the context of which what we have seen in *Hamlet* is easily explicable. But Shakespeare's career is located at the end of Europe's
age of faith, and it is important to note that the kind of duality
that defines his work is built crucially into the greatest literature
of a more confidently Christian period, where it has nothing to
do with the dialectic between faith and doubt. It is the central
point in the *Divine Comedy*, the supreme poetic embodiment of
Christian vision, that no event can be looked at from a single
point of view. The journey in time must be seen in the light of
the journey beyond time; every moment achieves full sense both
in time and out of time, both as historical fact and as figure. In
so structuring his poem, Dante, as Charles Singleton has taught

us, imitates that God who creates a world in time at a historical moment in a timeless universe.³ The power of Dante's vision resides in his ability to make us believe as fully as Shakespeare or Homer makes us believe in the reality of a created world while making us know simultaneously that in terms of another and fuller understanding of being, that world, in which we live, has only a very limited kind of reality. Dante changes our way of seeing by doing through art what can really be done no other way: fusing as complementary to one another and simultaneously valid total responses to life that would seem to be contradictory.

Such tension is central in the work of another Christian poet who is not explicitly concerned with an exploration of the paradoxes of the Christian vision. In the *Troilus* Chaucer subjects us to the tension between the equal forces of a view, explicit only at the end but implicit in the irony of the whole, that the hero's mistake is taking seriously the objects of his sublunary desires, and a view of Troilus as hero, with desires that we want to see fulfilled. In the *Canterbury Tales* Chaucer's irony is more profound and subtle, and it is omnipresent. It arises from the very situation of the poem, a journey which is both a pilgrimage and an end in itself and which reflects allegorically a life whose essence, as Chaucer's characterization constantly tells us, is its precarious location between conflicting goods. Chaucer's Christianity is not confused: he knows and teaches us what Christian judgments must be made on each of his characters, and we have no doubts about how to assess the Pardoner or the Parson. Chaucer is completely in control of our responses to the less exemplary characters. But those responses are almost never allowed to be simple. The commanding irony of the *Tales* is implicit in the dual meaning of nature at the very beginning of the General Prologue: is it really and only man's nature to long for pilgrimages in the springtime when it is the nature of all other living creatures to turn to sexual activity? And that irony introduces each of the characters in Harry Bailly's company. It controls our dual attitude towards the Monk, who is of the earth earthy but for his calling ought not to be. Like Chaucer we condemn the Monk's failure as a monk while we admire his success as a different sort of man. A more profound instance of the irony of the *Tales* is at work in the presentation of the Wife of Bath, who gloriously epitomizes the love of sheer physical and intellectual existence, yet from the viewpoint of a simultaneously dramatized standard is damned, and rightly so, for everything we admire in her. Chaucer's particular genius in respect to his presentation of character is his awareness of the dichotomy between the standards on which he builds and judges it. This awareness makes possible the most exquisite of judgments—like the implicit and delicate judgment of the Prioress, for example, who is compounded of a refined and genuine religious sensibility and of worldly longings she hardly recognizes. But Chaucer's aim is not so much, like Dante's, the arousing of our moral sensibilities and the finality of judgment as it is the amused and affectionate imitation of human personality unstably composed of basic elements that in all but the saint seem almost irrelevant to one another. The dichotomy underlying the Chaucerian vision is most beautifully evident in the first two ideal types portrayed in the General Prologue. Without comment Chaucer introduces the exemplary Knight, orderly and dutiful, who represses all impulse toward worldly pleasure and does not even take the time to change his spattered military uniform before embarking on the pilgrimage which fully expresses his desire, and his equally exemplary son, the Squire, who epitomizes the joyous, sensual, and disorderly indulgence of an untrammeled and poetic youth. Both of them reflect the same ambiguous "nature" described at the outset. The good life, the moralist must say, is one or the other; yet for Chaucer and for all of us living in his world the two ways of life coexist as goods. Not the Knight or his son, but both of them; not the Parson's devotion to the next world or the Wife's to this, but both of them; not the Wife's ideal and lovable hedonism by one set of standards or her sure damnation by another, but both of them. The result is art. We study Chaucer in the context of a faith which provides positive answers to all questions, but we experience him with that sense of the palpability and the ultimate mystery of the world that we share with all great writers.

Whatever it is, then, that brings about the kind of vision we have observed in Shakespeare is not fundamentally changed by so broad and deep a cultural phenomenon as the Christian transformation of the west, and in fact we find that kind of vision recurring continually in modern literature. We encounter it in Cervantes' masterpiece, with its unresolvable tensions between the compelling idealism of Don Quixote and the equally compelling intransigence of the world;[4] in Goethe's *Faust*, with the tension—one of many—between being and becoming; in Stendhal's ironic romances of the heroic conquest of a world not worth conquering by free heroes imprisoned in themselves. We watch Tolstoy staving off the capitulation to despair or to his ultimate conversion, fighting the temptation to see the world as simple and without tensions, by embodying the opposite principles he would have us live in the two heroes of *War and Peace*: the driving and finally nihilistic egoism of Prince Andrew on the one hand, the acquiescent and almost egoless affirmation of Pierre Bezhukov on the other. And in our own century, to cite only the most notable example, we see the fundamentally dialectical nature of Mann's novels and recognize that in that respect this most original of writers is in a long tradition. Wherever we first encountered it, the mode of vision I have been describing becomes for all of us I think the ineffable quality that enables many of the greatest fictions to maintain their hold over us, that tells us that the artist and his audience know a reality incapable of being supplanted, alas, by the kind of intellectual formulation we would like to be able to make about life. Because this vision draws its power not from the validity of a poet's particular beliefs—Olympian gods or Christian eternity or enlightened skepticism or historical determinism—but rather from its embodiment of a perennial sense of conflict between human ideals at any moment in time, we find ourselves learning as much about ourselves and the world we live in from writers whose ages have little else to teach us as we do from our closest contemporaries. Consciousness changes enormously from one age to another; yet, as the great anthropologist Levi-Strauss has been telling us,[5] certain facts about our interaction with the world remain eternally true, and it is with those facts that much of the most enduring literature deals.

◄§ III §►

Now surely it can and should be objected that what I am saying sounds like the pernicious aestheticism which sees literature as laudably unconcerned with finding answers to life's problems because those problems are incapable of solution, and which leaves the artist and his audience open to moral dangers: a quietistic and essentially despairing inability to make commitments, a turning away from the business of life to the "appreciation" of the literary artifact as a thing in itself, with its built-in consolation prize for abandoning the struggles in which moral and political life should engage us, an awe for "vision" at the expense of decision and action, a deeply emotional recognition and justification of the status quo in a world so far from simple. Certainly many in our time, both creators and consumers of art, have used literature precisely to these ends. Moreover, it is significant that every one of the artists I have described lived at a revolutionary moment in history when the vision he created in his art was the only alternative to despair or to a narrow and activist kind of commitment.

But the activist charge against the aesthetic vision we are discussing does not do it justice. If poets indulged in paradox for its own sake—merely, that is, to provide pleasure or to give their works internal unity and form (as formalistic critics sometimes assume they do), their achievements, no matter how estimable, would be fair game for such attacks. But reading Shakespeare and Homer, Chaucer and Tolstoy, we know differently. When at the center of their work we find such paradoxes and contrarieties as I have been describing, we experience that startled awareness in which the power of art resides: we recognize that we are seeing the world through the artist's vision as our deepest experience tells us always the world really is. The justification of an art which refuses to come to simple and logically consistent terms with the world then is precisely that it refuses to do so, for in imitating the only world available to that subjective experience in which we are imprisoned every moment of our lives it enables us to understand, with a luminosity and concentration that life provides only at rare moments, the nature of the world we experience. "The enrichment which art can give us originates in its power to remind us of harmonies beyond the grasp of systematic analysis," a modern writer has said. "Literary, pictorial and musical art may be said to form a sequence of modes of expression, where the ever more extensive renunciation of definition, characteristic of scientific communication, leaves fantasy a freer play. . . . emotionally uniting manifold aspects of human knowledge." One turns to art, then, not to gratify a subjective hedonism, but, to find a mirror of experience nowhere else to be found. Great art is not a turning away from life's problems, but a facing up to what the real problems are.

What I have been describing in the litera y experience thus implies a quality, if not of the nature of objective reality, at least of the nature of our ability to understand and come to terms with reality. Now interestingly, artists—and men as artists' audiences— are not alone in their sense that the world we experience cannot adequately be described in a manner that is always logically consistent. The modern writer I cited in the last paragraph is neither an artist nor a literary critic, but the physicist Niels Bohr, attempting in an essay entitled "Unity of Knowledge" to explain that twentieth-century physicists who find themselves forced to live with apparently unresolvable paradoxes and contrarieties are, distressing though it may seem at first, in the mainstream of human experience.[6] The epistemological quandary in which physicists since Einstein have found themselves, in fact, has an immediately apparent relevance to what I have been describing in some aesthetic experience; and the way out of that quandary that Bohr and other physicist-philosophers have been taking is so remarkably similar to the implicit conclusions of the literary works we have been discussing that I want to digress briefly to describe it.

In a valuable popular exposition of the chief philosophical problems roused by the adventurous new investigation of matter and energy to which our century has devoted much of its best abilities, J. Robert Oppenheimer focuses our attention on a most perplexing set of questions.[7] These questions can be seen most conveniently in terms of one model, modern investigations of the nature of light. Classical optics, Professor Oppenheimer reports, had led physicists to tell us that light consists in continuous waves, but recent discoveries have seriously altered that belief. For the discovery of what Oppenheimer calls "the new symbol of the atomic domain," Planck's constant, was not in accord with the theory of light as waves, and

> it led Einstein to the bold, though at the time hardly comprehensible, conclusion that light, which we know as an electromagnetic disturbance of rapidly changing electrical fields, which we know as a continuous phenomenon propagating from point to point and from time to time like a wave, *is also and is nevertheless* corpuscular, consisting of packets of energy determined by the frequency of the light and by Planck's constant.[8]

Light is waves, yet it *is also and it is nevertheless* corpuscular. The new discoveries present what Oppenheimer properly calls a "radical . . . problem of understanding"[9] because the new fact of light as quanta, though incompatible with the idea of light as waves, does not do away with it. The problem is that there are phenomena which physicists can understand only by treating light as waves and others which they can interpret only by treating it as quanta, discrete packets of energy.

A related difficulty occurs when scientists attempt to describe the behavior of charged particles in motion: in a sense, we seem to know too much, and no classical or simple answer will do.

> To what appeared to be the simplest questions, we will tend to give either no answer or an answer which will at first sight be reminiscent more of a strange catechism than of the straightforward affirmatives of physical science. If we ask, for instance, whether the position of the electron remains the same, we must say "no"; if we ask whether the electron's position changes with time, we must say "no"; if we ask whether the electron is at rest, we must say "no"; if we ask whether it is in motion, we must say "no." The Buddha has given such answers when interrogated as to the conditions of

a man's self after his death; but they are not familiar answers for the tradition of seventeenth- and eighteenth-century science.[10]

The problem created by recent experience with subatomic particles is as surprising as that created by the new way of explaining light. The physicists had expected the hydrogen atom to act like a model of the Newtonian universe, and statistically in fact they found that hydrogen atoms—when many of them are considered —do conform fairly closely to the classical laws of Newtonian physics. But watched individually, no hydrogen atom will behave according to predictions. This discovery was a disturbing one; as Oppenheimer says, "We saw in the very heart of the physical world an end of that complete causality which had seemed so inherent a feature of Newtonian physics,"[11] Scientists had to assimilate the idea that the causality that operates for large objects in our familiar world does not seem to operate on the atomic level on which that world is built.

Out of this quandary came two principles. One is that of correspondence, developed by Bohr and others, which stipulates that the classical laws of Newton and Maxwell apply without modification to phenomena on a large scale, while on the tiny scale of the distances and masses involved in the activity of individual electrons they will apply only statistically. Thus one can predict the trajectory of a bullet as a certitude, but the movement of an electron only as a probability. The principle of correspondence acknowledges what the physicists' difficulties in dealing with the fundamental nature of light suggest, that there are serious limitations in our power to perceive reality on the level of its smallest and most basic entities. The other principle, which is in fact merely an implication of the first, is the principle of complementarity, and on it I should like to dwell for a moment.

The term "complementarity," which Oppenheimer defines simply and memorably as the idea "that an electron must sometimes be considered as a wave, and sometimes as a particle,"[12] was introduced by Bohr in a lecture at the International Physical Congress held in 1927 at Como. In 1961 Bohr reprinted a revised version of that lecture, "The Quantum Postulate and the

Recent Development of Atomic Theory," and in the introduction to the collection of essays in which he reprinted it he described complementarity as "a new mode of description designated as *complementary* in the sense that any given application of classical concepts precludes the simultaneous use of other classical concepts which in a different connection are equally necessary for the elucidation of the phenomena."[13] Oppenheimer's explanation is helpful:

> In a little subtler form this complementarity means that there are situations in which the position of an atomic object can be measured and defined and thought about without contradiction; and other situations in which this is not so, but in which other qualities, such as the energy or the impulse of the system, are defined and meaningful. The more nearly appropriate the first way of thinking is to a new situation, the more wholly inappropriate the second, so that there are in fact no atomic situations in which both impulse and position will be defined well enough to permit the sort of prediction with which Newtonian mechanics has familiarized us.[14]

The implication is that the physicist makes his definition of reality, or assumes a reality, according to what works in a particular experiment, and it is a legitimate inference from what has been said thus far that physicists must be skeptical of any idea of ultimate "truth"; but such is not the case, and for two reasons. In the first place, the physicist is modest enough to recognize that the need for a theory of complementarity says much about the perhaps insuperable problems involved in studying matter on so small a scale that our experimental methods must intrude on and shape the discovery that is being made, so that we can never examine a particle as it exists outside of our examination; like Eliot's roses, the particles have the look of particles that are looked at. Our inability to perceive the whole truth about electrons does not rule out the existence of such a truth. But second, and more important philosophically, complementarity tells us something about the nature of reality. A particular description of the atom is not the only way of talking about it. It is the only way appropriate to the information we have and the means that we have used to obtain it. It is the full account of this information and if the experiment was properly and scrupulously done it tells us all that we can find out. It is not all we could have found out had we chosen a different experiment. It is all that we could find out having chosen this.

And, most important, "this state [a given state observed in a particular experiment] is objective."[15] Our radically opposed descriptions of such phenomena as light are nevertheless objective, based on nature and not merely on the limitations or strengths of our minds. Taken together they suggest that reality when fully understood is more complicated than any simple, logical, and coherent reading of it, yet of such a nature that we find ourselves forced constantly to make, and to profit from, simple, logical, and coherent readings.

Oppenheimer is careful not to make facile analogies from these implications of modern physics to problems that lie in other areas; nevertheless, striking analogies are immediately apparent, and he sees them clearly. I want to single out only one group that he suggests:

> Indeed, an understanding of the complementary nature of conscious life and its physical interpretation appears to me a lasting element in human understanding and a proper formulation of the historic views called psycho-physical parallelism. For within conscious life, and in its relations with the description of the physical world, there are again many examples. There is the relation between the cognitive and the affective sides of our lives, between knowledge or analysis and emotion or feeling. There is the relation between the aesthetic and the heroic, between feeling and that precursor and definer of action, the ethical commitment; there is the classical relation between the analysis of one's self, the determination of one's motives and purposes, and that freedom of choice, that freedom of decision and action, which are complementary to it.[16]

Our deepest consciousness, that is, is almost inevitably complementary. I need cite only one example, suggested above and developed in several essays by Bohr and Oppenheimer. Consider, they suggest, our habitual resolution of the ceaseless debate between theories of free will and of determinism. We live easily with complementary answers. In creating the concept of law, we hold men responsible for their actions, ruling outside the law those who can be demonstrated by virtue of insanity or certain kinds of passion not to be free so that we can call all others innocent or guilty. In the court, that is, we know that men are free and responsible agents—and we know our freedom of choice. But thinking of what psychology and sociology and anthropology have taught us, we do not really believe at all in freedom. We know that criminals do what they do because they are the victims of their genetic make-up and of their environments and of accident; we see them trapped in the repetition of acts which are responses to what they cannot escape in themselves. Now if one of these radically opposed ideas is true, the other cannot be. Yet we know that they both are. Contemplation of this anomaly leads us first to conclusions about the insufficiency of our knowledge; but it leads us also to a suspicion that there are truths less susceptible of rational formulation than the half-truths we are equipped to turn into discursive prose.

Now certainly the problem with which we are dealing is one more of phenomenology than of ontology. It would be wrong to extrapolate from the physicist's predicament to grandiose generalizations about the split nature of reality. As far as we know, our difficulty in reducing the present state of our knowledge to coherent and logically consistent statements tells us more about our own experience of nature than it does about the nature we experience. Bohr frequently explains the idea of complementarity by reminding us of our perennial consciousness of a double vision occasioned by the fact that we must simultaneously view the world as objective, existing outside and independent of us, and as filtered through our individual subjective consciousness. But to recognize that the problem is centered in consciousness is not to concede that it is any the less real than if it pointed to a fact of nature-in-itself. The problem is real because we live with it in virtually every aspect of our lives. (It is not without significance, by the way, that the most important psychologist of our century was drawn reluctantly to a complementary vision: Freud saw the psyche as the result of conflicting principles built into a single organism.) And it is precisely in imaginative literature that we should expect to find the most poignant awareness of the complementary nature of human experience, for experience, stripped of its irrelevant and unessential qualities perhaps but unmediated by the simplifying rational intelligence, is the stuff of art. Only men of a certain extraordinary kind of religious faith find in literature a vehicle for expressing a recognition of absolute truth (I think of those who believe that the force and value of poetry inhere in its eternal return to myths that, regardless of the poet's intentions, embody existential truths); most of us, I dare say, are drawn to poetry because in it as in nothing else we are enabled to re-experience in such a way as to come to understand it the unresolvable complexity of life as life presents itself to the fullest human consciousness.

◦§ IV §◦

There is another reason why such a vision is not in great poets the program for irresponsible escape and dilletantism it might seem to be. The reason is implicit in the fact that the writers I have named are quite different from one another in every other respect. The differences begin in personality, but they eventuate in world-views as different as their creators. Homer seems hardly more than an eye, aloof and elusive; Vergil's characteristic melancholy infuses and dominates every line of his work. Chaucer presents his world in all its complexity, and in all the complexity of his attitude toward it, in the always comfortable tone of a man whose faith is utterly secure no matter how much he appreciates its ambiguities; Tolstoy, for all the objectivity of his presentation, makes us constantly aware of the intense quest, the deliberate backing away from doubt, which he shares with more than one of his protagonists. Stendhal is rooted in the sense experience of the world; Mann is always the intellectual in search of the right abstractions. Dante's eye leads us always away from immediate detail to its manifold significance, Shakespeare's always to the perception of the object itself. And what generalization can one make about Shakespeare? For is he not almost as different from one play to the next as other writers are one from another?

What I am saying is that the aesthetic presentation of the world as complementary is not in itself a whole vision. It is only a beginning, the groundwork on which a work of art can be constructed. It provides a writer with the basis of a mimesis which appeals to the common understanding because it recalls the unresolvable tensions that are the fundamental conditions of human life. It is a mode of awareness, an option for a certain and essential kind of openness to human experience. It is not a final dogma —any more than the principle of complementarity is a dogma for physicists. If it suggests on one level of awareness that facile commitment is a mistake, it can suggest on another that living as full men in a real world makes demands on us for commitment and action that can never be satisfied. We might end where we began: When we learn with Hamlet the tragic coexistence of two opposed ideals of behavior, we do not despair because of our knowledge. We do not surrender our attachment to the values of civilization because we have come to see their ultimate fragility, but rather we come to prize them more because we know what they mean. In *Hamlet,* that is, complementarity leads us to renewed and poignant affection for certain traditional values; and in each other play it leads in as particular a direction.

I propose to examine a number of Shakespeare's plays which are built on visions of complementarity. I hope to demonstrate that the poet's perhaps intuitive, certainly habitual understanding of the truth as in some sense complementary and of poetry as the proper vehicle for the conveyance of that sense of the truth is a constant in his work. But such a demonstration is only a beginning, for it is much more interesting that Shakespeare develops in this respect as in all others; and I shall want to discuss ways in which the Shakespearean vision grows in depth and changes in nature while remaining true to the principle which underlies it. If my argument develops through the discussion of individual plays and poems rather than through an overview of the entire canon, it does so because each play is a discrete entity which cannot safely be talked of as simply or primarily an example of something generic to them all or to a group. Shake-speare's vision is a historical phenomenon, responsive to his cultural situation; it exists in time, and each of its manifestations must be discussed by itself.

NOTES

1. The view of Hamlet as diseased intruder is that of G. Wilson Knight in "The Embassy of Death: an Essay on *Hamlet*," *The Wheel of Fire*, first published in 1930. Some recent interpretations of *Hamlet* which develop aspects of what I am describing are to be found in Helen Gardner, *The Business of Criticism* (Oxford, 1959), pp. 35–51; Maynard Mack, "The World of Hamlet," *Yale Review*, XLI (1952), 502–523; John Lawlor, "Agent or Patient," *The Tragic Sense in Shakespeare* (New York, 1960), pp. 45–73; Fredson Bowers, "Hamlet as Minister and Scourge," *PMLA*, LXX (1955), 740–749; C. S. Lewis, "Hamlet: The Prince or The Poem," *Proceedings of the British Academy*, XXVIII (1942), 139–154; D. G. James "The New Doubt," *The Dream of Learning* (Oxford, 1951), pp. 33–68; Harry Levin, *The Question of Hamlet* (New York, 1959); and L. C. Knights, *An Approach to Hamlet* (Stanford, 1961).

2. See, for example, E. H. Gombrich, *Art and Illusion: A Study of the Psychology of Pictorial Representation* (New York, 1960) and Leonard B. Meyer, *Emotion and Meaning in Music* (Chicago, 1956).

3. Charles S. Singleton, *Commedia: Elements of Structure, Dante Studies*, I (Cambridge, Mass., 1954).

4. See Leo Spitzer, "Perspectivism in the *Don Quijote*," *Linguistics and Literary History* (Princeton, 1948), pp. 41–73, for a provocative account of some of the ways in which Cervantes' technique serves "to break up a multivalent reality into different perspectives" (p. 57).

5. Claude Levi-Strauss, *Tristes Tropiques* (New York, 1961).

6. Niels Bohr, "Unity of Knowledge," *Atomic Physics and Human Knowledge* (New York, 1961), p. 79.

7. J. Robert Oppenheimer, *Science and the Common Understanding* (New York, 1954).

8. *Ibid.*, p. 43; italics added.

9. *Ibid.*, p. 43.

10. *Ibid.*, p. 40.

11. *Ibid.*, p. 47.

12. *Ibid.*, p. 69.

13. *Atomic Theory and the Description of Nature* (Cambridge, 1961), p. 10.

14. *Ibid.*, p. 70.

15. *Ibid.*, pp. 71–72.

16. *Ibid.*, p. 81. See also Niels Bohr, "Natural Philosophy and Human Cultures," *Atomic Physics and Human Knowledge,* pp. 23–31. Here as elsewhere Bohr discusses the wide range of crucial matters on which our thinking is complementary: thought and feeling, instinct and reason, free will and causality, etc.

Self Against Self

⋖ I ⋗

COMPLEMENTARITY IN SHAKESPEARE, I HAVE ARGUED, IS A WAY OF seeing, not an idea or an ideology. But like other ways of seeing things, it arises from the demands made by the age, by the inadequacies of available intellectual modes to provide simpler and rationally more satisfactory answers to the questions Shakespeare might ask. The first example of such a question we considered was *Hamlet*, where we found Shakespeare posing his problem, the definition of man's best nature, in the traditional terms— reason and unreason—offered him by his culture, and developing his tragic account of the human situation in terms which thus make dramatically poignant the antinomies implicit in the traditionally double view of human nature. As we shall see in later chapters, Shakespeare responds and asks us to respond to a large number of such antinomies, and, as I have suggested, it would be a mistake to attempt to locate the center of Shakespeare's concerns in the polarities of a single idea. On the other hand, the problem explored in *Hamlet* is too rich to have been exhausted, and Shakespeare returns to it several times, posing it each time in a new way, suggesting each time a new answer. In every play in which rationality is one of the answers to a fundamental question, its complementary opposite is something new, something not considered in the same way in any other play, and we are made to see the problems built into the complexity of human nature in a novel way. So freshly does Shakespeare confront the situations he dramatizes that at times the plays themselves seem to contradict one another, giving us the sense that the canon itself is a complementary phenomenon. In this chapter I intend to deal with two such plays, *Troilus and Cressida* and *Othello*. Thematically as rich and independent as any that Shakespeare wrote, each of these plays sets the rational faculties against the heart's faith, and in the course of doing so they lead us to opposed valuations of the psychological and ethical powers they dramatize. By considering these plays, both separately as attempts to focus on aspects of the problem defined in *Hamlet* and together as reflections on each other, we may come to a new understanding of the richness of the Shakespearean vision.

◆§ II §◆

To many in each generation *Troilus and Cressida* must seem, as it did once to Tennyson, " 'perhaps Shakespeare's finest play.' "[1] On the stage it has had memorable if all too infrequent successes; in the study its muscular and irridescent intellectuality, its language and characterization have earned it the constant attention of Shakespeare's critics. Yet critics repeatedly imply their sense that *Troilus and Cressida* is a failure, and find themselves obliged either to denounce its apparent idiosyncrasies or to explain them by seeing the play as a special phenomenon— an exercise for law students, a comical satire—not to be judged by the canons that we normally apply to Shakespeare. The range of statements that have been made about the play is as broad as can be imagined. Thus, for example, S. L. Bethell locates the problems of the piece in its "consciously philosophical" nature and Shakespeare's failure to merge the "story" and the "philosophy," so that "the story is an excuse for thought rather than the embodiment of thought";[2] Robert Kimbrough, on the other hand, explains what he finds anomalous in the play by arguing that "the plot has no central drive, no consistent argument": Shakespeare has been too little willing to sacrifice the conventions which he has inherited from several traditions to achieve an intellectually coherent whole. "War and lechery generally confound all, but this overall theme has no general reverberation or universal ring as developed in this play. It opens in confusion and merely moves through more confusion to less confusion."[3] The play is damned on the one hand for the primacy of its theme, on the other for its themelessness.

For both these critics the heart of the problem is the relation of "theme" or animating idea to action; and it should be noted that such critics as have achieved a measure of success with the play—Una Ellis-Fermor and L. C. Knights, for example— have done so precisely by confronting the question of the involvement of the theme in the play.[4] Not to recognize the extent to which an underlying idea relates the discrete elements of *Troilus and Cressida* to one another and explains Shakespeare's disposition of events is dangerously to misunderstand both the play's technique and its meaning. Ideas have a life in this play that they rarely have on the stage. What gives them that life is the way in which, built into a double-plot structure, they are made dramatic. *Troilus and Cressida* is perhaps the most brilliant of all instances of the double plot, that convention which gives a play the power to convey a complex theme implicitly through action and ironic language.[5]

Through the use of the double plot, as in other ways through other conventions, Shakespeare and his contemporaries turned ideas into theater so that the two could scarcely be separated. Our understanding of the significance of the double plot has long since enriched our understanding of a number of Shakespeare's plays.[6] It is interesting that two of the plays in which the parallelism characteristic of the double plot is dominant are *Hamlet* and *King Lear*,[7] in both of which we recognize the vision I have been calling complementary. The reason, I think, is clear. Parallels between events in a play make us ask why they are there. The double plot demands that we understand the principles underlying the implicit and often, as we shall see, explicit analogies between plots, that we ask and answer the question of why the two plots are in the same play. It demands, that is, that we make sense of the play, that we not think simply in terms of plot. In so doing, of course, the parallelism of the double plot serves as do many of the conventions of Shakespeare's theater, to provoke an experience in which understanding plays as large a part as emotional response and in fact is scarcely separable from it. But the double plot tends to complicate the issues while making them clearer: we learn something about Lear's inadequacies as father as we see Gloucester implicitly parodying them, but what we learn tends to make us both more sympathetic with the King's suffering and more annoyed with him. I am going to argue that if the "final effect" of *Troilus and Cressida* is "baffling" and "ambivalent,"[8] the reason is not, as Professor Kimbrough claims, that Shakespeare has failed to produce a coherent play, but rather that the meaning of the play can emerge only as we confront the complementary answers to the question it raises. Once we have recognized—in large part through the agency of the double plot— those answers, we are prepared to accept a new answer which is not complementary, and to discover intellectually what our experience has already told us, that *Troilus and Cressida* is one of its author's greatest plays and that it makes sense.

Despite the smoothness of the bond between them, *Troilus and Cressida* presents two distinct plots, as independent of one another as any in Shakespeare: the affair between Troilus and Cressida on the one hand, and the Greek ruse to bring Achilles back into the war and thus end it on the other. Each would in itself constitute a strong enough line for a play of its own; neither plot depends for its outcome on the course of the other. Even in such scenes as the Trojan council meeting, where Troilus irrelevantly speaks of the taking of a wife, or the exchange of the prisoners, which deeply concerns the progress of each action, the two plot lines remain separate. With its discrete plots which paradoxically seem to comprise a unified action, *Troilus and Cressida* resembles other plays in which Shakespeare modifies the convention of the double plot—*A Midsummer Night's Dream* and *King Lear*, for example, where we begin with a strong sense of separate plot lines only to learn that they are inextricably intertwined. Whether the illusion Shakespeare creates in a given play is that the actions are independent of one another or that they are, as in *Troilus and Cressida*, part of a complex and integrated whole, the result is always a structural sophistication so purely Shakespearean that perhaps we should not be surprised at the reluctance of centuries to recognize a shared convention in the double plots of Shakespeare and those of his contemporaries.

In *Troilus and Cressida* the double-plot structure makes possible a thematic exposition, aesthetic rather than conceptual despite the philosophizing for which the play is so remarkable, that makes one realize most poignantly the inadequacy of rational analysis. Only by observing particulars in the order in which they appear, by considering each moment of the play in the contexts of both the whole play and the point at which it occurs, and by recognizing the effects achieved by the parallels between the autonomous plots can we stay clear of the traps into which the critic tempted to make *a priori* statements may fall. My concern is thematic, to be sure. I am not, however, interested in formulating a "one- or two-word subject about which the [play] makes an ineffable statement," but rather with determining by an inductive reading of the whole play the principle which unifies and gives meaning to its discrete elements.[9] The analysis of a work whose genius is primarily structural must itself be structural.

Like a glittering and intricate spiderweb, the totality of the play seems implicated in its every node. Almost any point will do for a start. Let us take the end of the second scene, for example. Watching the heroes return from battle, Cressida and Pandarus have been fencing with each other, Pandarus maladroitly attempting to arouse his niece's interest in a young man toward whom she shows every evidence of indifference. As her uncle leaves, however, Cressida tells us that she actually prizes Troilus more than Pandarus can praise him:

> Yet hold I off. Women are angels, wooing:
> Things won are done; joy's soul lies in the doing.
> That she beloved knows nought that knows not this:
> Men prize the thing ungain'd more than it is.
> (I. ii. 312–315)

Conveyed in the first sententious speech of the play, Cressida's pessimism comes as a greater shock than the more conventional cynicism she has been demonstrating to her uncle, and is an important touch in a character study which will attempt to explain a notoriously inexplicable infidelity. But, like many such speeches in Shakespeare, Cressida's scene-ending soliloquy does not merely characterize: It raises a question. Is she right? Has a moment no value beyond its duration? Is expectation more satisfying than fulfillment? Is there no survival value in achievement?

As might be expected, Shakespeare is not overtly setting out the thematic conclusion of the play, but he is preparing us for the exposition, sounding his theme in the minor so that we will think back, often and crucially, to Cressida's statement as new facets of the theme are revealed. Already we may be called back by the odd similarity of Cressida's self-justification to a remark that Troilus has just made, with savage irony, in the only other soliloquy so far in the play:

> Peace, you ungracious clamours! peace, rude sounds!
> Fools on both sides! Helen must needs be fair,
> When with your blood you daily paint her thus.
> (I. i. 92–94)

Helen's value, that is, lies in the doing: If so many men fight for her, she must be worth fighting for. Like Cressida's soliloquy, Troilus' sardonic jibe merely foreshadows the arguments to come as to the subjectivity of value;[10] but like hers it has a dramatic significance that no one can miss who knows the old story, for, finding the fickle Helen "too starved a subject" for his sword, Troilus immediately and ironically turns to the praise of Cressida.

His theme adumbrated in the love plot, Shakespeare now begins to develop it in the war plot. Listening to the elaborate argumentation of the first Greek council scene (I. iii), the audience may be rather surprised to recognize in a discussion of matters that seem far removed from the love life of the Trojans a concern with the same questions that have already been raised within the walls of Ilium. Why have the gods prolonged the war for seven years? asks Agamemnon. The answer: because Jove wants to make trial of men. When fortune smiles all men seem alike in quality,

> But, in the wind and tempest of her frown,
> Distinction, with a broad and powerful fan,
> Puffing at all, winnows the light away;
> And what hath mass or matter, by itself
> Lies rich in virtue and unmingled.
>
> (I. iii. 26–30)

With comic alacrity the aged Nestor catches his commander's drift. Whatever it tells us about his intellectual independence, Nestor's repetition of the idea clarifies and reinforces it. He is neither the first nor the last Shakespearean character to make a statement which we must take more seriously than we do its speaker, and his performance here exemplifies Shakespeare's capacity simultaneously to strengthen dramatic illusion and to advance the theme. When the sea is smooth all boats seem equally competent, Nestor observes, but when it storms only the stoutest survives: "Even so/ Doth valour's show and valour's worth divide/ In storms of fortune" (I. iii. 45–47).

Again a metaphysical question underlies the speeches: What is the value of a man? When can one be sure of that value? The answer suggested by Agamemnon and Nestor is that, as the medium in which fortune distributes adversity, time will ultimately distinguish true value. As the play develops, the idea of time as a process which defines and identifies value will grow increasingly complex and important as its role in both actions becomes clear; here it is being suggested for the first time, and as yet it may not seem particularly relevant.[11]

What follows immediately has all too often been taken as a formulation of the play's theme. Ulysses' great sermon on "the specialty of rule" delights the ear and lingers in the memory; it is a gorgeously imagined setting of an Elizabethan commonplace. Moreover, it is crucial in the play. Seldom if ever, however, does such a set piece explicitly enunciate the theme of a play by Shakespeare, and we should not assume that it does here. Brief reflection, in fact, should be sufficient for the realization that Ulysses' remarks do not hit dead center. What he does is to make us aware of the urgency of the Greeks' situation, of the dire condition of a society which has lost its old order, and of the dangers of surrendering reason to will, passion, and power. These concerns are indeed highly relevant to what goes wrong in both plots, and parallel in philosophical assumption to the debate about reason and passion; but they do not comprise the ultimate statement to be made about the universe of the play. When Ulysses so persuasively pictures the shaking of degree he is merely describing, not explaining; one might similarly account for juvenile delinquency by pointing out that many young people have lost their respect for established values. Ulysses' speech carries our attention from seven years of stalemate and the concern of the great generals to the delinquency of Achilles without allowing us to think of the latter as less important than the former. This is a significant function: If the crucial understanding of Achilles' own attitude, at the center of the subplot, is reserved for a later point, its significance has at least been clearly signaled. But the comfortable ideas about order and disorder so often cited—most notably by Tillyard—as the chief importance of the speech do not really begin to answer the questions the play has been asking.

The idea which most looks forward to vigorous development in the play is that of time, whose winnowing function has been described by Agamemnon and Nestor. Already in this scene Ulysses, who is to make the play's most famous speech about time, speaks of it in an odd fashion as he proposes his trick to Nestor:

> I have a young conception in my brain;
> Be you my time to bring it to some shape.
>
> (I. iii. 312–313)

Time is thus a midwife, attendant at an organic process. As he unfolds his plan, Ulysses continues to talk in the language of birth and growth:

> Blunt wedges rive hard knots: the seeded pride
> That hath to this maturity blown up
> In rank Achilles must or now be cropp'd,
> Or, shedding, breed a nursery of like evil,
> To overbulk us all.
>
> (I. iii. 316–320)

The imagery of the nursery takes us back to Agamemnon's account of the seven years' failure:

> Checks and disasters
> Grow in the veins of actions highest rear'd,
> As knots, by the conflux of meeting sap,
> Infect the sound pine and divert his grain
> Tortive and errant from his course of growth.
>
> (I. iii. 5–9)

Ulysses' organic description of time finds its echo almost immediately in Nestor's response. Proposing an encounter between Hector and Achilles, the old man suggests that the success of the event

> shall give a scantling
> Of good or bad unto the general;
> And in such indexes, although small pricks
> To their subsequent volumes, there is seen
> The baby figure of the giant mass
> Of things to come at large.
>
> (I. iii. 341–346)

Thus, by the end of the first council scene our attention has been drawn to a question of value and to a notion of time. How these matters are to be related to the play's theme is a larger question that in characteristically Shakespearean fashion withholds its answer until later. But after the scurrilous interlude in which we first see Achilles, Ajax, and Thersites, the play takes up these matters again. Once again the scene is a council meeting, this time within Troy. And once again, as if to underline the symmetry between I. iii and II. ii, rational men make a mockery of reason. As Ulysses in the Greek camp both praised and exemplified the reason that stands in opposition to the universal wolf of appetite, yet found no better use for his reason than to trick Achilles, so Hector in Troy sees and rationally understands what action is necessary, yet impulsively acts against his own decision. Like the scene before Agamemnon's tent, the scene in Priam's palace concerns the war plot; but at a crucial moment in the argument Troilus reveals that his own attitude toward the return of

Helen is based on his attitude toward Cressida, and at this moment the developing theme of the play begins to coalesce.

Like the Greeks, the Trojans are reassessing their situation; and like them they discover almost immediately that the attempt to justify what is happening to them leads to a discussion of value.

> *Hect.* Brother, she is not worth what she doth cost
> The holding.
> *Tro.* What is aught, but as 'tis valued?
>   (II. ii. 51–52)

During the course of the argument, Troilus lets us understand what he meant, in the play's first soliloquy, by his jibe at Helen. To Hector, Helen's value is an objective quantity which, measured against the manhood lost in her defense, makes her surrender a moral necessity: "What merit's in that reason which denies/ The yielding of her up?" (II. ii. 24–25). Reason is the key word here, for objective evaluation is a rational process. And Troilus recognizes that reason is precisely the challenge he must answer:

>   Nay, if we talk of reason,
> Let's shut our gates and sleep: manhood and honour
> Should have hare-hearts, would they but fat their thoughts
> With this cramm'd reason: reason and respect
> Make livers pale and lustihood deject.
>   (II. ii. 46–50)

Distrustful of reason's ability to find excuses for selfish behavior—as indeed it does later when Hector backs out of his fight with Ajax on rational grounds—, Troilus self-consciously espouses an irrational position:

> I take to-day a wife, and my election
> Is led on in the conduct of my will;
> My will enkindled by mine eyes and ears,
> Two traded pilots 'twixt the dangerous shores
> Of will and judgement: how may I avoid,
> Although my will distaste what it elected,

> The wife I chose? there can be no evasion
> To blench from this and to stand firm by honour.
>   (II. ii. 61–68)

Judgment may err in choice; will is changeable. All that is left is commitment, fidelity to the choices one has made regardless of the consequences; and committed behavior actually creates the worth of the object to which it is committed. From the sarcastic "O, theft most base,/ That we have stol'n what we do fear to keep" (II. ii. 92–93) it is a short distance to "But I would have the soil of her fair rape/ Wiped off, in honourable keeping her" (II. ii. 148–149). Helen has only such value as her defenders create—but that value is absolute.

Heroic, faithful, selfless, touching as Troilus' asseveration is, our accord with it is shortly to be subjected to considerable strain when we first meet Helen. From Euripides—perhaps even from Homer—to Giraudoux, the story of Helen's rape has captivated the literary imagination because it so neatly puts the question: Should the Trojan war, or any war, have been fought? This is the question that Shakespeare too is asking. Having set up Troilus' justification for the keeping of Helen, Shakespeare dramatically demolishes it within the same debate, even before Helen is introduced. "No marvel," Helenus remarks acidly to Troilus, "though you bite so sharp at reasons,/ You are so empty of them" (II. ii. 33–34); and Hector makes a similar charge:

> Or is your blood
> So madly hot that no discourse of reason,
> No fear of bad success in a bad cause,
> Can qualify the same?
>   (II. ii. 115–118)

Opposed to reason, after all, is will, almost synonymous in Shakespeare's English with blood. "The reasons you allege," Hector points out, "do more conduce/ To the hot passion of distemper'd blood/ Than to make up a free determination/ 'Twixt right and wrong" (II. ii. 168–171). Hector objects that in rejecting reason in evaluation Troilus is committing himself to the dangers of subjectivity. "But value dwells not in particular *will*," he argues, because the value of an object resides within the object:

> 'Tis mad idolatry
> To make the service greater than the god;
> And the will dotes that is attributive
> To what infectiously itself affects,
> Without some image of the affected merit.
> (II. ii. 56–60)

Will is the issue, then. Is Hector right in arguing that reason perceives value, or is Troilus in proposing that will projects value upon the object? Shakespeare insists that we be at least aware of the consequences of Troilus' belief, for the hero's most persuasive argument (II. ii. 61–96) is ended by the unanswerable screams of Cassandra:

> Our firebrand brother, Paris, burns us all.
> Cry, Trojans, cry! a Helen and a woe:
> Cry, cry! Troy burns, or else let Helen go.
> (II. ii. 110–112)

The compressed argumentation of II. ii, then, has spelled out a dialectic that we have already seen developed in the first council scene; even more interestingly, it has translated that dialectic from its first adumbration in the initial soliloquies of the hero and heroine of the love plot to parallel arguments about will by Ulysses and Hector in the political world of the war plot. Most interestingly of all, through a bold device Shakespeare calls attention to the symmetrically matched investigations of a single metaphysical question in the two plots. At the climax of Troilus' argument, the moment at which he must most convincingly advocate his proto-existentialist ethic, the willful hero makes an analogy between the two actions in which he is concerned:

> I take to-day a wife, and my election
> Is led on in the conduct of my will,
> My will enkindled by mine eyes and ears. . . .

As a recent editor shrewdly notices, "the analogy between Troilus' choosing a wife and the rape of Helen as an act of revenge is, of course, a very false one."[12] But—as it will take the rest of the play to show—the analogy has a point. Immediately one sees the similarity between Helen and Cressida as foci of action who by one standard are worthless, and by another infinitely valuable.

In the main plot Cressida is going to remain the focus of the question of value. In the subplot, however, the same question is going to be asked most insistently not about Helen, but about Achilles. Thus, avoiding the symmetry another dramatist might have attempted, Shakespeare creates the illusion of a universe that is not only coherent but also multitudinously rich. The kaleidoscopic fashion in which the dramatist begins to formulate the theme in his subplot in terms of one character only to complete it in terms of another is one of the marks of his genius in the play.

The next scene begins as another depressing interlude in which Achilles, Ajax, Thersites, and company revile each other (note how little of the Troilus-and-Cressida plot has been generated so far), but the scene grows more significant as Troilus' question, "What is aught but as 'tis valued?" becomes Achilles' question. The warrior has "much attribute," Agamemnon concedes to Patroclus (II. iii. 125); yet, because Achilles does not regard his own virtues virtuously, because he is "in self-assumption greater/ Than in the note of judgment" (II. iii. 133–134), because he overvalues himself, Achilles is losing the respect of his colleagues. There is a fatal disparity between the actual, inherent value of the hero and the opinion of that value which Achilles holds. "Imagin'd worth," in Ulysses' words,

> Holds in his blood such swoln and hot discourse
> That 'twixt his mental and his active parts
> Kingdom'd Achilles in commotion rages
> And batters down himself.
>   (II. iii. 182–186)

Like Hector talking of Troilus, Ulysses identifies overvaluation with blood, and the notion of will runs through his entire criticism of Achilles; even Hector's charge of idolatry ("'Tis mad idolatry/ To make the service greater than the god") finds an echo in Ulysses' "Shall he be worshipp'd/ Of that we hold an idol more than he?" (II. iii. 198–199). The question "What is Achilles?" has not yet been formulated as it will be in coming scenes; but the materials have been gathered to make it possible.

In terms of both plot and theme, the exposition of the play is now over in both actions and the development section about to begin. Each plot has presented a woman who, because of the attitudes of those about her, raises the metaphysical question of value; and each has introduced as central male character a man whose patently exaggerated evaluation—of Cressida in Troilus' case, of himself in Achilles'—has been attacked as willful, a matter of blood, by a character notably concerned with reason and its relation to social order. As the third act opens, Shakespeare leads us back to the love plot. He does so, however, in such a way as to keep alive in his audience's mind its similarity to the war plot, for the scurrilous episode between Helen and Pandarus plainly parallels the similar episode with which the preceding scene opened. Two passages (others might be cited) exemplify Shakespeare's technique:

II. iii

Ther. Agamemnon is a fool; Achilles is a fool; Thersites is a fool, and, as aforesaid, Patroclus is a fool.

Achil. Derive this; come.

Ther. Agamemnon is a fool to offer to command Achilles; Achilles is a fool to be commanded of Agamemnon; Thersites is a fool to serve such a fool, and Patroclus is a fool positive.

Patr. Why am I a fool?

Ther. Make that demand of the prover. It suffices me thou art.

(62–73)

III. i

Helen. In love, i'faith, to the very tip of the nose.

Par. He eats nothing but doves, love, and that breeds hot blood, and hot blood begets hot thoughts, and hot thoughts beget hot deeds, and hot deeds is love.

Pan. Is this the generation of love? hot blood, hot thoughts, and hot deeds? Why, they are vipers: is love a generation of vipers?

(139–146)

The alacrity of many readers to agree with Thersites that in *Troilus and Cressida* "all the argument is a cuckold and a whore" (II. iii. 78–79) is easy enough to understand when in contiguous scenes, set in the play's two worlds, reason is so symmetrically travestied.[13] But it is important to observe that the milieux of

Achilles and Ajax and of Pandarus and Helen are, though strikingly similar, only one level of a play in which moral seriousness
is almost ubiquitous: even Cressida's betrayal, it is clear, has its
philosophical basis.[14]

As the scene in which Troilus and Cressida finally get together, III. ii stands at the center of the play. Not surprisingly, it
picks up and develops the still emerging theme of the piece, once
again simultaneously exposing a number of that theme's facets,
but this time fully revealing it. In the first place, as everyone has
noticed, the sensuality of Troilus' language gives away the quality of his love; more interestingly, it affirms the accuracy of Hector's unanswered charge that Troilus is moved by will, or blood,
rather than by reason:

> I am giddy; expectation whirls me round.
> The imaginary relish is so sweet
> That it enchants my sense: what will it be,
> When that the watery palate tastes indeed
> Love's thrice repured nectar?
> (III. ii. 19–23)

But this is not all. In his fear that expectation must exceed fulfillment—"This is the monstruosity in love, lady, that the will is
infinite and the execution confin'd, that the desire is boundless
and the act a slave to limit" (III. ii. 87–90)—the lover shows himself in precise agreement with Cressida's initial reason for with-
holding herself from love: "Men prize the thing ungained more
than it is."

Again, what is the relation between the thing and the value
men place on it? Such repeated asking of the question—in relation to Achilles, his reputation, and his opinion of himself; to
Helen, her intrinsic worthlessness, and the value that has already
produced seven years of war; and now to the love of Troilus and
Cressida—makes us recognize the justice of the epithet "problem
play." As Troilus suggests a position new for him, the crucial
scene hints at the play's answer to its basic question:

> Praise us as we are tasted, allow us as we prove; our head
> shall go bare till merit crown it: no perfection in reversion

shall have a praise in present: we will not name desert before his birth, and, being born, his addition shall be humble.

(III. ii. 98–103)

With its suggestion that time will tell, Troilus' speech recalls
the words of Agamemnon and Nestor at the Greek council meeting; moreover, it picks up the organic metaphors in which first
Agamemnon, then Ulysses, and finally Nestor couched their discussions of time. In a climactic scene of the love plot Shakespeare
is beginning to draw such images together in a significant pattern.
Though its meaning does not yet become clear, the pattern
emerges dramatically in the words of Troilus. We have heard
once before, in Agamemnon's opening speech, of the winnowing
function of time. Now, hopefully, Troilus inquires as to the
probability of a fidelity in Cressida that might withstand the
decay of the blood: he wishes that his

> integrity and truth to you
> Might be affronted with the match and weight
> Of such a *winnow'd* purity in love;
> How were I then uplifted! but, alas!
> I am as true as truth's simplicity
> And simpler than the *infancy of truth*.
> (III. ii. 172–177; italics added)

The connection between Troilus and "unpractised infancy" (I.
i. 12), the establishment of Troilus as one who "with great truth
catch[es] mere simplicity" (IV. iv. 106), and the notion of
Troilus as innocent and faithful remain constants throughout
the play. But of far greater significance is the picture of truth, like
time, as an organic entity, something that has an infancy and a
maturity. We shall hear more of it.

Immediately, however, follows one of the most striking dramatic moments in the play, and here it is that the argumentation
of the play moves from dialogue into staged action as, through
the use of a dramatic irony powerfully grounded in his audience's
familiarity with the old story and the terms it has lent their language, Shakespeare allows a ritualistic tableau to act out for us
what will happen when time, now in its infancy, shall grow old:

Tro. True swains in love shall in the world to come
Approve their truths by Troilus: when their rhymes,
Full of protest, of oath and big compare,
Want similes, truth tired with iteration,
As true as steel, as plantage to the moon,
As sun to day, as turtle to her mate,
As iron to adamant, as earth to the centre,
Yet, after all comparisons of truth,
As truth's authentic author to be cited,
'As true as Troilus' shall crown up the verse,
And sanctify the numbers.
    Cres.   Prophet may you be!
If I be false, or swerve a hair from truth,
When time is old and hath forgot itself,
When waterdrops have worn the stones of Troy,
And blind oblivion swallow'd cities up,
And mighty states characterless are grated
To dusty nothing, yet let memory,
From false to false, among false maids in love,
Upbraid my falsehood! When they've said 'as false
As air, as water, wind, or sandy earth,
As fox to lamb, as wolf to heifer's calf,
Pard to the hind, or stepdame to her son,'
'Yea,' let them say, to stick the heart of falsehood,
'As false as Cressid.'
    Pan. Go to, a bargain made: seal it, seal it; I'll be
the witness. Here I hold your hand, here my cousin's.
If ever you prove false one to another, since I have taken
such pains to bring you together, let all pitiful goers-
between be called to the world's end after my name;
call them all Pandars; let all constant men be Troiluses,
all false women Cressids, and all brokers-between Pandars! say, amen.

                                     (III. ii. 180–211)

The debates in *Troilus and Cressida* may well be the most
magnificent staged argumentation since Aeschylus. But the real
measure of the play's greatness is to be taken at such moments
as this, where an argument which originates as an abstraction
from human experience is re-embodied in such experience to give
the illusion of life. Shakespeare is not telling us about time's

function in determining value: he is showing us, and what he shows us is the theme of the play. The Troilus who has seen "the infancy of truth" will live to see his Cressida betray him before his eyes, and to exclaim, "O wither'd truth" (V. ii. 46). And what will have happened in the time in which truth passes through its life-cycle will be the ironic fulfillment of each of the prophecies at the ritualistic ending of III. ii.

To suggest the nature and role of time in *Troilus and Cressida*, let me, recalling the notion of the spiderweb-like structure of the play, move forward for a moment to the beginning of IV. iii, when Paris announces that the day of Cressida's removal to the Greek camp has arrived.

> It is great morning, and the hour prefix'd
> Of her delivery to this valiant Greek
> Comes fast upon.
>
> (IV. iii. 1–3)

Steevens glossed "great morning" as "*Grand jour;* a Gallicism," and Delius noted in 1856 that the same phrase occurs in *Cymbeline*, IV. ii. 61.[15] No other explanation of the lines has ever been offered. Editors might well have referred us to another sense of "great" in *Pericles*, V. i. 107: "I am great with woe, and shall deliver weeping." In the passage in *Troilus and Cressida* as in the one in *Pericles*, "great" means "pregnant," indicating a condition that culminates in "delivery." The incessant personification of time in *Troilus and Cressida* is astonishing. Time is a monster, a witch, an arbitrator, a robber, a fashionable host; it is envious and calumniating, grows old and forgets itself, and walks hand in hand with Nestor. To recognize such a treatment of time, one need not agree with Professor G. Wilson Knight that time is the "arch-enemy," the issue on which the "love-interest turns";[16] but one must note the play's peculiar emphasis on the organic, almost personal nature of metaphysical process. The answer to Troilus' optimistic faith in the world's ability to meet his expectations of it is roundly answered by what the end of III. ii tells us: Cressida, like Troilus and Pandarus, is defined not by wishful thinking but by what each will become in time, and action which is not guided by that realization is going to come a cropper.[17]

At the center of the play, then, the theme which has been taking shape from the beginning has become full and clear. Shakespeare chooses this moment to stage the turning point in the action of the main plot, the making of the bargain which will send Cressida to the Greeks. The trade of prisoners naturally involves the war as well as the private affairs of Troilus, and so we are back in the war subplot almost immediately. Again, if the play's structure is not a matter of conscious design, one must marvel at the intuitive genius which arranges that, immediately after the climactic exposition of the theme of the relation of time to value in the main plot, that theme should be dramatized with equal emphasis and clarity in the subplot. Thematically, III. ii and III. iii, one in the main plot, the other in the subplot, are the crucial scenes of the entire play.

Ulysses' trick has worked, and the neglected Achilles is driven to investigate the cause of the derision he sees aimed at him. Merit, he sees, has little to do with reputation:

> And not a man, for being simply man,
> Hath any honour, but honour for those honours
> That are without him, as place, riches, favour,
> Prizes of accident as oft as merit:
> . . .   I do enjoy
> At ample point all that I did possess,
> Save these men's looks; who do, methinks, find out
> Something not worth in me such rich beholding
> As they have often given.
>   (III. iii. 80–83, 88–92)

Claiming like Hamlet to paraphrase the book he is reading, Ulysses offers Achilles an explanation of his predicament that Cassius had once given to Brutus in *Julius Caesar* (I. ii. 52ff.): Man "Cannot make boast to have that which he hath,/ Nor feels not what he owes, but by reflection" (III. iii. 98–100). One perceives one's own value, that is, by seeing it reflected in the opinions of others. Pretending to find the position difficult to accept, Ulysses continues its exposition: If value is subject to the judgment of others, then "no man is the lord of any thing . . . Till he communicate his parts to others" (III. iii. 115–117). Therefore, Achilles' qualities are forgotten, while those of Ajax, "a very horse," receive universal admiration. "What things again most dear in the esteem/ And poor in worth!" Ulysses exclaims (III. iii. 129–130). Having noticed that his deeds do seem to have been forgotten, Achilles cannot deny what Ulysses has been saying, and he is ready to hear his shrewd opponent's explanation of the shortness of reputation:

> Time hath, my lord, a wallet at his back,
> Wherein he puts alms for oblivion,
> A great-sized monster of ingratitudes:
> Those scraps are good deeds past, which are devour'd
> As fast as they are made, forgot as soon
> As done: perseverance, dear my lord,
> Keeps honour bright: to have done is to hang
> Quite out of fashion, like a rusty mail
> In monumental mockery.
>
> (III. iii. 145–153)

How many moments of the play crystallize here: not only what Agamemnon and Nestor have already told us about time's determination of value, but also all that we have learned in the last scene; not only Achilles' discovery that what he has done will not retain its luster but must be constantly renewed, but also Cressida's intuition of the ultimate reality of process ("Things won are done").

> O, let not virtue seek
> Remuneration for the thing it was;
> For beauty, wit,
> High birth, vigour of bone, desert in service,
> Love, friendship, charity, are subjects all
> To envious and calumniating time.
>
> (III. iii. 169–174)

Ulysses' speech is profoundly pessimistic. For if the love plot has been telling us that value resides not in the valuer (Troilus, Achilles), but in the true nature of the object (Cressida, Achilles), the war plot makes explicit what the ritual at the end of III. ii dramatized: Even the value in the object itself will be defined—generally through the process of erosion—by time. By the kind of irony that the double plot in the hands of a master makes possible, the point is dramatically reinforced. As Achilles laments the course his career has taken in time, arrangements are in the making to take Cressida away from Troilus while simultaneously the lovers are enjoying what they take to be the sealing of their love's compact. When we next see Troilus he will be unaware of his impending loss, and the irony will recur. And when Troilus discovers the grim irony of his happiness, he will respond to it in a terse remark that Achilles might as well have made to Ulysses: "How my achievements mock me!" (IV. ii. 71).[18]

His theme established, Shakespeare will vary it for the rest of the play in ways that it is not necessary, after so much analysis, to describe. A few points, however, in which the double-plot structure continues to make itself felt deserve brief notice. One is a new version of the question of merit, noteworthy because it applies—and is applied by the audience—even more vividly to a character in the main plot than to the subplot character it ostensibly describes. Paris asks Diomedes whether Menelaus or Paris himself "deserves fair Helen best." Diomedes, who as everyone in the audience knows is going to be Cressida's next lover—her Paris, as it were—answers as follows:

> Both alike:
> He merits well to have her, that doth seek her,
> Not making any scruple of her soilure,
> With such a hell of pain and world of charge,
> And you as well to keep her, that defend her,
> Not palating the taste of her dishonour,
> With such a costly loss of wealth and friends.
> He, like a puling cuckold, would drink up
> The lees and dregs of a flat tamed piece;
> You, like a lecher, out of whorish loins
> Are pleased to breed out your inheritors:
> Both merits poised, each weighs nor less nor more;
> But he as he, the heavier for a whore.
>
> (IV. i. 54–66)

The words precisely describe Cressida as the play's Thersites-voice might describe her in transit between Troilus and Diomedes. The predominant and unpleasant imagery of eating and drinking is only a version of Troilus' characteristic language in love.[19] The dregs to which Helen is reduced in masculine opinion hark back too neatly to be overlooked to an earlier prophecy:

> *Tro.* What too curious dreg espies my sweet
> lady in the fountain of our love?
> *Cres.* More dregs than water, if my fears
> have eyes.
>
> (III. ii. 70–72)

And, in the dazzling manner in which *Troilus and Cressida* works, giving the impression of a blinding flash, a single aesthetic moment, rather than of a discursive composition, Cressida's last note has already had its significant echo in Achilles' pain in the scene that follows her remark:

> My mind is troubled, like a fountain stirr'd;
> And I myself see not the bottom of it.
>
> (III. iii. 311–312)

By its last acts the play vibrates at almost every point with this sort of cross-reference. Thus IV. v, a scene crucial to both plots, is larded with variants of the theme. Let two excerpts speak for themselves. Agamemnon greets Hector:

> Understand more clear.
> What's past and what's to come is strew'd with husks
> And formless ruin of oblivion;
> But in this extant moment, faith and troth,
> Strain'd purely from all hollow bias-drawing,
> Bids thee, with most divine integrity,
> From heart of very heart, great Hector, welcome.
>
> (IV. v. 165–171)

And Hector says a few moments later:

> The end crowns all,
> And that old common arbitrator, Time,
> Will one day end it.
>
> (IV. v. 224–226)

The last two acts consist primarily of the working out of the ironic prophecies in both plots. In the war plot the decision to keep Helen eventuates not in the glory that Troilus predicted, but in her continuing degradation (recall Diomedes' opinion) and in the utterly ignoble death of Hector himself, presaging the final catastrophe Cassandra has announced. Like a vengeful deity, time has decided the debate in the Trojan camp. And in the love plot we have watched Cressida, in a ritualistic prefiguration of her future, passing lightly from the kisses of one Greek to the next. With Troilus we look on at her final act of betrayal; and we watch him arrive at a state, in which reason has become useless, that Ulysses has long since identified as the consequence of the behavior of Troilus' alter ego, Achilles:

> O madness of discourse,
> That cause sets up with and against itself!
> Bi-fold authority! where reason can revolt
> Without perdition, and loss assume all reason
> Without revolt: this is, and is not, Cressid.
> (V. ii. 142–146)

As "the dragon wing of night o'erspreads the earth" (V. viii. 17) —again time is a personal force, the monster of ingratitudes, all too eager to gobble up human achievement—Achilles has ironically regained a reputation which his Myrmidons have stolen for him, and once again, even in the rush of the denouement, we are asked to contemplate the value of reputation. Troilus' last words reveal that he has learned at last the harsh reality that a man is what time proves he is, not what the optimist wishes him to be:

> Hence, broker-lackey! ignomy and shame
> Pursue thy life, and live aye with thy name!
> (V. x. 33–34)

Perhaps it is a signal of the difference between *Troilus and Cressida* and most of Shakespeare's plays that the idealistic hero, with whom for all our awareness of his error we have been led consistently to sympathize, should utter as a last speech words that so clearly reveal the diminution of his stature. Similar reduction affects us in the last appearance of other leading characters whose careers we have followed with concern: Cressida feebly chastizing herself for a disposition to follow Diomedes that she is scarcely capable of recognizing as contemptible, Achilles wretchedly crying the triumph won in fact by his rough-neck vassals, Pandarus suddenly aged and bequeathing to the audience his venereal disease. Pandarus, whose coarse and heart-less grumbling ends the play, is a paradigm of all the play's characters. In the magical conclusion of III. i we have virtually seen etymology staged as Pandarus ironically prophesies the way in which he will become his name, and at the end we see the process complete. Regardless of their own intentions and the best potentialities within them, the major characters of the two plots have been transformed by a process over which none of them has control. That process is time, a time presented so con-sistently in organic terms that one comes finally to understand its inevitability: It grows according to its own will, not according to the desires of any individual. And that process is the play's answer to the question of value: Value exists not in the subjec-tive will of the valuer or, as the play's rationalists would have it, in the object he sees, but only in that object as time disposes of it. As in *Hamlet*, this is to say, Shakespeare has asked a meta-physical question and offered mutually exclusive answers to it, each of which we are tempted to accept and both of which we are ultimately forced to reject. But as he does not do in *Hamlet*, Shakespeare allows us to perceive a third answer which lies be-yond the terms in which the first two are posed: Value is a func-tion of time. If this is not a satisfactory answer to a legitimate philosophical question, one must admit that very few readers have suspected that it was Shakespeare's intention in *Troilus and Cressida* to satisfy their skepticism or dispel their pessimism. But the play provides another kind of satisfaction which one seeks more legitimately perhaps in the theater, the aesthetic satisfaction of recognizing a structure brilliantly animated and made coherent by its complex relation to a thematic center.

⋘ III ⋙

But what is that "thematic center"? In discussing *Troilus and Cressida* I have tried as much as possible to let the play

speak in its own explicit terms; to avoid special pleading or dis-
tortion I have not talked about complementarity. But looking back
at what we have seen, we may find it impossible to avoid the
notion any longer. If I began with the record of confusion the
play has caused, I must finish by pointing out what by now is
clear: That confusion is the result of Shakespeare's strategy. For
what we have at the end of our experience of the play is not a
thematic bromide about the omnipotence of time, but an unresolvable complex in which the undeniable truth about time's
effect on value walks the stage of our memories in the company
of other actors equally demanding of our attention and our belief, and in effect contradictory to what we have seen prove true.
The play does not deny Troilus' asseverations of faith even
though it proves them foolish; that is, it does not allow us not
to admire Troilus for a position that is in some respects more
heroic than any other position taken in the play. It does not deny
the rationalism of Hector and Ulysses; they, too, we must admit,
make convincing arguments, though Hector's refusal to acknowledge the claims of passion and Ulysses' inability to transcend a
career of petty trickery except in his rhetoric make their program
unrealistic even for themselves. Even Achilles' concern for glory,
essentially as we have seen a parody of Troilus' hopes for Cressida, cannot be erased from the consciousness the play leaves us
of what is finally valuable, and our concern with reputation is if
anything intensified by our mortification at Achilles' failure at the
end to live up to his own. Whatever the intellectual judgment
the play brings us to, we have no choice but to recognize the
complementarity of the values it would seem by the end to have
demolished.

We find ourselves thus in an odd predicament when we
discuss this play—or any play by Shakespeare, or perhaps any
work of literary art. The by now unrevolutionary kind of analysis
I have made of *Troilus and Cressida* tells us in a number of ways
that the play is organized and made coherent by a theme.[20] I
have suggested that the theme is the idea that a time which has
its own purposes indifferent to ours determines the meaning and
value of events without regard to our hopes or fears or even our
actions. Doubtless the theme could be stated more precisely and

authoritatively, but that is not the issue as long as we agree that the play lends itself to thematic analysis of this sort. The predicament to which I have referred is that, because of the complementary nature of the play, the theme is not identical with that total communication which we call the meaning of the piece. The meaning is more an area of turbulence than a sententious moral; it is a complex question about the nature of value and an interrelated group of incompatible answers.

Now is it not nonsense to expend so much effort on the analysis of a play and to come up with the demonstration of a theme which we then say is not what the play is all about? I believe that the answer is no, and for a very simple reason. The present generation of critics, and several generations to come, I venture to say, are deeply indebted to the movement we call the New Criticism. Our chief debt is what we have learned about the means of discovering the theme, the principle of coherence, in a literary work: the techniques of the New Critics have made possible a kind of rational investigation into the ways in which poetry conveys meaning that earlier generations simply could not formulate. But in the process of their revolution, the New Critics generally tended to stop short in their analysis. Despite their warnings about the "heresy of paraphrase," such critics as Cleanth Brooks and L. C. Knights tend often to leave us with the sense that the themes they have brilliantly exposed are identical with, or are the summary of, the works under analysis, and this is particularly ironic because these critics have been especially concerned to avoid precisely such simplifications.

The theme of a play or a poem is not its meaning because a play or a poem says what cannot be said discursively. *Troilus and Cressida*, like *Hamlet*, and like every play by Shakespeare, refuses to satisfy us with a simplistic statement about experience. Rather, it makes clear to us the ways in which an aspect of experience is problematic, and makes it impossible for us to resolve the problem. In *Troilus and Cressida* the meaning centers about the problems time creates for value and moral action; in *Hamlet* it centers about the tragic predicament of reasonableness in a world that may be based on realities that undercut that ideal. Each play, that is, is a world, or rather a subjective vision of an objective world. Each world lures us into a sense of its reality by all the devices of literary illusion. One of the chief devices is the way in which everything in a particular dramatic world must be considered in certain terms: the question of value is ubiquitous in *Troilus and Cressida,* the question of passion in *Hamlet;* and this is part of what we mean when we speak of the unity of a play. We demand such artifice in a play for the simple reason that we see the objective world in the same way, focused through a subjective vision and projected onto a subjective consciousness. Our minds tell us that the world is manifold, perhaps chaotic, but we can never escape from the unitary impression formed by our subjectivity; and the work of art, subjectivity incarnate, pleases and instructs by imitating that impression.

If this is so, then the role played by the theme is apparent. In the objective world we view we have a unitary impression of a manifold reality; inevitably rationalizing our sense of unity, we constantly attempt to reduce experience to formulated law, to understand the order we feel intuitively in verbal terms. We believe that the world makes sense and we try to express that sense; yet we also know that the world consistently eludes the sense to which we reduce it. "In each case," Niels Bohr says, describing the nature of complementary accounts of the same reality, "we are concerned with expedients which enable us to express in a consistent manner essential aspects of the phenemena."[21] We live with moral truths—expedients—and with the complex experience that led us to them. So it is in the literary work: the theme, the principle of coherence which seems upon analytic reflection to underlie the bewildering experience we confront, emerges as one strand, perhaps dominant, in the tapestry of the whole; "only the totality of the phenomena exhausts the possible information about the objects" on which we experiment.[22] Like the physicist who confronts a reality so much more complex than his ability to account for it from a single point of view that only complementary descriptions can do it full justice, yet who must make the descriptions demanded by particular experimental conditions, so the audience of such an artist as Shakespeare participates in an imitated nature which cannot be reduced to a single "theme" but must be understood in terms of "the totality of the phenomena." And analyzing the works which thus imitate nature, the critic finds himself in a position much like that of the speculative physicist. In Bohr's words once again:

> We are here at a point where the question of unity of knowledge evidently contains ambiguity, like the word "truth" itself. Indeed, with respect to spiritual and cultural values we are also reminded of epistemological problems related to the proper balance between our desire for an all-embracing way of looking at life in its multifarious aspects and our power of expressing ourselves in a logically consistent manner.[23]

◄§ IV §►

> If there be rule in unity itself,
> This is not she. O madness of discourse,
> That cause sets up with and against itself!
> Bi-fold authority! where reason can revolt
> Without perdition, and loss assume all reason
> Without revolt: this is, and is not, Cressid.
> (V. ii. 141–146)

Extrapolating from his subjective understanding of the unity of experience, Troilus has misjudged the nature of objective reality. No matter how much more we like his youthful intensity than we do any other moral quality we have seen in the play, no matter how much his brave willfulness lingers in our minds as tragically admirable, we have no doubt that he is wrong. The plot, framework of the play's illusory reality, proves his mistake in believing that his fidelity alone is sufficient to make Cressida what he wants her to be. For better or for worse, faith and will, commitment and passion, the principles on which Troilus' acts are aspects of one psychological complex in the world of the play, and that complex fails because it is opposed to reason. The final acknowledgment of that failure is Troilus' helpless contemplation of the split reality to which his mistake has bound him: "This is, and is not, Cressid."

Now Troilus is not the only character in Shakespeare who finds himself in such a predicament. Similarly confronting the discrepancy between what he has believed and wanted to be true about the woman he loves and what she seems actually to be, Othello too finds his reason yielding to an insupportable sense of a split reality:

> By the world,
> I think my wife be honest and think she is not;
> I think that thou art just and think thou art not.
> (*Othello*, III. iii. 383–385)

In all of Shakespeare's work there is perhaps no clearer demonstration of the complementary nature of his vision than these two plays taken together. Their situations are remarkably similar; moreover, as we shall see, the questions they raise are virtually identical. In the hands of an artist more, in Isaiah Berlin's phrase, a hedgehog than a fox, more committed to a single reading of reality, more convinced of the "rule in unity," the two plays would doubtless constitute proofs of one thesis. In Shakespeare, however, they are resolutely opposed in theme. Though the world is problematic in the same way in both, the thematic resolutions offered are mutually incompatible. This is not because Shakespeare "matured" between 1601 and 1604, or because he changed his mind, for examination of other works composed in the same years will show no such direct progress; rather, it is because he remained faithful not to a conclusion, but to a complementary vision true to the inner logic of each situation with which he deals.

Like *Troilus and Cressida*, *Othello* has been attacked for what is most obvious in it. It is a useful principle, as the critical history of *Hamlet* should have taught us, that the most troublesome large questions provoked by a Shakespeare play generally point to the heart of the play, to what is most certainly its intention. The most telling attack on *Othello*, renewed often from Thomas Rymer in the seventeenth century to Bernard Shaw in our own, decries the play for its melodrama, for its hinging on such a device—appropriate to the "bloody farce" Rymer describes and the Italian opera that Shaw sees in *Othello*—as a handkerchief, and for putting at its climax a crime motivated by unbelievable evidence.[24] It would be foolish to deny that the plot depends singularly on coincidences such as Cassio's innocent interview with Bianca, which Iago can turn so neatly to his own purposes without being discovered, and Emilia's failure to put two and two together. A related attack, anticipated by Rymer, is on the time scheme of the play, which later initiated the theory of "double time" in Shakespeare:[25] Iago depends for the plausibility of his story on a time lapse of months when only days have gone by, and the turn in Othello's attitude occurs in a horrifying rush which some critics find difficult to accept in a hero. These matters of plot are of course related to the character of the protagonist, and significantly Rymer and Shaw save their loudest salvos for the Moor himself, a character the former finds fit only for comedy and the latter incapable of talking sense. What troubles Othello's critics most, I think it fair to say, is the speed, the infuriating single-mindedness, with which he throws his pearl away. What kind of tragedy is this, whose plot is based on the devices of bedroom comedy and whose hero is so quickly destroyed by his fatal flaw?[26]

Let us once again begin by confronting these problems head on. From the earliest stories we heard as children we know that plots built on coincidence tell us something very specific about the world in which their action occurs, and our experience with Shakespeare repeats our earlier discovery. Coincidence in a Shakespeare play conveys a strong sense of inevitability—comic providence in *The Comedy of Errors* and *The Tempest*, for example; tragic destiny in *Hamlet*. Similarly the coincidences in *Othello* should lead us neither to an embarrassed conclusion that Shakespeare is a naïve dramatist nor to Rymer's assumption that the poet's ingenuity manipulates a chaotic reality for the sake of symmetry and surprise, but rather to the conviction of a significant shape in events, of an inner logic which makes such a word as "coincidence" virtually irrelevant. That *Othello*—unlike *Antony and Cleopatra* and *King Lear*, like *Macbeth* and *Romeo and Juliet* and *Hamlet*—is a tragedy of destiny is made abundantly clear by the constant dramatic irony which tells us from the beginning that the worst potentialities in events are going to be fully revealed.[27] Thus we hear in the first scene Brabantio's threatening dream (143), and in the third repeatedly ironic speeches in which Othello and others hint at the tragedy shortly to unfold. Nowhere outside the opening scene of *Macbeth* does Shakespeare so clearly involve his audience through dramatic irony in an awareness of impending and inevitable catastrophe as he does here:

> *Brab.* Look to her, Moor, if thou hast eyes to see:
> She has deceived her father, and may thee.
> *Oth.* My life upon her faith!
>
> (I. iii. 293–295)

The first act ends with a threat by Iago—"Hell and night/ Must bring this monstrous birth to the world's light"—that puts us in the universe of *Troilus and Cressida*, in which a time described in organic terms moves at its own pace to determine events over which the actors themselves do not have final control. One more instance, multiply ironic, will serve to exemplify Shakespeare's technique. It is Cassio's innocent and joyous outburst at the news that the ship which bears both Iago and Desdemona to Cyprus has been almost miraculously preserved in the storm, as if to preserve Desdemona for a blessed life:

> Has had most favourable and happy speed:
> Tempests themselves, high seas and howling winds,
> The gutter'd rocks and congregated sands,—
> Traitors ensteep'd to clog the guiltless keel,—
> As having sense of beauty, do omit
> Their mortal natures, letting go safely by
> The divine Desdemona.
>
> (II. i. 67–73)

In the context of tragedy such statements are signals of a controlling destiny, and viewed in the light of that destiny the handkerchief is awesome rather than comic.

But to have said that a fictional world is thus controlled is only to have begun. *Oedipus Rex* and *Tom Jones* depend alike on the use of coincidence to suggest destiny, but Sophocles' nemesis is very different from Fielding's providence, which is in turn a much more benevolent force than that to which Hamlet sadly resigns himself. What can we say about the universe of *Othello*?

First of all we must note, as many critics have done, that of all
Shakespeare's tragedies it is the least concerned with the evocation
of a cosmic universe, depending precariously on the microcosm
of domestic tragedy in a way that reminds some of *A Woman
Killed with Kindness* more than it does of *Macbeth. Othello*, that
is, does not provoke us to the metaphysical speculation that *Hamlet* does; it does not ask us to determine the conditions of the
world in which its characters play out their fates. It is, as Hazlitt
perceived,[28] essentially a tragedy of character. The fatality in the
play's universe is the fatality of character itself. In *Othello* more
exclusively perhaps than anywhere else except *Coriolanus*, Shakespeare seems to be dramatizing the notion that character is destiny. It is worth remarking that critics who find themselves
dissatisfied with the plot of *Othello* find themselves equally ill
at ease with its characters. To understand this play we must understand its characters.

And thus we are back at the largest question: Why must
Othello collapse so easily under Iago's temptation? With characteristic insight and industry Professor Heilman summarizes traditional critical solutions of the problem and advances a useful
thesis of his own:

> According to one view, the problem is insoluble: Othello
> believes Iago only "by virtue of the convention of the calum-
> niator credited." Among the analysts of character, the older
> tradition is that Othello is the victim of Iago and remains
> pretty much the "noble Moor" throughout; he is guilty only
> of being too innocent or foolish or simple or trusting or of
> losing his usual self-control. According to the other main
> approach through character, Othello is not the "noble Moor"
> at all but has serious defects of character which cause his
> downfall—defects such as habitual flight from reality and
> as pride.[29]

Noting that he began his own study holding the orthodox, Brad-
leyan "view of Othello's 'nobility,'" Professor Heilman reports
that his work on the play led him to a new view, which sees the
hero's virtues coexisting with his defects from the very start, and
he suggests a complementary approach to Othello's character:

> There is something in Othello's own rhetoric, I suspect,
> which can simultaneously support conflicting impressions
> of his personality. The sweep, the color, the resonance, the
> spontaneity, the frequent exoticism of the images—all this
> magniloquence suggests largeness and freedom of spirit, and
> it is at first easy to forget that self-deception, limitedness of
> feeling, and egotism may also inhabit this verbal expan-
> siveness.[30]

Wisely choosing to avoid schematism in his reading, Heilman
analyzes Othello in pluralistic terms. His searching analysis should
be read by all students of the play, and I do not pretend to anything like the exhaustive analysis of *Magic in the Web*. On
the other hand, as often in Shakespeare, the characterization of
Othello, while being complex enough to justify the kind of analysis Professor Heilman performs, is in its largest features simple
enough to demand a more schematic reading. Though many
qualities exist side by side in *Othello*, a single principle underlies
Shakespeare's conception of the character, and I should like to
suggest the principle.

The central and fatal fact of Othello's life is his love for
Desdemona; to understand him we must understand the love
that defines and destroys him, and the play gives us ample opportunity to do so. Though the psychology of love is essentially
constant in Shakespeare, he emphasizes a different aspect of love
in each play in which it figures importantly. In *Troilus and
Cressida*, as we have seen, he focuses on its willful sensuality;
in *Twelfth Night* we are made most aware of its comic madness
and its mad rightness; in *Antony and Cleopatra*, its transcendence
and its escapism; in *A Midsummer Night's Dream*, its kinship
with poetic imagination; in *Romeo and Juliet*, the poignance and
totality of its commitment. Now all these qualities coexist in
every treatment of love in Shakespeare, and, particularly in their
opposition to reasons, they are closely related to one another. Each
one of them is simply an abstraction brought about by a dramatic
presentation which suggests them all but stresses that one which
most enables us to understand the universe of the play and the
particular nature of the characters' predicaments. Every quality
of love I have named is present in Othello's love. But Shakespeare

so combines them and sets them in such a context that the configuration takes the shape of one variety of love in particular: the
faith of the religious man. As Helen Gardner observes in a rich
and suggestive study, "the tragic experience with which this play
is concerned is the loss of faith."[31] To understand Othello and
his love is to understand both the psychology and the existential
predicament of the Christian.

This is to say not that Shakespeare is concerned in *Othello*
with the historical situation of Christianity or with the sociology
of faith, but rather that he focuses his play on the problems implicit in belief and fidelity, and in so doing carries to its fullest
development a concern he has manifested already in *Hamlet*
and *Troilus and Cressida* and *King Lear*. Nowhere else in Shakespeare are we led to think more explicitly in Christian terms. Of
all the tragic heroes Othello is the most emphatically Christian.
He is a soldier in the wars against the Turks, as we are reminded
even in his last speech. His language is rich with allusion to
Christian eschatology. He sees his life not as the wandering of
Lear in the dark or the flight of Antony in pursuit of immortal
and fleshly longings or the leap of Macbeth's vaulting ambition,
but simply as a "pilgrimage" (I. iii. 153).[32] These are merely
signals. What really matters is not the fact that Othello is a
devoted Christian, but the fact that his love for Desdemona is
a version of Christian faith.

Like all Shakespearean love, Othello's is fundamentally irrational. To Lodovico, as the hero begins to crack, it may seem
that he has been the perfect stoic, governed always by reason:

> Is this the noble Moor whom our full senate
> Call all in all sufficient? Is this the nature
> Whom passion could not shake? whose solid virtue
> The shot of accident, nor dart of chance,
> Could neither graze nor pierce?
>
> (IV. i. 275–279)

But he has not, or should not have, seemed so. The armor in
which his virtue is dressed when first we see him is never the
dispassionate contemplation of the stoic, but rather the serene
self-confidence of a man secure in his commitment:

Let him do his spite;
My services which I have done the signiory
Shall out-tongue his complaints.
(I. ii. 17–19)

Not I; I must be found:
My parts, my title and my perfect soul
Shall manifest me rightly.
(I. ii. 30–32)

Keep up your bright swords, for the dew will rust them.
(I. ii. 59)

Vouch with me, heaven, I therefore beg it not,
To please the palate of my appetite,
Nor to comply with heat—the young affects
In me defunct—and proper satisfaction,
But to be free and bounteous to her mind:
And heaven defend your good souls, that you think
I will your serious and great business scant
For she is with me.
(I. ii. 262–269)

My life upon her faith.
(I. i. 295)

As in A *Midsummer Night's Dream*, the first presentation of the love that is to comprise the play's action is through the eyes of a heavy father, and Brabantio like Egeus sees his daughter's passion as the product of "witchcraft." In *Othello* as in A *Midsummer Night's Dream* the sorcery that makes lovers love is ironic for a multitude of reason. Actual sorcery turns out to be unnecessary; the mysterious processes that control the lovers make their love seem more valuable than the unsympathetic reason which opposes it, especially since we are given rational grounds to approve it; but we are also made to realize, when rational men can understand love only in terms of witchcraft, that the causes of love are entirely subjective and unreasoning. The rational Rymer has only contempt for Othello's account of the wooing that won Desdemona. His response is wrong, but as is often the case with readers who

respond strongly to moments in Shakespeare, it is occasioned
by something that ought to be noticed:

> She thank'd me [for my stories],
> And bade me, if I had a friend that loved her,
> I should but teach him how to tell my story,
> And that would woo her. Upon this hint I spake:
> She loved me for the dangers I had pass'd,
> And I loved her that she did pity them.
> This only is the witchcraft I have used.
>   (I. iii. 163–169)

Much of Othello's behavior as the play progresses is to constitute
a search for "the cause"—of what he hardly knows; but Shakespeare wants us to understand that his love and Desdemona's,
like Romeo's and Juliet's, Demetrius' and Helen's, Ferdinand's and
Miranda's, has, in a rational sense, no cause. Hence the language
of witchcraft, magic, drugs, drams, charms, minerals, enchantment, conjuration, and arts inhibited recurs throughout the entire
exposition of the romance in the first act. It tells us that the central
commitment of Othello's life is mediated through his passions.

In this aspect Othello's love is no different from that of
another Shakespearean lover, but certain qualities in its configuration constantly make us think of the love of this Christian
soldier in terms of faith. One of them is its alliance in his own
mind with all that he takes to be virtuous. Hence his blandly
ironic assurance to the Duke of Venice that his "disports" will
never "corrupt and taint my business" (I. ii. 272): Desdemona
is at one in Othello's mind with the "serious and great business"
of fighting the enemies of Christendom; she is the center of the
universe in which he lives. Now again this is true of other lovers in Shakespeare, but with a difference. Adonis knows that to
commit himself to Venus is to abandon all that he holds valuable.
Romeo embarks on a marriage forbidden by both his familial and
his legal situation, and must throw away the world and soon his
life to have Juliet. Antony must find out new heaven, new earth
to measure his life because the world he builds around it is
tragically opposed to the political world in which he lives. But
Othello begins with a marriage, and in that marriage its hero

finds the solid center not only of the worldly structure in which he lives—his home, unlike Antony's, becomes the seat from which he rules his state—but also of all his belief in the benevolent political and cosmic order of which he sees himself the servant. Nothing could state the meaning of his commitment more economically than his serene and ironic public announcement, "My life upon her faith." When he ceases to believe in Desdemona, "chaos is come again" (III. iii. 92).

As there are kinds of love, so there are kinds of faith. Dante's faith in Beatrice, so much a figure for his faith in God that in the Earthly Paradise Beatrice and Christ are virtually merged, transcends reason as Othello's does, yet is supported by a rational substructure that would make Dante immune to Othello's predicament. But Shakespeare is dealing with what might have seemed to some of his contemporaries a purer type of faith, a fideism in which reason plays no part. Othello is the least analytic of Shakespearean tragic heroes. In his unquestioning and swift allegiance to what he believes, in the lack of division between belief and act, he manifests a quality which one sees only in the saint or the fool. The speed and fullness with which he alters his beliefs to fit his situation once Iago has entered it indicate a character which can exist only in terms of total commitment. Other men may pause to distinguish between what seems and what is; for Othello the analytic mode scarcely exists until, to his loss, he is trapped into it. Appearance and reality are one: "My parts, my title and my perfect soul/Shall manifest me rightly" (I. ii. 31–32); outer and inner are identical. Desdemona's faith is of a different order, more finely perceiving because more tainted by reason; she does not balk at the Moor's color, because "I saw Othello's visage in his mind" (I. iii. 253). But Othello's sense of Desdemona is characterized by a radical simplicity; the alabaster of her body incarnates the purity of her soul. In such a vision there is no place for reason or for the dialectic that doubt might create. Either Othello loves, giving himself totally, or he does not. There is no middle alternative: "No; to be once in doubt/ Is once to be resolved" (III. iii. 179–180).

For the singleness of purpose and meaning that his love can

give him, Othello has traded all the mobility he had before the play began:

> But that I love the gentle Desdemona,
> I would not my unhoused free condition
> Put into circumscription and confine
> For the sea's worth.
>
> (I. ii. 25–28)

In a play in which the sea is the constant standard of the spaciousness of the world and the word "free" a dominant motif, such a passage suggests the degree to which Othello allows the moment of his falling in love with Desdemona and the fact of his marriage to her to become the defining fact of his life. Paradoxically, in his commitment he finds a new freedom, the freedom to live confidently among men not of his race, to govern majestically, to give himself fully to the most fulfilling of experiences. The paradox of freedom—and the word "free" is repeatedly applied to Othello—through total commitment of the self is, of course, one of the most familiar Christian paradoxes. But Othello's freedom is short-lived. While Desdemona keeps her faith until the end, praying in the last moments of her life, Othello betrays his in a ritual in which he announces the birth of a new religion as he kneels with Iago and pledges murder, and his own end is the suicide of a man in despair. The logic of his fate becomes apparent as soon as we contemplate the rest of the play.

Othello's characterization is narrower than is generally the case in Shakespeare. He is what he is by virtue of what he is not. And what he is not, what he excludes from himself, rises quickly to the surface in the person of Iago. Whatever formulations we make about it, each reader senses the intimacy of the relationship between these mighty opposites, the degree to which they form halves of a personality that neither possesses in full. The unusually schematic nature of *Othello* has been explained in part by Bernard Spivack's fine study, which demonstrates that Shakespeare gave to the play's original audience the unmistakable sense that they were watching a version of the morality play, a moribund but still active influence on dramatists of Shakespeare's generation.[33]

In such a play one expects a radical separation between good and evil, and in particular the symbolic embodiment of evil in that fascinating creature of long tradition, the Vice. Spivack has shown us how carefully Shakespeare has drawn Iago to create the impression that, whatever else he is, he is a perfectly traditional Vice in manner and function.

Now we learn a good deal about the world of *Othello* by seeing it in terms of the morality play. We can understand, for example, why it is natural in a play of this kind that a good hero can be attracted by an evil tempter whose perfidy does not fool us for a moment; we can understand why the play makes the distinction between angelic good and diabolic wickedness so schematically clear, yet so tragically difficult for the protagonist to perceive. But this is not enough, for Shakespeare never uses a major convention without making it his own, exploring its implications and using it for the purpose of something new. In a play whose characterization and texture are much more complex than what one ordinarily finds in the morality play, Shakespeare is obviously using the schematism provided by the morality convention for more interesting ends than the simple moral which the origin of the convention might suggest, and which in fact the play suggests to the contemptuous Rymer:

> First, This may be a caution to all Maidens of Quality how, without their Parents consent, they run away with Blackamoors.
> Secondly, This may be a warning to all good Wives, that they look well to their Linnen.
> Thirdly, This may be a lesson to Husbands, that before their Jealousie be Tragical, the proofs may be Mathematical.[34]

What Shakespeare has done to disqualify such criticism lies in the meanings he has built into the polarized characterizations given to him by the morality scheme. It is not merely that Othello is the good man torn between good as represented by Desdemona and evil as represented by Iago, for the particular form of Othello's evil is the loss of the particular form of his good, his faith in his wife; and Iago's evil must be understood therefore as what makes Othello lose his faith.

What is the principle that Shakespeare opposes to Othello's faith? We must notice immediately that in several respects Iago is not unattractive, and one of them is especially disturbing: he often speaks the truth. Like Polonius, he is the source of some of the most proverbial wisdom in Shakespeare. There are several reasons for this. In the first place, the convention of the moralities makes the Vice an engaging fellow (if he were not, he would not to be effective) and makes him honest with the audience; Iago does not lie to us about what he is up to. Second, we see in the device of an evil character making very good sense about the absolute value of reputation, for instance, another demonstration that Shakespeare does not think that a special few have a corner on wisdom; Nestor and Polonius, Claudius and Edmund are capable of telling us things we ought to know in ways that make it impossible to forget them. It is perhaps the most familiar mark of Shakespeare's complementary sensibility that he recognizes how from any subjective position there is a kind of truth; each man's world makes sense to him, and all his intelligence serves what he is— even if he is a scoundrel. Third, for the meaning of the play the most important fact: *Othello* is a tragedy in which though we have no question about moral good and moral evil, the principles represented by the main figures are not simply good or evil in themselves as they would be in a morality play. Othello's fate is proof itself that his kind of faith has its defects as well as its virtues, and Iago's frequently convincing speeches suggest that the principle espoused by his evil nature is of itself no more absolute in a moral sense than his victim's faith.

That principle is the recurrent polar opposite to love in every play in which Shakespeare is centrally concerned with it: reason. Now it is quite clear that the kind of reason Iago uses does not have the discipline or the responsibility to its own methods that we find in the thought of a Christian rationalist like Thomas Aquinas or Hooker, and therefore that Terence Hawkes, whose reading of *Othello* resembles mine in some crucial respects, is justified in calling it a "lower" reason.[35] On the other hand it may appear to the audience more like what we ordinarily think of as reason than the theologian's rational method, which assumes its conclusions and holds itself always responsible to a suprarational authority. The paradox of freedom in *Othello* contributes to this sense of Iago: If on the one hand Othello is most free in his commitment to unquestioning faith and loses his freedom in allowing himself to listen to Iago—"I am bound to thee forever" (III. iii. 213) is his response to the ensign's false information— Iago on the other, who loses his freedom because of his commitment to the particular goal of destroying Othello, is most free in the unhampered play of rational process in which he indulges throughout the main part of the action. "Low" though his reason certainly is, Iago uses both syllogistic, deductive processes and empirical, inductive "proofs" of his hypotheses at every. moment. I have already alluded to his famous rationale for the importance of reputation, "Who steals my purse steals trash" (III. iii. 157); it is not accidental that, with equal reason, he attacks reputation and things of the spirit from the materialist's viewpoint, or that the Iago who argues to Othello, "Who steals my purse steals trash" should insist to Roderigo, "Put money in thy purse" (I. iii. 345). In a fine study of *Othello* Albert Gerard reads Iago as a consistent materialist, but in order to do so he must claim a more persistent interest in "selfish practical achievement" than most critics can find.[36] Iago's real consistency is his ability to begin with any premise—Cassio's affection for Desdemona, his own self-interest, the value of money, the role of reason itself (I. iii. 322–337)—and brilliantly reach a reasoned conclusion. Like other evil characters who pride themselves on their rationality— Edmund, Goneril, Richard III—Iago is driven by murky impulses that have nothing to do with reason. But the form that his diabolism takes, both in maliciously bringing others down and in explaining himself to himself, is intellectual process separated from belief and from instinctive virtue.[37]

As in *Hamlet* and *Troilus and Cressida*, the background of the tragic action in *Othello* is thus a war between values, but uniquely in *Othello* Shakespeare has chosen to embody those values in opposed characters whose interaction destroys them both. What happens to Othello is most instructive in Shakespeare's understanding of faith. Trapped by Iago's apparent reasonableness, which presents all the "ocular proof" that Othello needs to shatter the unexamined image of Desdemona he has lived with, and by all the verbal tricks which the subtle mind can impose on the simple, Othello plunges almost directly from his total belief in Desdemona to a new belief just as total that she is false. The journey is a passionate plunge; the Moor who could not dote yet doubt demands such proof as will have "no hinge nor loop/ To hang a doubt on" (III. iii. 365–366), and precisely like Hamlet in his least rational and most committed moments, vows to have none but "bloody thoughts" (III. iii. 457) until he accomplishes his revenge. He watches with horror as his passion begins to control him:

> Now, by heaven,
> My blood begins my safer guides to rule;
> And passion, having my best judgment collied,
> Assays to lead the way.
>
> (II. iii. 204–207)

We watch with equal horror, but with more understanding, as he disintegrates. What we are able to see, and what may in the long run disturb us most, is that this sudden and radical submission to passion is not a change in Othello's character, but rather the emergence of what has been its fundamental quality from the start. I have already cited the irony of Lodovico's comment on the earlier, apparently stoical and therefore dispassionate Othello, and we have seen that irrationality is the essence of his nature. What happens to him is different from what happens to Hamlet in the months during which he must change his nature to accomplish his assignment, and Shakespeare underlines the fact by emphasizing the short time in which the action transpires. As Arthur McGee has argued, Shakespeare

> was undoubtedly careless of time except when it was important dramatically, but in presenting *Othello* . . . he was just as careful to have Desdemona murdered on the second night in Cyprus as he was to ensure that his Caesar was murdered on the Ides of March.[38]

In this remarkably short time we see not a change in character, but rather the full and painful revealing of the implications of a character already fully formed but heretofore not fully tested in the world.[39] Mr. McGee may be right in arguing that Iago's calumny about Desdemona and Cassio refers to the time of spousal rather than of marriage in Cyprus, but the other arguments that Othello allows Iago to convey to him are scarcely more plausible than the charge of months of adultery during one night of marriage. It is the completeness of his submission to passion, not the rational attractiveness of what Iago has to say, that drives Othello to believe that his wife has given the handkerchief to Cassio and that Cassio's assignation with Bianca is proof of the affair with Desdemona. We watch the entire play in little as Othello refuses to answer Emilia's knock at the door and thus to accept the argument that would destroy his resolve to kill Desdemona. Like the passionate atheism of a former zealot, Othello's murder of Desdemona is of a piece with his former reverence for her; it is the fruit of a relationship which is at all times completely inaccessible to reason.

One can hardly quarrel with Rymer's wry suggestion that before killing one's wife one must be sure that the proofs of her guilt are "Mathematical." On the other hand, given Iago's alarming skill in marshalling convincing pseudo-evidence, Othello seems to have but little choice.[40] His mistake is not merely in crediting the kind of evidence and reasoning that he does, but more fundamentally in exposing a love based on faith to tests irrelevant to faith; not in allowing false reason to weaken his trust in his wife, but in conceding even for a moment that his love has more to do with "facts" and proof and with any kind of reason than with his intuitive sense of Desdemona. Iago himself ironically voices this idea when, in an unmistakable allusion to the Pauline definition of faith as "the substance of things hoped for, the evidence of things not seen," he reminds the Moor that Desdemona's "honour is an essence that's not seen" (IV. i. 16). It is Othello's tragedy that he tries to validate his faith.

As many critics have said, and some of them not very sympathetically, Othello is not very intelligent. But surely Shakespeare arouses our greatest sympathies for Othello, and equally surely he is not merely trying to tell us that the Moor should have been smarter. Rather, that weakness, that extraordinary irrationality, is Othello's most admirable strength. The paradox of the tragedy is that the faith which makes Othello great makes him helpless as well, and that that faith is superior to what subverts it. We find ourselves rejecting not the faith that Othello abandons, but the mental process that enables him to do so.

The argument implicit in *Othello* is a compelling one. We can easily imagine it as the enduring ideology of another poet. But we need only look back once more at *Troilus and Cressida* to realize that *Othello* is not Shakespeare's whole view, *for Troilus fails precisely because he does what Othello fails by not doing*: He allows the faith of the lover to weigh more than the measurable worth of the beloved. Othello fails because he credits appearances, Troilus because he refuses to do so; and in each case the relation between appearance and reality is so tortuous, at least for the protagonist, that the right choice is almost impossible to make. By looking simultaneously at these two plays in which reason is pitted against the irrational drives of the man in love, and by recognizing how brilliantly the plays oppose each other in theme while presenting worlds dichotomized in precisely the same way, we may achieve a startling and disquieting sense of Shakespeare's perennial complementarity.

᪥ V ᪥

Because Shakespeare sees man in the terms his culture affords him, we should not be surprised that he conceives character consistently in ways that must be explained in terms of such traditional categories as reason and will. But the truest constant in the plays is the complementary view of human personality. Ben Jonson is equally concerned with the rational and irrational in character, but invariably criticizes behavior from a single point of view, that of the man who can praise only the freedom from psychological disorder, vice, and social affectation that reason makes possible. Shakespeare has no single answer of this sort. Recognizing that human problems arise from a nature which he sees with considerable continuity of vision, he would have us understand that the cause of these problems is not in the violation of a single most laudable element of personality, but rather in the complexity of an unstable configuration each of whose several aspects has its own validity in different situations. In the two plays we have been discussing, reason has radically different parts to play. It is appropriate for Troilus, inappropriate for Othello; a faith that denies the need for empirical demonstration and logical proof is what makes Othello great and would save him if he could maintain it, while it makes Troilus foolish and destroys him. In *A Midsummer Night's Dream* Shakespeare opposes reason to the folly of lovers whose choices are often magically induced and always willful, only to make us realize that those choices are ultimately right and of the same order as that anti-rational illusion-mongering, the performing and watching of plays, which, depending on the charitable suspension of disbelief and the product of the charlatanry which can make the moon shine indoors, nevertheless tells us truths of which reason is incapable. Nowhere does Shakespeare ask us to ponder the nature of the self and of its role in the world without in some way raising the question of the place of reason in that self, and we shall find ourselves reverting to the question very shortly as it intrudes on other considerations. But the cultural ideal of reasonableness is never a fixed ideal in Shakespeare's vision; rather it is always a dynamic term in the dialectic of his dramaturgy.

NOTES

1. Jerome H. Buckley, *Tennyson: The Growth of a Poet* (Cambridge, Mass., 1960), p. 193.

2. S. L. Bethell, *Shakespeare and Dramatic Tradition* (London, 1944), pp. 98–105. Professor Bethell's commitment to Eliot's dramatic practice leads him to regard what sounds like a vice in my paraphrase as a special virtue. The fact that he happens to be attracted to a drama that demands "dual consciousness" on the part of an audience attending to a story and a "philosophy" that work in opposite directions is not the issue with which I am concerned here, though it is challenging. The point is rather that Professor Bethell sees a conflict between the play and its theme.

3. Robert Kimbrough, "The *Troilus* Log: Shakespeare and 'Box Office'," *SQ*, XV (1964), 205–206. Professor Kimbrough elaborates his argument in *Shakespeare's Troilus and Cressida and Its Setting* (Cambridge, Mass., 1964).

4. Una Ellis-Fermor, " 'Discord in the Spheres': The Universe of *Troilus and Cressida*," *The Frontiers of Drama*, 3rd ed. (London, 1948); L. C. Knights, "The Theme of Appearance and Reality in *Troilus and Cressida*," *Some Shakespearean Themes* (London, 1959). A convenient summary of recent criticism of *Troilus and Cressida* can be be found in Mary Ellen Rickey, " 'Twixt the Dangerous Shores: *Troilus and Cressida* Again," *SQ*, XV (1964), 3–13. Professor Rickey's own argument, that the unifying theme of the play is a corruption which consists in mistaking "prideful will and appetite" for honor and glory, will be seen to have its parallels to my own reading, though it stops short of seeing the uses to which this idea is put in the play, and the larger theme which it serves.

5. I have attempted to formulate a statement about the nature and history of the convention in "The Double Plot: Notes on the History of a Convention," *Renaissance Drama*, VII (1964), 55–69.

6. William Empson's "Double Plots" in *Some Versions of Pastoral*, first published in 1935, has been seminal, particularly with respect to *Troilus and Cressida and Henry IV*, though his discussions of those plays are more valuable for the avenues they open than for the conclusions they reach. Two recent studies which exemplify the kind of light double-plot analysis can shed on Shakespeare are Cecil C. Seronsy, " 'Supposes' as the Unifying Theme in *The Taming of the Shrew*," *SQ*, XIV (1963), 15–30, and R. W. Dent, "Imagination in *A Midsummer Night's Dream*," *SQ*, XV (1964), 115–129.

7. In a purely technical sense, I should prefer not to call *Hamlet* or even *King Lear* double-plot plays, reserving the term for plays in which the actions are fully independent of one another, so that the story of one can be told without the necessity of telling the other. *Troilus and Cressida* is an example in Shakespeare, though it does not seem to be; so are *Measure for Measure* and *The Taming of the Shrew*. But the purely technical use of the term tends to obscure an important fact, that the techniques of parallelism which Shakespeare and others employ most strikingly in the double plot are primary techniques of their dramaturgy. The clear and insistent comparisons and contrasts between Hamlet and Laertes and Fortinbras affect us in much the same way as those between Hotspur and Falstaff or, to cite characters in a purer instance of the double plot, Achilles and Troilus, and Helen and Cressida.

8. Kimbrough, "The *Troilus* Log," p. 205.

9. Sheldon Sacks, *Fiction and the Shape of Belief* (Berkeley and Los Angeles, 1964), p. 3. Professor Sacks's strictures against the casual use of the concept of "theme" are valuable (e.g., pp. 55–60). Like him, I find myself most concerned not with a writer's beliefs but with the "discernible and vital shape" such beliefs take in his works. Employing Professor Sacks's critical terminology, one might usefully study Shakespeare's plays in terms of their varying uses of the techniques of "represented action" and "apologue"; one of the things one might discover is that *Troilus and Cressida* disturbs its critics and inspires the kind of criticism it does because it is more like an "apologue" than most of Shakespeare's other plays. The debates, followed by episodes which seem to "prove" one or another position taken in them, are unusual in Shake-

speare. So is the fact that most readers, I suspect, though moved by the play's outcome, care less about the individual fates of the characters than they do about the thesis that has been made so painfully operative in the play's world by the end. Since my study is not taxonomic, however, I am not here concerned with proving *Troilus and Cressida* is an "apologue."

10. The most lucid summary of the arguments over value in *Troilus and Cressida* is Miss Ellis-Fermor's. Her conclusion, that Shakespeare is attacking all value, is not mine.

11. L. C. Knights, *loc. cit.*, p. 82, calls attention to the importance of time in the world of *Troilus and Cressida*.

12. *Troilus and Cressida*, ed. Alice Walker (Cambridge, 1957), p. 169.

13. O. J. Campbell, *Comicall Satyre and Shakespeare's Troilus and Cressida* (San Marino, 1938), pp. 202ff., argues against the suggestion that Thersites is Shakespeare's spokesman.

14. See Empson, *op. cit.*, p. 39, on the function in *Troilus and Cressida* of "the comic character's low jokes" in establishing the play's unity.

15. *Troilus and Cressida*, ed. H. N. Hillebrand, New Variorum ed. (Philadelphia, 1953), p. 212.

16. *The Wheel of Fire* (New York, 1957), pp. 65, 68.

17. The view of A. S. Knowland, in "*Troilus and Cressida*," SQ, X (1959), 353–365, that time is identical in the play with mutability is an oversimplification, failing to note the organic metaphors constantly used to describe time's nature and action.

18. It is significant that Ulysses has already complained that Achilles and Patroclus mock Greek "achievements" (I. iii. 181).

19. Though her interpretation of the phenomenon attempts, as often, to say more about Shakespeare than about what he is doing in a particular play, Miss Spurgeon astutely notices the "extraordinary number of food and cooking images in Troilus," in *Shakespeare's Imagery and What It Tells Us* (Cambridge, 1935), Chart VII. Troilus' speech as he awaits Cressida *chez* Pandarus (III. ii. 20ff.) is typical.

20. The term "theme" is by now so generally used that definition may be supererogatory; on the other hand, as with every term in general use, it means various things to various critics. I use it in what I take to be its most commonly accepted meaning: a simple and generalized statement about the world which may be abstracted from a literary work, to which the larger part of the work contributes, and with which the rest is generally consistent.

21. *Atomic Theory and the Description of Nature* (Cambridge, 1961), p. 12.

22. Bohr, "Discussion with Einstein on Epistemological Problems in Atomic Physics," *Atomic Physics and Human Knowledge* (Cambridge, 1958), p. 40.

23. "Unity of Knowledge," *Atomic Physics and Human Knowledge*, p. 80.

24. Thomas Rymer, *A Short View of Tragedy* (London, 1693), in *The Critical Works of Thomas Rymer*, ed. Curt Zimansky (New Haven, 1956), pp. 131–164. Shaw's most comprehensive and useful statement on *Othello*

occurs in an article on Verdi, "A Word More about Verdi," which appeared in *The Anglo-Saxon Review*, March, 1901, pp. 221–229, and runs as follows:

> The composition of *Otello* was a much less Shakespearean feat; for the truth is that, instead of *Otello* being an Italian opera written in the style of Shakespeare, *Othello* is a play written by Shakespeare in the style of Italian opera. It is quite peculiar among his works in this aspect. Its characters are monsters: Desdemona is a prima donna, with handkerchief, confidante, and vocal solo, all complete; and Iago, though slightly more anthropomorphic than the Count di Luna, is only so when he slips out of his stage villain's part. Othello's transports are conveyed by a magnificent but senseless music which rages from the Propontick to the Hellespont in an orgy of thundering sound and bounding rhythm; and the plot is a pure farce plot: that is to say, it is supported on an artificially manufactured and desperately precarious trick which a chance word might upset at any moment. With such a libretto, Verdi was quite at home; his success with it proves, not that he could occupy Shakespeare's plane, but that Shakespeare could on occasion occupy his, which is a very different matter.

Useful summaries of criticism of *Othello* are to be found in Robert Heilman, *Magic in the Web: Action and Language in Othello* (Lexington, 1956) and Marvin Rosenberg, *The Masks of Othello: The Search for the Identity of Othello, Iago, and Desdemona by Three Centuries of Actors and Critics* (Berkeley and Los Angeles, 1961).

25. The doctrine of double time was first developed independently in 1849 by Nicholas Halpin and John Wilson in *Blackwood's*; Rymer had criticized the time scheme of *Othello* in *A Short View of Tragedy*, pp. 146, 148, 151, 153, 154, and 156. The fullest study of the time problems in Shakespeare's plays, and my source for the information about Halpin and Wilson, is Mable Buland, *The Presentation of Time in the Elizabethan Drama*, Yale Studies in English, XLIV (New York, 1912). For further discussion of the time problem in *Othello*, see A. F. Sproule, "A Time Scheme for *Othello*," *SQ*, VII (1956), 217–226. More recently, Arthur McGee, "Othello's Motive for Murder," *SQ*, XV (1964), 45–54, has attempted to rationalize the time scheme of *Othello* by arguing that Iago deceives Othello about Desdemona's behavior not in the time since the marriage, but since the earlier betrothal in which, by Elizabethan custom, the two were as good as married.

26. The most articulate of recent attempts to demonstrate that Othello is the victim of a flaw which vitiates whatever greatness he may possess is Leo Kirschbaum's "The Modern Othello," *ELH*, XI (1944), 283–296.

27. For a detailed study of dramatic irony in *Othello*, see Heilman's *Magic in the Web, passim*. This invaluable book is a searching commentary on the play which makes the writer of a shorter essay uneasy, and its bibliography is useful. My view, though more schematic than Professor Heilman's and though in ultimate disagreement with his largest conclusions, agrees with

his at literally hundreds of points, large and small, though I arrived at my own reading independently.

28. William Hazlitt, *Characters of Shakespeare's Plays* (London, 1817), pp. 42–60.

29. Heilman, *op. cit.*, p. 137.

30. *Ibid.*, pp. 137–138.

31. Helen Gardner, "The Noble Moor," Annual Shakespeare Lecture of the British Academy, 1955, *Proceedings of the British Academy*, XLI (1955), 197.

32. This is not to suggest that I consider *Othello* a "Christian tragedy." For a stimulating discussion of this issue see Robert H. West, "The Christianness of *Othello*," *SQ*, XV (1964), 333–343.

33. Bernard Spivack, *Shakespeare and the Allegory of Evil* (New York, 1958). Spivack's convincing argument that Iago is a fusion of the unmotivated Vice, whose evil is radical and gratuitous, with a naturalistically presented man who has real problems and motivations, suggests another aspect of Shakespearean complementarity. The fusion of two kinds of character allows Shakespeare to suggest in Iago two understandings of evil: the subjective view of the villain himself, in which judgment is to a certain extent waived, and the objective view provided by our knowledge that as Vice Iago represents metaphysical evil.

34. Rymer, *A Short View of Tragedy*, p. 132.

35. Terence Hawkes, *Shakespeare and the Reason* (London, 1964), pp. 100–123.

36. Albert Gerard, "Alack, Poor Iago! Intellect and Action in *Othello*," *Shakespeare Jahrbuch*, XCIV (1958), 218–232; p. 225.

37. Gerard agrees with Leavis that it is wrong to see Iago as diabolical (p. 220), but Spivack has said the last word on the subject. I should make it clear that though reason is Iago's mode, his reasons for being what he is are as mysterious and passional as Othello's; the motive force behind Iago's rationality is irrationality. See Paul A. Jorgensen, " 'Perplex'd in the Extreme': The Role of Thought in *Othello*," *SQ*, XV (1964), 265–275 for an excellent study of Iago as a compulsive "thinking man." See also Rosenberg, *The Masks of Othello*, for a provocative study of Iago as character.

38. McGee, *op. cit.*, p. 54. McGee's thesis is that Othello and Desdemona were bethrothed *de praesenti* before their formal marriage, and that Iago's accusations are not of impossible adultery in Cyprus but rather of infidelity in Venice after the betrothal. The argument is reasonable, though like Ernest Schanzer's similar argument about *Measure for Measure* in *The Problem Plays of Shakespeare* (London, 1963), it assumes that the audience will be listening hard for hints about a complex legal situation. At any rate, the fact remains that the apparent transformation of Othello takes place itself in a remarkably short time.

39. See Appendix for a discussion of the relation between elapsed time and growth of character in Shakespeare and contemporary drama.

40. It is an odd fact about the world of *Othello* that despite the utter mendacity of Iago's charges they require very little substantiation to begin to look most reasonable. Interestingly, at least one modern critic, Margaret L. Ranald, "The Indiscretions of Desdemona," *SQ*, XIV (1963), 127–139, finds Desdemona responsible for behavior that gives a good deal of plausibility to Iago's argument. As Mrs. Ranald observes, it is Desdemona's finest qualities that thus serve Iago. The clear implication is that sophistry such as Iago's can make anything serve its purposes; Desdemona is immune to Othello's morbid suspicion only so long as he accepts her unquestioningly.

The Polity

◄§ I §►

IT IS A TRUISM IN CERTAIN SCHOOLS THAT SHAKESPEARE'S PLAYS
are the defining embodiment of Elizabethan ideals of order and
degree, the Tudor myth of the polity as beehive and history as the
working out of a providence that sanctions kings as divine agents
and condemns regicide or anything that might lead in its direction as sacrilege. For this view, promulgated with eloquence,
learning, and insight by E. M. W. Tillyard and others, there is
much to be said, and innumerable passages and incidents from
the plays leap to mind in support of it. There can be no doubt
that with the possible exception of Dante no great western writer
has so dearly loved the ideal of hierarchical social order as Shakespeare, whose vision of it helped England through its severest
trials in the twentieth century and has given to English-speaking
peoples a local habitation and a name for much that we hope
for in the state. On the other hand, many readers have realized
for a long time that this reading of Shakespeare's politics is too
simple. One need not go so far as Jan Kott, who sees the history
plays as embodying "the image of the Grand Mechanism,"[1] an
image in which the precepts of Machiavelli and the blind move-

ment of the wheel of fortune are fused to reflect a cruel and meaningless process in which only power counts, to recognize that against ideal and wishful dramatic images of Tudor political ideals Shakespeare poses a powerful sense of *Realpolitik*. In politics as in everything else Shakespeare incites contradictory readings in men of different natures, showing to the modern British patriot, with his nostalgia for good old days that may never have existed, the vision with which he would shore up the last days of England, and to the east European participant in the revolutions of our century a vision of the morbid police state cast up on the tides of brutal historical process. Both images are in the work; taken together they suggest a complementary approach to the problems of history.

I am not going to suggest that politics is any more one substance for Shakespeare, one set of givens toward which he expresses one attitude, than love. Apart from the fact that we can find, as we would expect, cultural sources for all the attitudes on which Shakespeare bases his political plays, that he appeals to a certain stock of political ideas of various kinds—just as he appeals to demonstrably traditional ideas of love—there is only one constant in Shakespeare's political plays: the view of politics as problematic. Every political play that he wrote, without exception, shows the state in crisis—crisis of the sort that calls all into question, forces us to examine all our political assumptions and ideals, and leaves us finally with a resolution that does not allow for simplistic adherence to particular political ideals. And because politics is the art of managing the social world in which we live and attempting to solve its insoluble problems, Shakespeare's politics is tragic. As I hope to make clear, this is not to say that Shakespeare leaves us with the comfortable conclusion that because action is necessarily simplistic and therefore inevitably wrong, we may simply avoid action. Shakespeare's politics is tragic precisely because he will not allow us the luxury of evading action, because he shows us why we must act in history, and err.

⊸§ II §⊶

E. W. Talbert does not exaggerate when he claims, in his useful study of the cross-currents of sixteenth-century political thought as *Richard II* reflects them, that "*Richard II* is as much of a problem play as any of the later 'problem comedies.'"[2] Had he attempted to design a situation more nearly embodying the moral ambiguities he develops in *Richard II*, Shakespeare could scarcely have equaled the opportunities he finds ready-made in his material. Here as in *Julius Caesar* he seizes on a historical event whose meaning was a matter of dispute and of inescapable concern to the unstable moment of history in which he composed his plays. *Richard II* is all problem. Written in a day so close to insurrection that its performance had to be blocked by the state and within less than fifty years of the great civil war that was to question and for a time even to abolish the very idea of monarchy, yet only a handful of years before the first English-man was to ascend his throne supported by a claim of his divine right to it, Shakespeare's first mature essay into the mimesis of historical crisis could hardly have been anything but problematic.

As always, the problem shapes the structure of the play. The question that *Richard II* poses is the question of what to do about a king whose continuance on the throne is essential to the continued order of a state governed by hereditary monarchy, but who is manifestly unfit personally for what is required of him. Shakespeare plunges us immediately into the problem by setting it up in the opening scene in a debate—its circumstances and issues veiled both because they are too dangerous even to be discussed in public in the play's fictional world and because they are familiar to an audience which knows the history and has re-cently seen it performed on the stage. Richard has secretly em-ployed Thomas Mowbray, Duke of Norfolk, to murder the Duke of Gloucester, uncle to the King and possibly dangerous to his control of England; and Richard's cousin Henry Bolingbroke, ob-viously unable to suggest the King's complicity even if he is aware of it, has challenged Richard's position by attempting to expose Mowbray. It might serve the purpose of immediate stabil-ity in the realm for Bolingbroke to keep silent, but he is an irascible and ambitious man, who can only profit by Richard's capitulation, and moreover—as ever in Shakespeare and the world, the elements are mixed in him—he is a patriotic and righteous man whose own father, brother to the murdered Duke, is im-

plicitly threatened by the King's ruthless act. Though it is not
often in Bolingbroke's nature to be deeply disturbed by the moral
implications of the actions he contemplates, he has a problem,
and he shares it with the audience.

The problem is explicitly stated, and one traditional answer
to it given, by John of Gaunt, Duke of Lancaster and father to
Bolingbroke, as he responds to the plea of his widowed sister-in-
law that he avenge the crime:

> God's is the quarrel; for God's substitute,
> His deputy anointed in His sight,
> Hath caused his death: the which if wrongfully,
> Let heaven revenge; for I may never lift
> An angry arm against His minister.
>
> (I. ii. 37–41)

In a sense Gaunt shares the view of Mowbray, who is not presented as a blackguard, yet has served the wishes of a monarch
who felt the murder necessary to uphold his own position as
king. If the unthreatened rule of the King is the principle of the
state's survival, there may be some justification for what he has
caused to be done. At any rate, to take arms against God's minister is to Gaunt an even more egregious crime than Richard's.
And if history is providentially governed, then to oppose its
course is sacrilegious. What happens in history is what heaven
wants.

An obvious answer to Gaunt's position underlies all the action; ironically Shakespeare puts it into advice delivered to Richard himself as in the deposition scene the King helplessly falls
back on the idea that God controls history and will protect his
minister: "Fear not," the Bishop of Carlisle instructs the King,
now mournfully yielding to passive anticipation of impending
disaster;

> Fear not, my Lord: that Power that made you king
> Hath power to keep you king in spite of all.
> The means that heaven yields must be embraced,
> And not neglected; else if heaven would,
> And we will not, heaven's offer we refuse,
>
> (III. ii. 27–32)

And Aumerle, son of the Duke of York and loyal to Richard, immediately translates Carlisle's meditative statement into practical power politics: Bolingbroke is growing strong while we hold ourselves back. Richard's advisors, then, share Gaunt's belief in providence's stake in history, but they oppose to his and Richard's passive fatalism the notion that providence depends on the actions it makes available to individuals who know how to use power.

To their advice Richard responds with a deeply felt statement of his belief that heaven will take care of him:

> Not all the water in the rough rude sea
> Can wash the balm off from an anointed king;
> The breath of worldly men cannot depose
> The deputy elected by the Lord.
>
> (54–57)

The statement is clearly presumptuous and ultimately wrong in terms of the plot, yet difficult to refute, since Bolingbroke and England will have to pay dearly for what happens to prove it wrong. No matter how much Shakespeare makes us understand that Richard is here whistling in the dark, playing at being kingly instead of defending his threatened crown, he will not allow us to think of the problem entirely in terms of power politics. Again, simply on the level of plot, the play's world reacts precisely as Richard believes it will to the deposition of a king whose legitimacy is a matter as much of religion as of politics. At the moment that Richard officially yields all to Bolingbroke, the same Bishop of Carlisle pronounces a curse against those who strike out against "the figure of God's majesty,/ His captain, steward, deputy-elect,/ Anointed, crowned, planted many years"/ (IV. i. 125–127) and predicts, as Richard will do shortly again (V. i. 55–68) in language which his successor will ruefully remember later (II *Henry IV*, III. i. 67–79), the bloody civil wars that all the audience is fully aware of. If Richard argues in surrendering his throne that "With mine own tears I wash away my balm" (IV. i. 207), we know that he cannot. Divinity does seem to hedge the seat of royal power and to punish those who oppose it with power no matter for how good a reason. Yet it allows Richard himself to be destroyed; and to make the paradox even more unsettling, providence will, in the fullness of time, place on the throne a son of the usurping Bolingbroke who will save England from its enemies, within and without, as the sacrilegiously deposed Richard could not.

Thus Gaunt's "God's is the quarrel" states the question of the play and the tetralogy but does not answer it. The question is inevitable in a state whose political stability is defined in the light of a benevolent providence that places absolute sanctions on the power of fallible rulers. It is no wonder that, given such postulates, historiography and political theory should find themselves caught in almost insuperable contradictions and conflicts in the age that most explicitly defines the royal prerogatives and puts them to the test; the problem is built into the European idea of kingship. The same contradictions are implicit in the version of the myth that first defines that idea, and explicit in Samuel's advice to the Hebrews not to demand a king. As the authors of the books of Samuel are fully aware, men are simply incapable of creating the kind of political stability that the Tudor myth envisions. The very first King of Israel was a tragically bad one, and if his mistakes can be explained in large part by the fact that he had not learned how to make the transition from the statecraft of a judge to that of a monarch, the fact remains that David confronting Saul was faced with a problem identical to Bolingbroke's. Like Bolingbroke he was motivated both by the drive to power and by love of country; like him he discovered that regicide must follow deposition in order to bring about a new legitimacy, and like him he had to spend a tragic life trying to atone for an inexpiable sin. Like Richard, Saul recognized immediately that to yield an inch to his challenger, even to let him cut off a corner of his garment, was to have given up all his power. And like Israel, England discovers that the new and benign order brought about by the creation of monarchical stability has legitimized in the process of its creation a kind of permanent challenge to the crown that will ultimately destroy kingship itself.

This is the insoluble problem of history as the chronicle plays make us see it. Shakespeare poses it brilliantly in little in the scene (III. iv) in which the gardeners, employing a familiar analogy, discuss the state as garden and Richard II as incompetent caretaker. The well-tended garden, in which natural process properly controlled brings forth flower and fruit in their appointed season and the community of the whole lives in wholesome balance, is the ideal to which we must contrast the disorder and disease rampant in the England of *Richard II*, and with its appeal to nature the analogy conveys the Elizabethan sense that the well-ordered polity is both a reflection of cosmic order and the product of a benevolent providence. But the ideal is only an ideal; the terms of the analogy do not provide adequate guidelines for translating it into statecraft. Reproaching Richard for not having acted as a king should, the gardeners suggest only that he should have been more autocratic. Through the myth of the garden Shakespeare suggests the King's providential function, his sacred place in the natural order, and the inevitable ruin of those who attack it, but he does not allow us to share Gaunt's momentary and Richard's perennial sense that with the aid of providence the garden will somehow take care of itself as long as the King retains his power. The problem of *Richard II* is the problem of England; it is not accidental that the most moving hymn to England ever composed occurs here in the passionate words of the dying Gaunt. Shakespeare does not solve the problem—only history and a new set of assumptions unimaginable in the sixteenth century were to do that; rather, he understands it as few of his contemporaries did, and he makes us fully and painfully aware of it.

The primary technique of *Richard II* is that of keeping our sympathies in suspense. The structure of the play demands that we choose: Is our allegiance to Richard or to Bolingbroke? If to the former, then we have resolved the play's problems along the lines set out by conservative Tudor thinkers like Thomas Elyot and Richard Hooker, who consistently evade the issue of the problems created by a bad monarch by wishing he were better and by refusing to countenance the legitimacy of usurpation. If we feel final allegiance to Bolingbroke and what he represents, no matter how much feeling for the great tradition we may have, we find we have opted for the new men who see the polity as a contract in which bad kings must be replaced and who see politics as an arena of perpetual conflict where only power counts. But Shakespeare does not let us make the choice. A good index to the play's intentions is the role played by Gaunt's brother, the Duke of York, perhaps the first of Shakespeare's "reflector" characters, who, like Casca and Horatio and Kent and Enobarbus in later plays, epitomizes and directs our shifting sympathies. Like us York begins with a poignant sense of loyalty to the crown; like us he soon finds his sympathy virtually exhausted and declares an end to his former approval. When Richard rejects his advice, we come quickly to question the King's legitimacy (II. i). In the next scene York finds himself wavering between the conflicting principles represented by Richard and Bolingbroke:

> If I know how or which way to order these affairs
> Thus thrust disorderly into my hands,
> Never believe me. Both are my kinsmen:
> The one is my sovereign, whom both my oath
> And duty bids defend; the other again
> Is my kinsman, whom the king hath wrong'd,
> Whom conscience and my kindred bids to right.
> Well, somewhat we must do.
>
> (II. ii. 109–116)

York is still undecided when Bolingbroke, illegally violating the terms of his exile, arrives at Berkeley castle; he denounces him but nevertheless puts him up for the night. In the deposition scene which ensues almost immediately, York's sympathies have become more defined. Horrified by what is happening, he declares his fealty to the King, and by the beginning of the fourth act he is Richard's ambassador to Bolingbroke, unhappily assisting his nephew's abdication. The sequence of events has fully awakened and crystallized York's allegiance to the principle of sacred kingship. In the last act it is his account, to his wife, of Richard's disgrace at Bolingbroke's hands that turns us most against the usurper, and when he denounces the ruthless new King, we find it hard to disagree with him. Torn morally as at the outset, York decides to pledge fealty to the new King. But now comes a final turn: York discovers that his son Aumerle is part of a conspiracy against Henry IV, acting out his father's sympathies. With all the anger of a father who has reluctantly made his decision against a large part of his own moral feeling to support a principle in which he only half believes, and now finds his son actively engaged in supporting the position he has reluctantly ruled out for himself, York turns on Aumerle and rushes off to Windsor to denounce him before the King. At this final juncture Shakespeare is able to use York in order to make us admire and respect the usurper who throughout has so offended the conscience of this indecisive epitome of our own feelings; for after hearing out the opposed pleas of the Duke and Duchess of York and Aumerle's contrite petition for pardon, the usurper about to have Richard murdered in the Tower becomes the wise, humane ruler, aware like David of his own limitations, that his predecessor could not be, and at the play's close York is loyal servant to the new King.

York thus calls to our attention the ambivalence upon which the play is structured. That ambivalence arises immediately from the fact that Bolingbroke is embarked on an action simultaneously good and evil and must in the course of time be regarded both as patriotic citizen righteously avenging the dual outrage to his country and himself and as regicide, both as the savior of the English polity and as plotter against its crown. But ultimately, and this is why *Richard II* is more than simply a sensitive account of a peculiar and local political problem, the play's ambivalence originates in a tragic understanding of man as political animal which expresses our gravest doubts about the possibility of human virtue in the public world.

I have indicated that the ambivalence of *Richard II* is built into its structure. But that structure, even as I have thus far described it, depends entirely on character, for our response to the politics of the play is a response not to theory but to the men whose lives and actions make theory necessary in the world. Bolingbroke's situation as Shakespeare dramatizes it almost necessitates an ambivalent response, but it is his character that makes it difficult for us to reach conclusions about him easily. At once patriotic and ambitious, manly and ruthless, he is above all always mysterious. We simply do not know for sure what his motives are at any point in the play. Interestingly, Shakespeare denies him soliloquies, so that we never see him from within.[3] What we see is what the world sees: a powerful man who says and does the right thing at the right moment to reach the throne, and who—whether out of virtue or of a tough political astuteness we cannot know—has always the most convincing reasons for what he does. Like Julius Caesar's desire to become king, Bolingbroke's ambition is a question, not a given. His decisiveness and strength, his possession of the mental and political talents required for the management of the king's office, mark him as more efficient, in a certain sense more kingly, than the King he replaces; but though Richard's offences against him put us on Bolingbroke's side early in the dispute, we are never sure of the kind of man we are dealing with.

One characteristic device will show how Shakespeare creates a sense of moral uneasiness about Bolingbroke. Immediately upon hearing of the death of John of Gaunt, one of the play's most affecting moments, Richard dismisses his dead uncle with a heartlessness for which the audience will never fully forgive him, and to York's horror and ours seizes all of Gaunt's possessions, now rightfully Bolingbroke's. There is no doubt in our minds that Bolingbroke is being robbed, or that in simple justice he has a right to reclaim what Richard thus cynically takes from him. As the royal party leaves the stage, however, a small party remains behind, a knot of malcontent lords whom the Earl of Northumberland quickly binds into a conspiracy against the King. Shakespeare elicits our sympathies for their mission by showing us Richard at his worst, and by putting in their mouths worried speeches about the mistakes of more national import that the King is committing, to England's disaster. Now, if ever, we are ready and eager to have Bolingbroke return to England and save it. But at this point, in the very scene in which Gaunt has died and Richard stolen his property, Northumberland reveals to the patriots whose confidence he has tested that Bolingbroke, already sailing with confederates and three thousand men, has virtually reached the northern shores of England. In Holinshed's chronicle account of these events, most immediate source for Shakespeare's version, time is not so telescoped: Gaunt dies, England suffers under Richard's rule, messages are sent abroad to Bolingbroke, and finally the Duke undertakes his voyage.[4] Shakespeare's strategy makes Bolingbroke's return morally ambiguous. To our outraged sense of justice it is an appropriate response to Richard's high-handedness, while it is simultaneously apparent from the chronology that the voyage must have other purposes than the regaining of what Bolingbroke does not know he has lost. By not showing us the mobilizing of forces and the making of the decision to come back to England, Shakespeare leaves us in doubt as to what Bolingbroke is really up to, and we retain that doubt to the end. If Bolingbroke's motives are thus obscured, the play's conclusion, on the other hand, shows us a king able to deal, as Richard was not, honorably and wisely with the assassin he has employed. By the end we know that—for whatever reasons—Bolingbroke is going to be a good king.

The presentation of Richard is similarly ambiguous, but as the play's tragic center he is a far more complex character, and the extremes of our response to him are farther apart. Where Bolingbroke is adequately competent and strong, Richard is appallingly incompetent. Where Bolingbroke earns our rational admiration and at times our moral approval, Richard commands our deepest emotions. It is a notorious fact that productions of *Richard II* which stress the King's faults while playing down his virtues make the play fail; for the real power of this historical tragedy lies in its ability to elicit our increasing sympathies for the King whose fall we recognize as inevitable and even desirable. Richard begins the play as a man unwilling to stand behind the immoral commitments his power struggle has necessitated, and his dismissal of Mowbray, whose only hint of complaint is the tactful suggestion that he had expected better treatment than banishment, puts him in a bad light. Moreover, he uses his power to make a humiliating charade of a conflict he would do better to settle amicably and out of the public eye; the chivalric duel he stages between Mowbray and Bolingbroke, only to break it off melodramatically and banish the contestants, is a wanton show of power calculated to offend all, and his canny fear that the opponents may get together abroad to conspire against him tells us that he suspects the foolishness of the game he is playing. Followed by the disgraceful dishonoring of the dead Gaunt, whose

whole concern was the preservation of England, Richard's behavior at the beginning of the play makes it clear that he is unfit
to be king, and his never self-possessed and sometimes hysterical
response to Bolingbroke's successive challenges confirms our sense
of his unfitness. On the other hand, Shakespeare begins early to
work on our sympathies, not only by making us suspicious of
Bolingbroke and by engaging us in York's problems, but more
poignantly by showing us the loyalty of the Queen. And simultaneously with the movement of the play toward an awareness
of the horror of Bolingbroke's action, climactically conveyed in
the curse the Bishop of Carlisle utters at the moment Richard
surrenders all to Bolingbroke, we begin to see the richness of
sensibility, language, and imagination in the King that leads some
to see in him the prototype of Hamlet. His helpless struggles in
the machine in which he is caught do not make us wish a different end to the play, but they do make him the most sympathetic
character in the play. In the last act, where we finally come to
admire the newly crowned Henry IV, we also come to admire
Richard, for entirely different reasons. At the beginning of the
act he is a new man, strong and able to bear his adversity with a
manliness not apparent before; he has been instructed by his
suffering. And for the first time he shows some political astuteness, making the prediction that Henry IV will recall years
later (II *Henry IV*, III. i. (67–79). The new King's wise behavior
at the end of *Richard II* suggests that he has already acquired a
sense of the sins by means of which he has ascended the ladder
to the throne, but like Claudius he is unwilling to give up that
whose possession causes him grief; Richard, however, reaches by
the point of his death a full acceptance of his responsibility for
his demise that requires a moral courage more impressive than
anything demanded of Bolingbroke in *Richard II*.

So much is built into the political problem with which Shakespeare is dealing, and into the dynamics of chronicle plays. Similarly in Marlowe's more schematically structured *Edward II* we
come to admire a disastrous king only as the woes he brings
down on his head and his country overwhelm him, and finally
to disdain the forces that necessarily replace him. But, unlike
Marlowe, Shakespeare uses the tragic situation as a platform on

which to stage a greater tragedy, and this is the genius of *Richard II*. The complementarity of the play does not rest in its opposition of ideas of the commonwealth, but makes us understand the perennial tragedy of politics, a tragedy not of systems but of men. From Aeschylus to Ibsen and Camus, great dramatists have found in politics the kind of problem which enables them to examine the human condition as only art can examine it, but always when their art is great it is so because it uses politics not to tell us about the polity what the historian and the political scientist can tell us with greater precision and knowledge, but to make us understand man in politics and therefore in the world. A historian might rest content with the knowledge that Henry IV saved England and managed to pass on his crown to his more successful son. Shakespeare recognizes all this and would not have us underestimate its importance, but he is more concerned with the human loss involved. For the fact, as Shakespeare constructs it in *Richard II* and the history plays that follow it, is that the man who succeeds is, though better constituted for success, farther from our deepest ideals as a man than the failure he must displace. On one level *Richard II* is a play about political success and the ideal of the commonwealth, and on that level Bolingbroke is admirable; on another it is about what it is to be a fully sentient human being, and on that level only Richard commands our respect. Shakespeare perennially distrusts success and the men who achieve it. Mark Antony is Brutus' inferior, Fortinbras Hamlet's, Aufidius Coriolanus'.

What Bolingbroke lacks, and the lack accounts in good part for his success, is inwardness, the capacities to suffer and to dream.[5] At the play's first crisis we become aware of the lack, and we recognize it as a source of his strength and a concomitant of his political resoluteness. Banished by his high-handed cousin, Bolingbroke is advised by his sensitive father to ignore the conditions under which he will have to live abroad, to "Think not the king did banish thee,/ But thou the king," and to imagine wherever he is that that is where he should be, "For gnarling sorrow hath less power to bite/ The man that mocks at it and sets it light." To this stoic commonplace, the advice that a man's mind is his kingdom, Bolingbroke responds with a scornful rejection

of the poetic imagination that transforms the world for its possessor:

> O, who can hold a fire in his hand
> By thinking on the frosty Caucasus?
> Or cloy the hungry edge of appetite
> By bare imagination of a feast?
> Or wallow naked in December snow
> By thinking on fantastic summer's heat?
> O, no! the apprehension of the good
> Gives but the greater feeling to the worse:
> Fell sorrow's tooth doth never rankle more
> Than when he bites, but lanceth not the sore.
>
> (I. iii. 294–303)

Of course he is right, and his literalistic insistence on what he is
and what is his keeps his will focused on the goal he finally
achieves. But in his answer to Gaunt Bolingbroke dissociates
himself from those "wrong" characters in Shakespeare—Troilus
and the unfallen Othello are their tragic, the lovers in A *Midsummer Night's Dream* their comic archetypes—whose vision points
higher than material fact. In declaring his fidelity to realistic
clarity of vision Bolingbroke gives us his first insight into the
stuff he has to bring him power, but ironically he suggests to us
at the same time what makes us care more at the end for Richard.

Now there can be no denying that imagination is Richard's
disease, or that in politics it is for him, as shortly we shall see
that it is also for Brutus, a fatal one. His famous meditation, "Let's
talk of graves, of worms and epitaphs" (III. ii. 144–177), is a
perfect example. It is a mortifying piece of self-dramatization and
self-pity, and as an answer to Aumerle's simple question, "Where
is the duke my father with his power?" it is, as the Bishop of
Carlisle remarks, totally inappropriate. On the other hand, it is
one of the most moving and memorable speeches in the play, and
for good reason. For Richard's response to adversity is simultaneously a retreat within and probing outward, a questioning of the
meaning of all things in the face of the fact of mortality. His
medieval *ubi sunt* leads him to a contemplation of the dance of
death. Such a meditation is inappropriate to his political respon-

sibilities, but it deals with issues fundamental to the growth and understanding of man, who, as even Henry IV's fruitless later quest of Jerusalem will demonstrate, is nothing if he does not come to see himself and politics in these terms.

> For within the hollow crown
> That rounds the mortal temples of a king
> Keeps Death his court and there the antic sits,
> Scoffing his state and grinning at his pomp,
> Allowing him a breath, a little scene,
> To monarchize, be fear'd and kill with looks,
> Infusing him with self and vain conceit,
> As if this flesh which walls about our life
> Were brass impregnable, and humour'd thus
> Comes at the last and with a little pin
> Bores through his castle wall, and farewell king!
> (III. ii. 160–170)

On the verge of failure, a matured and more sympathetic Henry IV will come later to such thoughts in a midnight revery that ends "Uneasy lies the head that wears a crown" (II *Henry IV*, III. i. 4–31); and his son on the eve of Agincourt will recognize like Richard the anomaly that common mortality makes of ceremony. If the burden of the history plays is the tragedy of history, it is Richard who comes closest to our understanding, to what the plays would have us think of as wisdom. But that wisdom seems in *Richard II* incompatible with the other kind of human greatness by which a man can function as he must. Shakespeare, Yeats remarked,

> . . . saw indeed in Richard II the defeat that awaits all, whether they be Artist or Saint, who find themselves where men ask of them a rough energy and have nothing to give but some contemplative virtue, whether lyrical phantasy, or sweetness of temper, or dreamy dignity, or love of God, or love of His creatures. He saw that such a man through sheer bewilderment and impatience can become as unjust or as violent as any common man, any Bolingbroke or Prince John, and yet remain "that sweet lovely rose."[6]

The tragedy of *Richard II* is the complementarity of its protagonists' virtues, which seem there incapable of being commingled.

Ꮽᔤ III ᏹᎡ

In one respect *Richard II* sets the terms for all the political plays Shakespeare will write after it: political success, defined in whatever terms the play's situation requires, will always be complementary to qualities of the human spirit incompatible with it. Shakespeare does not scorn such success—the harmonious commonwealth is an ideal he teaches us to value as few other writers do—but he makes us fully aware of the cost of achieving it. In the two plays that deal with the later fortunes of Henry IV Shakespeare frames the question of the value of political success in terms to which he will return with less optimism in *Antony and Cleopatra*, setting political responsibility against all that Falstaff represents. To call it hedonism is to make a judgment on it to which the play calls us more than once as the fat knight's constitutional inability and willful refusal to think in terms of his obligations come into conflict with what the patriotic ambiance and Hal's plight demand. But though he is a liar, Falstaff never misrepresents himself as a patriot, and even when we are angry at him for his monumental irresponsibility in raising troops, we can never reproach him for hypocrisy. Falstaff conveys the sense of life, sensual and unpurposive, life at any cost, life as the most absolute of values, in whose way no obstacle must be allowed to stand. His funniest moments invariably fill us with the joy of recognizing his preposterous insistence on remaining young despite his considerable age ("Young men must live"), on playing holiday like a truant schoolboy all year long, on cheating death with indefatigable vigor and inventiveness; his most poignant moments invariably remind us that he grows old, that finally death may make the claim on him that in life a sense of responsibility could not.

Yet for all that he must be rejected, in favor of an understanding of the world which allows little room for the spirit of perpetual play that Falstaff embodies. To be Falstaff one must turn away from the world of time, cease considering oneself as a participant in history. "What a devil hast thou to do with the time of the day?" asks Hal in his first speech to Sir John:

> Unless hours were cups of sack and minutes capons and clocks the tongues of bawds and dials the signs of leaping-houses and the blessed sun himself a fair hot wench in flame-coloured taffeta, I see no reason why thou shouldst be so superfluous to demand the time of day.
>
> (I. ii. 7–13)

But at the moment of his finest self-knowledge, Richard has already acknowledged that playing Falstaff's game in the world of men has been his undoing and England's:

> Music do I hear?
> Ha, ha! keep time: how sour sweet music is,
> When time is broke and no proportion kept!
> So is it in the music of men's lives.
> And here have I the daintiness of ear
> To check time broke in a disorder'd string;
> But for the concord of my state and time
> Had not an ear to hear my true time broke.
> I wasted time, and now doth time waste me. . . .
> (*Richard II*, V. v. 41–49)

Hal tells us in his first soliloquy that he is a man who knows time and therefore will ultimately redeem it, that all the year is not playing holiday, and he shares his father's skill in judging the propitious time for the conduct of affairs. What he knows is what Shakespeare tells us over and over: The movement of history has its own inexorable logic, and its medium is time. To succeed one must be able to seize the moment, to think always in terms of time. In *Troilus and Cressida* and *Othello* we have already noted passages, spoken by characters as different as Ulysses and Iago, in which time is described as if it were an autonomous organism; and such a passage we find at a crucial and retrospective moment in the Henriad, as Henry IV ruefully recalls Richard's prophecy that a time would come when the coalition supporting the new

king would break apart. His friend the Duke of Warwick answers
him in words that might be a motto for the entire tetralogy:

> There is a history in all men's lives,
> Figuring the natures of the times deceased;
> The which observed, a man may prophesy,
> With a near aim, of the main chance of things
> As yet not come to life, which in their seeds
> And weak beginnings lie intreasured.
> Such things become the hatch and brood of time;
> And by the necessary form of this
> King Richard might create a perfect guess
> That great Northumberland, then false to him,
> Would of that seed grow to a greater falseness;
> Which should not find a ground to root upon,
> Unless on you.
>
> (II *Henry IV*, III. i. 80–92)

No more a mystic than Shakespeare, Warwick roots the inevitability of the history he describes in the natures of the men
involved in it. But given that point of view, what we love in
Falstaff is no alternative to political commitment, and Hal has
no choice but to reject it. On the other hand, Shakespeare presents Falstaff so that we do love him, and by setting against him,
with his catechistic demolition of honor, a Hotspur who carries
the belief in honor to extremes that show its ultimate meaninglessness, by setting Hal symbolically and actually on the stage
between the dead Hotspur and Falstaff risen from his mock death,
and by making us recognize the unexpected inadequacy of Henry
IV and the uneasy compromise built into the life of his perplexing
son, Shakespeare suggests to us once again in the *Henry IV* plays
the welter of emotions with which we contemplate history, committed and detached, hopeful and despairing, sure that politics
can and must save us and at the same time contemptuously certain
that it is irrelevant to our realest lives. "The Buddha has given
such answers," says Oppenheimer speaking of our knowledge of
the movements of electrons, "when interrogated as to the conditions of a man's self after his death; but they are not familiar
answers for the tradition of seventeenth and eighteenth-century
science"[7]—or of rational historiography.

In only one play in his entire career does Shakespeare seem bent on making us believe that what is valuable in politics and in life can successfully be combined in a ruler as in his state, and it is curious that many readers cannot trust *Henry* V.[8] There can be no doubt that it is infectiously patriotic, or that the ideal of the harmonious commonweal, as expressed in the Archbishop of Canterbury's great speech on the beehive (I. ii. 183–213) and exemplified in the King's administration, reflects the highest point of Shakespeare's civic optimism. And Henry is clearly presented as the kind of exemplary monarch that neither Richard II nor Henry IV could be, combining the inwardness and the sense of occasion of the one and the strength and efficiency of the other with a generous humanity available to neither. Furthermore, he continues to manifest that ability to do the right thing at the right time whose absence undid his cousin. The tragic chronicle plays have demonstrated that political success is the fruit of a marriage between suitable character and luck. In contrast to both Falstaff and Hotspur, Hal bides his time, fights at the opportune moment, and finds providence always with him. As Henry V he would seem to be what the earlier plays might have made us think impossible: a flawless ruler, wise in the exercise of power which he possesses legitimately, and ever high on the wheel of fortune whose downward turn made Richard's "glory like a shooting star/ Fall to the base earth from the firmament" (*Richard II.* II. iv. 19–20).

But Hal, the only successful and fully heroic monarch in all of Shakespeare's ten chronicle plays, strikes us more as a wish than as a paradigm of political reality, and the joyous portrait is shaded by considerations we cannot ignore. An audience familiar with the history of its own nation, or even with the cycle of plays Shakespeare has already devoted to the tragic history that followed the short happy reign of Henry V must take the play's jolly assurance that all will now be well with England with more than a grain of salt; nothing could be more ironic than the play's final affirmations of that perpetual love between England and France which Henry's victory seems for one brief moment to have brought about, and of that stability, expensively bought by decades of struggle, which will crumble in the reign of Henry's son. And upon any reflection, we are forced by the play itself to question the happiness and virtue it seems to proclaim. Like Ulysses' great speech on "the specialty of rule" in *Troilus and Cressida*, the Archbishop of Canterbury's beautiful oration on the well-ordered state serves a nasty purpose, in this case to justify a war against France whose illegitimacy is underscored by the doubletalk in which he, the King, and all the King's ministers participate in the play's opening scenes. The order Henry achieves in England, for all the gallantry his own person lends it, is still a repressive one, achieved at the expense of the comedians whose antics have so delighted us, and few comments sum up our response to a play better than Dr. Johnson's note on "*Exit* Pistol" at V. i. 94:

> The comick scenes of the history of *Henry* the fourth and fifth are now at an end, and all the comick personages are now dismissed. *Falstaff* and *Mrs. Quickly* are dead; *Nym* and *Bardolph* are hanged; *Gadshill* was lost immediately after the robbery; *Poins* and *Peto* have vanished since, one knows not how; and *Pistol* is now beaten into obscurity. I believe every reader regrets their departure.[8]

Paradoxically, the joyous comic resolution of *Henry* V is purchased at the price of much that has before brought us comic joy.

And yet, the play's very form insists that it is a dream, for unlike the earlier plays in the cycle, unlike any other history play in the canon, *Henry* V is a comedy. Observing that "in creating Falstaff, Shakespeare fused the clown's part with that of a festive celebrant, a Lord of Misrule," C. L. Barber has convincingly argued that in *I Henry IV* Shakespeare balances "holiday" against "everyday," and Jonas Barish has shown us how in rejecting Falstaff Hal turns from the idyllic world of comedy to the grimmer realities of the workaday world.[10] It is Hal's adjustment to the reality principle which Falstaff denies to the end that makes him succeed where Richard, who cannot leave the world of play until too late, has failed. Unlike Richard, who believes that "the king's name" is "twenty thousand names" (III. ii. 85), Hal shares Falstaff's skepticism enough to be wary of the dangers of imagination and the vainglory of mere ceremony. But in *Henry* V Shakespeare would have us believe what hitherto his work in its genre has denied, that in the real world of the chronicles a man may live who embodies the virtues and experiences the fortune of the comic hero. Thus Hal-become-Henry is simultaneously Lord of Misrule, playing off his comical officers against one another for our diversion, and sober and legitimate monarch, and bloody general. Thus the hero of England's wars against France is also the hero of a perfectly traditional comedy which ends in peaceful solutions to the threatening problems of its world and in marriage. Always in romantic comedy we experience the joy of escape into a magic circle where the world's ills, to which the theater will soon release us once again, cannot touch us for the moment. Nothing is more poignant than the characteristic moment at the end of *Twelfth Night* when Shakespeare's sad and joyous spokesman the clown Feste voices what we already know in a song whose music carries us back to the comedy in whose sweet resolution we have just participated, but whose burden is the real world that awaits us beyond the charmed and charming circle the play has drawn: Our play is done, and "the rain it raineth every day." When Shakespeare translates history itself into the language of comedy, he reminds us, to our immediate joy and our continuing sadness, that such a moment as he thus presents is indeed a moment, that a unique combination of forces has made possible what cannot endure. In this respect *Henry* V is the most melancholy of the history plays.

The problem common to the four plays of Shakespeare's second cycle of history plays can thus be seen to arise from a view of man's tragic nature much like that of the psychoanalysts: Man is tragically torn between on the one hand the ethical demands made on him by his role in history and by that part of his personality which is compelled to accede to such demands, and on the other the instinctive sense that life is an amoral and absolute end in itself, and that only that matters which brings gratification to all the animal instincts, including the impulse to play. As we have seen, Shakespeare makes it finally impossible for his audience to choose the pleasure principle or the reality principle as the single basis of the good life, and he is no more optimistic than Freud about the possibility of living in a balance between the two. A version of the general dichotomy we have been observing in plays that deal with other problems, the view of human nature developed in the history plays reminds us that the roots of Shakespeare's psychology and ethics are planted in the neo-platonic and Christian tradition which sees man as an uneasy amalgam of opposed elements, soul and body, angel and beast. But unlike neoplatonists and Christians, Shakespeare does not resolve this problematic dichotomy by a resolution in favor of what tradition saw as the superior element in human nature, and this is why modern readers rightly recognize that his affinities are as much with the psychoanalytic as with the Christian under-standing.

◆§ IV §◆

A more simply explicable insight into the Shakespearean view of the tragic complementarity of human nature can be gained from *Measure for Measure,* a comedy concerned like the Henriad with man in the state in which all the problems of the history plays—the conflicting needs of law and freedom, order and libido, community justice and its sanctions concerning in-dividual will—are presented in terms of a fictitious society where Shakespeare is free to construct paradigms of the absolute state and Christian social order. Much has been written about the problems of this "problem play," and in some respects it will re-main troublesome; but in the clarity with which it sets up its problem, *Measure for Measure* illuminates the more tragic polit-ical plays, and I should like to discuss it briefly.

For modern audiences what seems most problematic is how to respond to Isabella's demand that her brother Claudio sacri-fice his life rather than allow Angelo to violate her chastity. To some critics it appears that Isabella has no right to make such a demand; Ernest Schanzer argues

> that it would be even more monstrous a perversion of justice
> for God to sentence her to eternal damnation for saving a
> brother's life by an act that has nothing whatever in com-
> mon with the deadly sin of lechery except its outward form,
> than it is for Angelo to condemn Claudio to death for an
> act which can only in the most legalistic sense be said to
> fall within the law against fornication.[11]

This is tempting, but one of the things that *Measure for Measure* makes clear is precisely that law is law, that the commission of a deadly sin for whatever reason is sinful, that in a Christian universe sin has absolute consequences. Claudio's own first response to Isabella's posing of the problem acknowledges the justice of her claim, and the play does not deny the theological framework in which the perdition of Isabella's soul is a greater evil than the loss of life which, under the Duke's eloquent instruction, Claudio has already admitted is only the gateway to eternal life. Significantly Shakespeare finds a happy resolution to the plot problem by educating his characters to a new understanding of law, by providing them a means of escape without necessitating their disobeying divine injunctions. *Measure for Measure* is not a naturalistic argument for sexual freedom.

And yet, as D. A. Traversi has argued in a persuasive study, Shakespeare opposes us to the kind of legalistic rigor that disturbs Schanzer by means of much of the substance of the play:

> In *Measure for Measure* the flesh acquires greater weight, more solid consistency, and to it corresponds a "law" which is "reason" made more personal, more immediately realized in answer to a more concrete sense of moral realities.[12]

As Traversi demonstrates, even the language in which the scurrilous Lucio mocks Claudio for his libidinous violation of the state's harsh law as wielded by Angelo conveys a vigorous sense, ironically poetic and appealing beyond Lucio's intentions, of the naturalness and attractiveness of the procreative function and the sensual impulses in general. In such an atmosphere, where man's animality is no less real or attractive than the ascetic spirituality which Angelo strains to absurdity and then finds too unreal as a definition even of his own nature, the audience of *Measure for Measure* finds itself deeply shocked by Isabella's crucial interview with her brother.

Her fault is not in what she asks, but rather in her failure to recognize the value of the sacrifice she demands. Though she is right she seems too right, acts as if what she asks of Claudio is easy to give; she is a prig. When in one of Shakespeare's most unforgettable speeches the masquerading Duke describes the ills

of that life he would have Claudio leave, we see the world from
Isabella's Christian point of view. *Contemptus mundi* teaches
us the importance of salvation, and Claudio agrees:

> I humbly thank you.
> To sue to live, I find I seek to die;
> And, seeking death, find life: let it come on.
>   (III. i. 41–43)

But Isabella uses the wrong strategy. Attempting to steel her
brother's resolution by denigrating the significance of death, she
reminds him that "the poor beetle, that we tread upon,/ In
corporal sufferance finds a pang as great/ As when a giant dies"
(III. i. 79–81). Claudio's first response is an irritable and proud
assertion that he is perfectly ready to die without such prodding:

> Why give you me this shame?
> Think you I can a resolution fetch
> From flowery tenderness? If I must die,
> I will encounter darkness as a bride,
> And hug it in mine arms.
>   (III. i. 81–85)

But his sister has planted in his mind the seeds of a doubt which
will suddenly erupt into full flower, for ironically she suggests
to him and to us the difference between a beetle's death and a
man's. She compounds her error by reawakening her brother's
moral outrage against his oppressor: Why should Claudio die for
Angelo's venality? Like Prince Andrew in *War and Peace*, Claudio
can be absolute for death only when he does not care about life,
and for him as for Prince Andrew anger against one who has
wounded him relumes a burning passion for life.

   Thus in response to Isabella's reminders of the reasons he
wants to live and to the heartless flippancy of her language in
making a demand both know she is right in making, Claudio
succumbs to a terrible fear of death:

> *Claud.* Death is a fearful thing.
> *Isab.* And shamed life a hateful.
> *Claud.* Ay, but to die, and go we know not where;

To lie in cold obstruction and to rot;
This sensible warm motion to become
A kneaded clod; and the delighted spirit
To bathe in fiery floods, or to reside
In thrilling region of thick-ribbed ice;
To be imprison'd in the viewless winds,
And blown with restless violence round about
The pendent world; or to be worse than worst
Of those that lawless and incertain thought
Imagine howling: 'tis too horrible!
The weariest and most loathed worldly life
That age, ache, penury and imprisonment
Can lay on nature is a paradise
To what we fear of death.

(III. i. 116–132)

Like Hamlet, who knows that the everlasting has set his canon against self-slaughter but knows not where one goes after death, Claudio is in one part of his being a good Christian, yet in another suspicious that life itself may be all life has to offer.

There is no answer to Isabella: She is right. But there is likewise no answer to Claudio, who is right in his own terms. The opposition between the Christian and the hedonistic-naturalistic views of life, so powerfully dramatized in the parallel speeches of the Duke and Claudio in III. i, is closely analogous to the opposition between the crown and Falstaff. And in *Measure for Measure* as in the Henriad, the conclusion is a paradoxical suggestion that the virtue in life is participating in both of these contradictory sets of values. In *Measure for Measure* the problem is solved—though many feel it is not—by tempering law with love, justice with mercy, by finding flexible judicial answers to questions that involve human passions, by divesting the self of that priggish self-assurance which taints Isabella as it almost destroys Angelo. Like Portia's use of the law to defeat Shylock's misuse of law, Isabella's bed trick reveals a sensibility able to endure the paradoxes of an imperfect world. But the happy endings of *Henry V* and *Measure for Measure* are imperfectly convincing enough to suggest that Shakespeare will not be satisfied with comic solutions to the insoluble problems man's nature inevitably creates in the public world. His two greatest political plays dramatize complementarity as the source of hopeless political tragedy.

❦ V ❧

Standing over the corpse of Julius Caesar at the climax of Shakespeare's tragedy, Mark Antony exclaims, "O, pardon me, thou bleeding piece of earth,/That I am meek and gentle with these butchers!" (III. i. 254–255). Most critics[13] have recognized in Antony's words an ironic refutation of Brutus' wishful imagining of the assassination:

> Let us be sacrificers, but not butchers, Caius.
> We all stand up against the spirit of Caesar;
> And in the spirit of men there is no blood:
> O, that we then could come by Caesar's spirit.
> And not dismember Caesar! But, alas,
> Caesar must bleed for it! And, gentle friends,
> Let's kill him boldly, but not wrathfully;
> Let's carve him as a dish fit for the gods,
> Not hew him as a carcass fit for hounds.
> (II. i. 166–174)

It should be noted that Antony refutes not only Brutus, but also Caesar. For the dictator, tempted by Calpurnia's dream not to go to the Capitol on the Ides of March, has been persuaded to ignore the dream by Decius' equally ritualistic and idealized interpretation of a spectacularly bloody incident:

> Your statue spouting blood in many pipes,
> In which so many smiling Romans bathed,
> Signifies that from you great Rome shall suck
> Reviving blood, and that great men shall press
> For tinctures, stains, relics and cognizance.
> This by Calpurnia's dream is signified.
> (II. ii. 85–90)

Two things interest us here, the emphasis put upon the blood at the turning point of the play and the surprising parallelism between Brutus' and Caesar's visions of it. The blood is a key to the meaning of the play. But in order fully to understand it we must first see the significance of the similarity between what Brutus and Caesar see in it. Like other such commanding touches in Shakespeare, the similarity is a crucially important element of an intricate and highly meaningful design. Before coming back to the turning point of the play, I should like to explore that design.

Part of the design is apparent already in the fact that in the first two scenes of Act II Brutus and Caesar make similar, and similarly ironic, statements about Caesar's blood. It is a remarkable fact which has escaped the notice of critics, though it must have occurred to innumerable audiences, that these two contiguous scenes are themselves extraordinarily like one another. Watching *Julius Caesar*, II. ii, the audience should be troubled by a sense of *déjà vu*; that sense, traced back to its causes, becomes increasingly troublesome. The scene presents the titular hero of the play for the first time as protagonist of a scene; the action focuses on him more than it has done heretofore. Similarly, the preceding scene has for the first time allowed the action to focus on the real hero of the tragedy. Though it is more than fitting that the play concentrate on its two great opponents on the eve of its climactic day, dramatic heightening alone will not explain the mysterious and graceful thoroughness with which the second scene repeats the action of the first.

II. ii begins, at the home of its protagonist, late in the night before the fatal Ides of March, as Caesar, his sleep disturbed, calls his servant:

> *Caesar.* Nor heaven nor earth have been at peace to-night:
> Thrice hath Calpurnia in her sleep cried out,
> "Help, ho! they murder Caesar!" Who's within?
>> *Enter* a servant.
> *Servant.* My lord?
> *Caesar.* Go bid the priests do present sacrifice
> And bring me their opinions of success.
> *Servant.* I will, my lord.   [*Exit*

Immediately we recall the opening of II.i:

> *Brutus.* What, Lucius, ho!
> I cannot, by the progress of the stars,

Give guess how near to day. Lucius, I say!
I would it were my fault to sleep so soundly.
What, Lucius, when? awake, I say! what, Lucius!
　　　Enter Lucius.
　　Lucius. Call'd you, my lord?
　　Brutus. Give me a taper in my study, Lucius.
When it is lighted, come and call me here.
　　Lucius. I will, my lord.　　　　　　　[*Exit*

As night gives way to morning in II. ii, Caesar, like Brutus in the preceding scene, greets as honored friends a group of conspirators. At the end of each scene, each antagonist has overcome his scruples and is asserting, in the presence of members of the conspiracy, his readiness to go to the Capitol. And in each scene the wife of its central figure, concerned about the consequences of her husband's behavior, assumes the position of suppliant: Calpurnia addresses Caesar "upon my knee" (II. ii. 54), Portia Brutus "upon my knees" (II. i. 270).

Striking enough; more so when we discover that Shakespeare has taken some pains to make his scenes appear thus constructed after a single pattern. Granville-Barker finds it necessary to apologize for the appearance of a conspirator at the end of II. i. "We may question," he remarks, "why, after a vibrant climax, Shakespeare so lowers the tension for the scene's end."[14] Only one advantage is gained by Brutus' departure in the company of Ligarius: the parallel with the end of the next scene. Moreover, Shakespeare has altered the material he found in his sources in such a way as to emphasize the similarity between the scenes. To cite a small instance, Plutarch describes Caesar as sending to the soothsayers after Calpurnia has spoken to him, but Shakespeare represents him doing so, in response to her talking in her sleep, before she enters the scene. Again no dramatic advantage is gained; the only importance of the change is that it allows Caesar's scene to open with a brief dialogue between protagonist and servant. More notable than these details, however, is the fact that the scene in Brutus' house does not exist in Plutarch's *Life of Brutus*; it is rather a composite of several scenes in which Brutus confers with the conspirators, decides who can be trusted, plans the assassination, *goes to visit C. Ligarius,* and fences with Portia's suspicion that something is in the wind. Even the dialogue with Portia, which Shakespeare bases closely on Plutarch, does not occur in the *Life* on the night before the Ides. The idea of parallel scenes in the two homes, then, is very much Shakespeare's own.

Such parallelism might of course be intended, like the scenes in the French and English camps on the eve of Agincourt in *Henry* V, to draw our attention to a contrast. We should expect to find dramatic differences between the characters of Brutus and Caesar, oppositions between notions and modes of behavior which might help point up the significance of the assassination. But when we begin to consider the Brutus of II. i and the Caesar of II. ii, we encounter some difficulty.

Watch Brutus, for example, as he refuses to join in an oath with the other conspirators:

> No, not an oath: if not the face of men,
> The sufferance of our souls, the time's abuse,—
> If these be motives weak, break off betimes,
> And every man hence to his idle bed;
> So let high-sighted tyranny range on,
> Till every man drop by lottery. But if these,
> As I am sure they do, bear fire enough
> To kindle cowards and to steel with valour
> The melting spirits of women; then, countrymen,
> What need we any spur but our own cause,
> To prick us to redress? what other bond
> Than secret Romans, that have spoke the word,
> And will not palter? and what other oath
> Than honesty to honesty engaged,
> That this shall be, or we will fall for it?
> (II. i. 114–128)

Here is Brutus the ardent republican, the ideal Roman, the man of action whose passionately maintained conception of honor makes him the first of a line of Shakespearean tragic heroes whose intensity of vision is almost their defining quality. Such a Brutus would be easy enough to contrast to a self- and time-serving Caesar. Brutus is right. What good is an oath which merely ornaments an action conceived in honor and love of country? Moreover, he is right practically. Any member of the band so inclined could break the oath to his own advantage and warn Caesar, and none does so in the absence of an oath. Oaths then are meaningless.

As Brutus' tirade goes on, however, a new note enters:

> Swear priests and cowards and men cautelous,
> Old feeble carrions and such suffering souls
> That welcome wrongs; unto bad causes swear
> Such creatures as men doubt; but do not stain
> The even virtue of *our* enterprise,
> Nor the insuppressive mettle of *our* spirits,
> To think that or *our* cause or *our* performance
> Did need an oath. . . .
>
> (II. i. 129–136)

The suggestion of vanity here increases immediately as Brutus mistakenly refuses to consider the possible aid that Cicero's oratory might give his cause. As Cassius, Casca, and Cinna advance arguments, Brutus says nothing. Then Metellus, not knowing his man, uses terms predictably repellent to Brutus to propose that Cicero might profitably be thought of by the populace as the leader of the conspiracy:

> O, let us have him, for his silver hairs
> Will purchase us a good opinion,
> And buy men's voices to commend our deeds;
> It shall be said, his judgement ruled our hands;
> Our youths and wildness shall no whit appear,
> But all be buried in his gravity.
>
> (II. i. 144–149)

Whether touched as under the circumstances he cannot afford to be by the crassness of Metellus' language, or wounded by the thought that Cicero will get credit for the leadership of the conspiracy, Brutus is wrong here, and his answer, that Cicero will not deign to join another man's cabal, is trivial, though his politic friends quickly agree with him.

Immediately follows what Plutarch, in North's translation, called Brutus' "first fault":[15] To the horror of every literate member of the audience, Brutus blithely rejects the proposal to murder Mark Antony. The speech in which he justifies his decision reveals a Brutus who parodies the sensible idealist of the preceding oration on honor, a man capable of blinding himself to practical realities through the casuistic use of analogy (Antony is merely the limb of a mystical body whose head is Caesar, and Antony will be unable to act once the head is off), and of a mystical mumbo jumbo whose foolishness is pointed up by Brutus' tolerant condescension immediately afterward to Cassius' superior worldly knowledge. The most famous lines in Brutus' speech describe his vision of the murder, and constitute the speech which is to be refuted by Mark Antony. The irony of Brutus' unworldly self-deception would be considerable in any context, but here, in an argument for the fatal preservation of Antony's life, it is unmistakable. The audience will recall these words shortly when Antony stands before the "dish fit for the gods" and calls the conspirators "butchers."

We have just seen Brutus then at his best and his worst, a virtuous man whose vices—not very serious vices, perhaps: vanity, inability to notice the vicious motives of those about him, a capacity to be deceived by analogies of his own making—undercut but do not vitiate the nobility of the character he demonstrates. Because his character is so mixed, it will be difficult to contrast him to the Caesar of any one scene; the expectations of contrast aroused by the parallelism between II. i and ii will have to be disappointed. What then can be the point of the symmetry?

Let us turn now to a central moment in II. ii. Caesar's servant has left to bring him the priests' opinions of success, and Calpurnia is imploring her husband to remain in his house. To her descriptions of the night's portents, lines calculated to terrify the audience as well as Caesar, the dictator wisely remarks that fate cannot be avoided, and that these predictions "are to the world in general as to Caesar" (II. ii. 29). Calpurnia replies that such portents obviously "blaze forth the death of princes," and Caesar responds with his most famous lines:

> Cowards die many times before their deaths;
> The valiant never taste of death but once.
> Of all the wonders that I yet have heard,
> It seems to me most strange that men should fear;

> Seeing that death, a necessary end,
> Will come when it will come.

> (II. ii. 32–37)

Like Brutus' speech against oaths in the preceding scene, Caesar's
stoical pronouncement is charged with Roman nobility. And like
that speech of Brutus', it degenerates immediately from magnificence to bluster, culminating in inflated self-adulation ironic in
the context. For as the servant returns with an absolute sign that
Caesar should not go forth, Caesar announces:

> The gods do this in shame of cowardice
> Caesar should be a beast without a heart,
> If he should stay at home to-day for fear.
> No, Caesar shall not: danger knows full well
> That Caesar is more dangerous than he:
> We are two lions litter'd in one day,
> And I the elder and more terrible;
> And Caesar shall go forth.

> (II. ii. 41–48)

For the rest of the scene Caesar's behavior alternates between
hyperbolic self-esteem such as this and suggestions of the sense
of dignity appropriate to the greatest of Romans. At Caesar's best
we see him, like Brutus earlier, ironically employing fine rhetoric
to support a mistaken decision.[16]

The resemblance between Brutus and Caesar is sketched in
other ways through these two scenes. In II. i we watch Brutus
succumbing to the skillful flattery of Cassius and company, who
gaily subscribe despite their trepidations to Brutus' refusal to kill
Antony. Ironically this episode is followed by Decius' account of
the way he flatters Caesar: by praising him for hating flatterers.
Already we may be noting the fact that both Brutus and Caesar
are—at least sometimes—susceptible to false praise. II. ii points
up the similarity when Decius' flattery finally persuades Caesar to
attend the day's exercises. Like the climax of Brutus' foolishness
in the preceding scene, in fact, Caesar's vanity is here demonstrated in his fatally capricious interpretation of the blood that
is about to be shed.

The juxtaposition of two such characterizations in two consecutive, crucial, and astonishingly similar scenes prods us to realize that Caesar and Brutus share a striking number of qualities. Both are great men who put country before self: Brutus' concern for the general good is dramatically mirrored in the crucial capacity for self-abnegation which Caesar shows when he refuses to hear Artemidorus' suit on the grounds—not those of his prototype in Plutarch—that "What touches us ourself shall be last served" (III. i. 8). Yet in both selflessness is intertwined with a self-destructive vanity and a tendency to play to the galleries: Witness the language of Caesar's rebuff to Artemidorus, or of Brutus' haughty remark to Cassius:

> There is no terror, Cassius, in your threats,
> For I am arm'd so strong in honesty
> That they pass by me as the idle wind,
> Which I respect not.
>
> (IV. iii. 66–69)

Significantly Brutus is perceptive enough at this point to see a falling off in Cassius, yet not perceptive enough to recognize worse failings in himself; thus he can reproach Cassius first for contaminating the bleeding of mighty Julius with money illegitimately raised, and second for not sending some of it to him ("For I can raise no money by vile means" [IV. iii. 71],).[17] A like balance of perception and self-righteous blindness is apparent in Caesar from the outset. Thus he sees better than Antony that the lean Cassius is not to be trusted, only to cancel out his observation with the fatuous "I rather tell thee what it is to be fear'd/ Than what I fear; for always I am Caesar" (I. ii. 211–212). Both sapient men, Caesar and Brutus alike sacrifice wisdom to egotism. Both generous men, Brutus with Cassius and Caesar with Metellus Cimber are alike predictably unable to relax a self-destructive moral rigidity.

In neither case is Shakespeare cynically deriding a great man for his weaknesses, large or small. Only a Cassius, never recovered from the shock of realizing that all men are mortal, could despise Caesar for being a poor swimmer. Shakespeare wants us rather to recognize them as flawed giants. Even in II. i and II. ii, where we learn more to their detriment than Mark Antony and Cassius ever know, Brutus and Caesar are presented to our admiration. Brutus is altruistic, courageous, compassionate and gentle with Ligarius, steadfastly noble in his recognition that oaths are superfluous and that honor should rule the conspiracy. Caesar too is courageous, contemptuous of cowards, a splendid Roman. If Brutus is unwilling to accept as a member of the conspiracy that Cicero who will "purchase us a good opinion," Caesar will not "send a lie" to the Senate to put a favorable light on his absence (II. ii. 65). More than their susceptibility to flattery and self-deception, their irrationality in deciding and rigidity in decision, and their posturing, we remember their largeness of soul, the courage with which they meet their ends, and—once again the strange link between them—their stoicism. Perhaps most startling of all the similarities, Caesar's famous expostulation on "death, a necessary end" looks forward directly to Brutus'

> Fates, we will know your pleasures:
> That we shall die, we know; 'tis but the time
> And drawing days out, that men stand upon.
> (III. i. 98–100)

and

> O, that a man might know
> The end of this day's business ere it come!
> But it sufficeth that the day will end,
> And then the end is known.
> (V. i. 123–126)

What can be Shakespeare's meaning in so carefully identifying Brutus with Caesar, slayer with slain? Ernest Schanzer has demonstrated how the ambiguity in Caesar's character fulfills the purpose of "show[ing] up the futility and foolishness of the assassination," and he argues persuasively that "the whole second part of the play is an ironic comment on Brutus' 'We all stand up against the spirit of Caesar,/ And in the spirit of men there is no blood. . . .'"[18] This is the function as well of an elaborate parallel which above all totally discredits Brutus' picture of the significance of the assassination. For if at best Caesar is to be replaced by his mirror image, what will the great eruption have accomplished? By making us see the similarity between Brutus and Caesar, Shakespeare has made the assassination rather a criminal mistake, as such recent critics as Palmer and Schanzer regard it, than an act of public virtue. The course taken by the events of the last acts implies that *Julius Caesar* is designed as a criticism of Brutus' action and as the embodiment of a despairing political quietism not evident in Shakespeare's earlier plays. But the similarly ambiguous presentations of the great antagonists are not the only key to the play's meaning: for by a brilliant manipulation of convention which no member of his first audience could have missed, Shakespeare brings us even more powerfully in the last acts to understand the meaning of Brutus' crime.

Let us return to the play's pivotal moment, where we began: Mark Antony's answer to Brutus' naïve idealization of the shedding of Caesar's blood. As everyone knows, *Julius Caesar* seems to start over as a new play at this point. Much recent criticism holds that the point of the second half of the tragedy is the triumph of "Caesarism"; Professor Schanzer has effectively refuted MacCallum, Dover Wilson, and the rest on this matter,[19] but his discussion of the ghost does not fully account for the events which comprise the last acts of the tragedy. What really happens at the moment of Antony's speech over Caesar's body is that the play changes its terms to those of a convention that at once gives new meaning to the reality with which Brutus thinks he has been dealing and informs the audience of the course events are to take. One is dubious about Brutus' grasp of the nature of things when he admonishes his fellow conspirators that the carving of Caesar can spill its victim's blood without constituting murder. He is deceived by his own logic, and, as we have already seen, this wishful self-deception is directly answered by Mark Antony's definition of the murderers as "butchers." At precisely this point in the plot, as Brutus bids his companions bathe their hands in Caesar's blood, the play changes its course:

> A curse shall light upon the limbs of men;
> Domestic fury and fierce civil strife
> Shall cumber all the parts of Italy;

> Blood and destruction shall be so in use
> And dreadful objects so familiar
> That mothers shall but smile when they behold
> Their infants quarter'd with the hands of war;
> All pity choked with custom of fell deeds:
> And Caesar's spirit, ranging for revenge,
> With Ate by his side come hot from hell,
> Shall in these confines with a monarch's voice
> Cry "Havoc," and let slip the dogs of war;
> That this foul deed shall smell above the earth
> With carrion men, groaning for burial.
>   (III. i. 262–275)

Mark Antony here calls up the world of revenge tragedy. No member of an audience remembering the *Ur-Hamlet* and *Titus Andronicus*, still in love with *The Spanish Tragedy*, and within a year of seeing the first performance of *Hamlet* could have missed Shakespeare's point; but nothing is more ephemeral than theatrical convention, and today only a familiarity with plays long dead and with such scholarship as Professor Bowers' *Elizabethan Revenge Tragedy* can make us understand what the first audience realized instantaneously. Antony reminds us, as we look at Caesar's blood, what blood on the stage can mean, and it is the moral law of that imaginary world that controls the rest of the play's events: The evil that men do lives after them; a bloody act committed to pay ambition's debt promptly incurs a further debt that must be paid; the ghost of a murdered man stalks his murderers; the sword of the revenger will not go up again "till Caesar's three and thirty wounds/ Be well avenged; or till another Caesar/ Have added slaughter to the sword of traitors" (V. i. 53–55). In the bloody world of revenge tragedy an audience knows precisely how to evaluate the part of each actor: Brutus, the first criminal, must trade his life for his crime; Mark Antony, the hero-revenger, is no sooner a hero than by the inner dynamics of his role he is the villain of the piece.[20]

The logic of the revenge conventions justifies the title of a play in which the titular hero is out of the way before the third act has barely got under way: Caesar is the moving force of the tragedy. The action of the play makes clear sense in terms of revenge tragedy. From the moment of the murder Brutus is marked as victim, and historical process will operate on the principle that blood will have blood. Morality is irrelevant. The efficient avenger must dissemble, disclaiming the very rhetoric he employs, urging indiscriminate mischief to take what course it will because the only way back to rest is through the spilling of blood. And because morality is irrelevant, the high principles on which the noblest of the conspirators moved become a mockery. Mark Antony is deeply and movingly touched by the death of his friend, but his responsive action is utterly without the lofty end of Brutus' bloody act. The principle of his action is opportunism. Where we know the populace to be "blocks, . . . stones, . . . worse than senseless things" (I. i. 40), he can appeal, as Brutus never deigned to do, to their vanity: "You are not wood, you are not stones, but men" (III. ii. 147). Whereas Brutus hesitates to kill Caesar despite what he takes to be an immediate danger to Rome, and refuses (however foolishly) to kill Antony himself, Mark Antony damns with a spot his sister's son, only to please a fellow triumvir for whom he has utter contempt. The point is clear. By committing an act that makes possible the dialectic of the revenge play, Brutus has automatically removed from history the feasibility of that high-minded governance to which he dedicates his life.[21] Because of his crime against established order, success will now go to the calculating. In such a world as he has made possible, one's chances for survival are in direct proportion to one's skill at seizing the main chance; moral passion is of no value. And so as *Julius Caesar* closes it is not even the hotblooded Antony, but the icily opportunistic Octavius who inherits Brutus' followers and makes the final disposition.

As he was to do, though with a difference, in *Hamlet*, and unlike his predecessors, Shakespeare used revenge tragedy to create the moral universe, the philosophical base, of his play. In the world of *Julius Caesar*, the conventions establish a dramatically convincing representation of a universe, governed by inexorable law, in which events are brought about not according to man's idealistic intentions but deterministically by their own logic. The ghost stalking Brutus at Philippi calls up a cosmic order in which Brutus' wishful planning is totally irrelevant.[22] "Indeed," the sage

Cicero has warned us at the outset, "it is a strange-disposed time:/ But men may construe things after their fashion,/ Clean from the purpose of the things themselves" (I. iii. 33–35). Caesar's superstition, his trust of his own personal majesty, his willing self-deception, and Brutus' naïve idealism, speciously leading him to the fatal sparing of Antony as well as to the unwarranted killing of Caesar,[23] are signs of such construing, answered finally by the irrefutable truth of historical fact played out in time. The lover, the lunatic, and the poet, Shakespeare has told us, see to the truth of things by the tricks of strong imagination, supplying through inner vision the sense and purpose that the seeing eye cannot provide. In the world of ancient history, he clearly implies, such vision is worse than futile. Troilus may argue that things are as they are valued, but Hector's contention that value lies not in the will but in the fact is confirmed by a world in which Cressida is what time proves her to be, not what Troilus posits her to be. Richard II may dream of the divinity that hedges a king, but Bolingbroke wins a crown because he understands political reality and acts only on what the moment offers.

Such a world, in which history, not man, is the determining force, is enunciated by Brutus when he erroneously uses his perception to justify battle at Philippi;

> There is a tide in the affairs of men,
> Which, taken at the flood, leads on to fortune;
> Omitted, all the voyage of their life
> Is bound in shallows and in miseries.
> On such a full sea are we now afloat;
> And we must take the current when it serves,
> Or lose our ventures.
>
> (IV. iii. 218–224)

The ironic fact that Brutus is wrong about the particular application of his insight serves only to support his generalization. His wisdom here is undercut only by his failure to realize that the flood cannot be gauged by the reasoning mind. In a world governed by necessity, plans, whether noble or otherwise, have little effect on the course of events. Brutus and Cassius believe that history is amenable to reason. Cassius' intuitions may tend to be more accurate and his plans more successful in the short range, but in the long range both men succumb to a historical process over which they have no control, while success, as we have seen, goes to the opportunist who does not plan but irresponsibly allows mischief to take its own course, and from him to Octavius, who initiates no action but simply waits to gather the fallen fruit.

Making his point in yet another way, Shakespeare shows us that even the man who attempts to live by reason is governed by irrational elements within himself that he cannot recognize. Thus the great soliloquy in which Brutus contemplates the killing of Caesar begins with a decision already made—"It must be by his death"—and proceeds through a set of rationalizations that reveal the utter absence of foundation for Brutus' fears.[24] The proud and independent Brutus—like the proud and independent Caesar subject, as we have seen, to skillful flattery—bases his action as much on the shrewd innuendo of Cassius as on the formulations of his own reason, and, noble though he is, shows by the eve of Philippi a degeneration—manifest in his querulousness, his new eagerness to finance his campaign with ill-got money as long as he has not raised the money himself, and his exaggerated priggishness with the newly sympathetic Cassius—which demonstrates clearly that even character is determined more by process than by abiding and shaping inner principles.

Brutus' ultimate wisdom, the only statement he ever makes to which the play offers no contradictory answer, is his recognition that the end is known only when the day has ended. Significantly this realization brings him precisely to Caesar's position: Death, the necessary end, will come when it will come. In the fact, not men's construing, is the meaning. Man is only actor, not playwright, and as actor he may not even, in the terms of *Julius Caesar*, know the conventions of the play in which he acts. In Cassius' ebullient words as the conspirators bend over the body of Caesar, Shakespeare makes mortifyingly explicit the fundamental irony of his tragedy:

> Stoop, then, and wash. How many ages hence
> Shall this our lofty scene be acted over
> In states unborn and accents yet unknown!
> (III. i. 111–113)

But by this point Shakespeare has made us party to his irony: He has let us see and consider before the assassination the identity between Caesar and Brutus which is at the center of the play. Confronted with a body of historical material which meant a great many things to a great many people, yet characteristically motivated by the artist's desire to transform the raw materials of historiography into the coherent form of significant art, Shakespeare has experimented with both structure and convention in *Julius Caesar*. By creating virtually *ex nihilo* a surprising parallelism between two crucial scenes, and by turning at its climax what promised to be a tragical history into a revenge play, he has twice directed our responses toward the meaning that is the vital principle of the play.

◄§ VI §►

Though the politics of *Julius Caesar* is essentially the same as that of the second tetralogy, setting visionary idealism against revolutionary *Realpolitik* and making a choice of one or the other a mistake, the Roman play is far more pessimistic. In *Julius Caesar* we find no statements like the Archbishop of Canterbury's portrait of an ideal state, no hint of an ideal polity such as Henry V approaches no matter how temporarily. Moreover, whereas Bolingbroke is a man in whom considerable virtue is merely qualified by the fact that his goal is power as much as the good of the state, Mark Antony's virtues are less easy to perceive, and Octavius, unlike those who triumph in the histories, is a selfish and unprincipled man from whom one can expect only evil. But what makes the politics of *Julius Caesar* hopelessly tragic is Brutus. Richard II is a man undone by vices which Shakespeare makes us understand have their virtuous aspects and would be attractive elsewhere. But Brutus is ruined by his virtues, and they are presented so much as such that many critics have found themselves unable to believe that Shakespeare really wants us to find fault with him. It is Brutus' hope for politics, his belief that reason and will can make history human rather than mechanical, his dream of Rome's good, that destroy him and the kind of world he generously wants. In his attractiveness is the true complementarity of the play. Once again, but more poignantly than in any previous historical play, Shakespeare has created a tragedy in which what we hope of the world is poised against what the world really is, and there is no possibility of the kind of world men with ideals and vision can be content with. Never again in a play dealing with history will Shakespeare allow us to believe even for a moment that such a state may exist as Brutus believed in and as Shakespeare himself for the moment of *Henry V* may have thought possible. The tragedy of the historical plays is based increasingly on Shakespeare's psychology, which sees human ideals and the virtue of reason set hopelessly against the fact of the human drive for power. One can understand history and participate actively in politics in the light of the first, *Julius Caesar* tells us, but one will be doomed to failure; or one can succeed by means of an understanding of the other, only to abandon the dream of a commonwealth devoted to the common good.

In his last political play Shakespeare carries the tragic pessimism of *Julius Caesar* to its conclusion. In *Coriolanus* as in the earlier plays he creates a protagonist whose virtues are his vices, whose moral assets disqualify him for political success. But here he goes even further than in *Caesar* to demonstrate that the virtue of the political idealist, though better than any other moral quality evinced in the play, is so self-destructive and so flawed in other ways as hardly to deserve the name virtue. In *Coriolanus* Shakespeare demonstrates bitterly that even the idealism we admired in Brutus is a pipe dream, and in so doing he comes closer than ever before to our least illusioned sense of what political reality may be. No modern dramatist has written a more despairing or a more convincing play about man and the state.

In a grim parody of the opening of *Julius Caesar*, the first scene begins with the passionate charge of a number of mutinous citizens that Caius Marcius, later to be named Coriolanus, is "chief enemy to the people" (I. i. 8). Like Othello and Antony, the hero is presented to us first from a hostile point of view, but the initial denunciation of Marcius is even more striking for its prophetic qualities. He is, after all, in the course of very little time, going to become Rome's hero and leader, get himself banished as chief enemy to the people, become what he has been accused of as he joins forces with Rome's enemy, the Volscian Aufidius, and ultimately die violently at the hands of his erstwhile friends. Whether or not the people's charge at the outset is true, however, its moral force is vitiated by their motivations: "Let us kill him, and we'll have corn at our own price. Is 't a verdict?" (I. i. 10–11). From here to the end of the play, shortsighted selfishness in those who surround him will be an important part of the moral background against which we shall have to construct our judgments of the hero himself.

The chorus of popular criticism of Marcius reaches its climax in a strange bit of dialogue:

> *First citizen.* I say unto you, what he hath done fa-
> mously, he did it to that end: though soft-conscienced men
> can be content to say it was for his country, he did it to
> please his mother, and to be partly proud; which he is,
> even to the altitude of his virtue.
> *Second citizen.* What he cannot help in his nature, you
> account a vice in him. You must in no way say he is covetous.
>
> (I. i. 36–44)

The most interesting thing about this description is its judicious-ness. The two men agree that Marcius has so many faults that one does not need to accuse him of the selfishness we have already seen the citizens manifesting; and strangely they suggest in their brief comments all the possible interpretations of Marcius' be-havior that the play will make available: He is motivated by honor, by the desire for fame, by patriotism, by the desire to please his mother, by pride. Moreover, his pride and his virtues are linked, and his pride can be seen as not so much a vice as a part of his nature that he cannot help, a tic, a neurosis. Again and again as the hero's character unfolds itself to us we shall find our minds returning to this strange mash of incompatible judgments and perceptions. We shall find ourselves disturbed about the relations of moral principle to personal psychology, of virtue and vice in action to inner compulsion in character; and we shall find that, like the character of Mark Antony, that of Caius Marcius grows more rather than less ambivalent before our eyes.

There is nothing ambivalent, however, in the presentation of the populace. Even a Stalinist critic of Shakespeare, who sees *Coriolanus* as reflecting Shakespeare's "profound disillusionment with absolutism, the court, the state officials, and the upper classes" and as a play in which "the plebeians constitute the only positive force," recognizes at least that Shakespeare is disturbed by the "political immaturity" of the people.[25] The populace is consistently presented as unstable, fickle, anarchical, deficient in vision. Our attitude toward them is defined in the first scene by the hero's friend Menenius Agrippa, an easygoing aristocrat who responds to their mutiny by telling his famous fable of the re-bellion of the body's members against the belly. Speaking in the traditional metaphor in which the state is a body, organically interdependent, nourished from a single source, Menenius uses the fable to his own ends, and Shakespeare uses it for effects that reach beyond this moment. Menenius' purpose, and the immediate effect of the account, is the degradation of the plebes. If the state is a body, the first citizen is the great toe of the assembly, his fellows mindless members who are fed but contribute nothing to the general welfare. The larger effect is the result of a limitation in Menenius' own vision. The notion of the state as organism is familiar to us from the earlier plays and part of the optimistic Renaissance myth of the state, but Shakespeare has changed the tone of the ancient fable he allows Menenius to tell so that the whole state comes to seem distasteful. The senate, center and source of the state's welfare, is only the belly; the sensual Menen-ius, who substitutes belly for brain in his own life, would find nothing wrong with such a picture, but the speech, taken as an ideal vision of the nature of the state, is repellent.

It is at this moment, when the populace has presented itself as selfish and utterly contemptible, and the voice of its aristocratic government has shown a good deal of wit but not much vision, that the hero of the tragedy first appears, railing. As Traversi has pointed out, Marcius' entry is a "masterpiece of irony," a "perversion of the traditional speech of warlike heroes."[26] Where we expect uplifting oration, we get rodomontade. If the nobility would lay aside its ruth and let him use his sword, says the military hero of Rome,

> I'ld make a quarry
> With thousands of these quarter'd slaves, as high
> As I could pick my lance.
>
> (202–204)

When word comes that the Volscians are planning war against
Rome, General Scrooge rejoices at the opportunity to reduce the
surplus population of his city, and sardonically observes that now
the Roman plebes can steal Volscian corn: "Take these rats
thither/ To gnaw their garners" (I. i. 253–254).

By the end of the first scene we are bewildered. Though the
populace is ugly enough to throw our sympathies to Marcius,
his undignified fury cools those sympathies. Unable to determine
whose side we are to be on, we may begin to think that this is
going to be the kind of play in which not sympathy but mocking
contempt is the playwright's aim; that is, we begin to expect that
the whole play will be a bitter satire.

The brief second scene makes us wonder, though, as it introduces us to Tullus Aufidius, Marcius' counterpart in the Volscian
world. For as we see Aufidius scheming in the Senate at Corioles,
planning deception against Rome, objecting because word has got
to the Romans that the Volscians are preparing for war, we realize
that the one political vice we have not seen in Marcius is a
willingness to use policy; he makes no pretense about his feelings. We learn moreover that Aufidius and Marcius are sworn
enemies. The play's structure thus leads us to qualify our initial
censure of Coriolanus, and to begin to be aware of the central
issue.

In the third scene Shakespeare adds to the uneasiness that
stems from our inability to decide what judgments to make as we
meet Volumnia, the hero's mother:

> I pray, you daughter, sing; or express yourself in a more
> comfortable sort: if my son were my husband, I should
> freelier rejoice in that absence wherein he won honour
> than in the embracements of his bed where he would
> show most love. When yet he was but tender-bodied
> and the only son of my womb, when youth with comeli-

ness plucked all gaze his way, when for a day of kings'
entreaties a mother should not sell him an hour from
her beholding, I, considering how honour would become such a person, that it was no better than picture-
like to hang by the wall, if renown made it not stir, was
pleased to let him seek danger where he was like to find
fame. To a cruel war I sent him; from whence he returned, his brows bound with oak. I tell thee, daughter,
I sprang not more in joy at first hearing he was a man-
child than now in first seeing he had proved himself
a man.

(I. iii. 1–19)

Surely this speech reflects our ideal vision of Rome. We may
carp at Volumnia's insistence that *she sent* her son to a bloody
war, but in the mother preferring her son's death to his lack of
honor, reflected in the next speech she makes, we recognize the
classic Roman matron.

As she goes on, however, a new note is sounded. Praising her
son's behavior in the battlefield she describes him oddly:

His bloody brow
With his mail'd hand then wiping, forth he goes,
Like to a harvest-man that's task'd to mow
Or all or lose his hire.

(37–40)

The picture, which will recur throughout the play, is of a terri-
fying automatic warrior, the inhuman mechanism of destruction
so well described by Traversi,[27] and it makes Volumnia's dream
somewhat less attractive. What Shakespeare is up to becomes
absolutely clear in the dialogue which follows. Marcius' gentle
and loving wife Virgilia objects, "His bloody brow! O Jupiter,
no blood!" and Volumnia responds in a speech reminiscent of
Lady Macbeth:

Away, you fool! it more becomes a man
Than gilt his trophy: the breasts of Hecuba,
When she did suckle Hector, look'd not lovelier
Than Hector's forehead when it spit forth blood
At Grecian sword, contemning.

(I. iii. 42–46)

Virgilia's reply, "Heavens bless my lord from fell Aufidius!" contrasts with the strange intensity with which Volumnia hopes her son will be wounded.

The final touch in the portrait of Volumnia is a speech by Virgilia's friend Valeria which Volumnia enthusiastically approves. "O' my word, the father's son," Valeria says of Marcius' little boy who prefers swords to schoolbooks;

> O' my troth, I looked upon him o' Wednesday half an
> hour together: has such a confirmed countenance. I saw
> him run after a gilded butterfly; and when he caught
> it, he let it go again; and after it again; and over and
> over he comes, and up again; catched it again; or whether
> his fall enraged him, or how 'twas, he did so set his
> teeth, and tear it; o, I warrant how he mammocked it!
>
> (62–71)

Volumnia's delighted answer, "One on's father's moods," may make us wonder whether perhaps our stomachs simply aren't strong enough for the necessary toughness of a Roman ideal Shakespeare wants us to admire. But eventually—not now, be it noted, when his aim seems to be our bewilderment—an ironic judgment will be made on this exchange. As the play begins its final movement, and news comes that the exiled and embittered Coriolanus, gone over to the Volscians, is making war against Rome, the admirable general Cominius, once Marcius' superior, describes the new enemy of Rome in a speech which unmistakably picks up the imagery of Valeria's fatuous reminiscence:

> He is their god: he leads them like a thing
> Made by some other deity than nature,
> That shapes man better; and they follow him,
> Against us brats, with no less confidence
> Than boys pursuing summer butterflies,
> Or butchers killing flies.
>
> (IV. vi. 90–95)

Here again is Coriolanus the heartless, perhaps mindless, mechanical man, the breaker of butterflies. Against Cominius' description of Coriolanus as his mother desires him to be our admiration for Volumnia is shattered.

In one other way our puzzled responses to the third scene will be clarified and redirected later. Throughout this scene, no matter how much we are tempted to find fault with Volumnia, we find ourselves at least equally tempted to wonder if the retiring Virgilia isn't too much the wife, too ready to put home and hearth before the moral necessity of war and country and the manly duties of her husband. But to our surprise it is Virgilia who impresses us most after her husband's banishment with her courage in standing up to and denouncing the craven tribunes who have engineered that banishment. Volumnia vituperates as we would expect her to, but Virgilia's cold, unblinking hostility comes as such a surprise to us that we are forced to re-evaluate her character, and therefore Volumnia's. I think it might be argued that though Shakespeare's men are each of them *sui generis*, his women are created in accordance with a formula. Every woman in the canon is a mixture of elements clearly distinguishable as masculine and feminine. The ideal type is perhaps born before our eyes when Petrucchio's Katherine learns to control and subordinate her masculine will, yet to keep it as a real if submerged element in her personality at the end of *The Taming of the Shrew*. The villainous woman is too much the man, the manager, the denier of her femininity: Tamora; Goneril; Regan; Lady Macbeth, who would be unsexed, who would pluck her nipple from the boneless gums of her smiling babe and dash its brains out. The weak woman lacks too much of man: Olivia, who moons away in a perpetual posture of ailing emotion; the helpless Ophelia ("I do not know, my lord, what I should think"); Gertrude; Bianca; Hero; and so on. The ideal woman in Shakespeare is always utterly feminine in charm and acceptance of her place in the social hierarchy, but equipped with a masculine will as strong as iron: General Cordelia, the two Portias, Viola, Rosalind, Beatrice, the matured Juliet, Isabella, Helena, Hotspur's Kate, and Desdemona. Significantly the ideal woman in Shakespearean comedy often disguises herself as a man, then reclaims her feminine identity. In *Coriolanus* Volumnia perplexes us at first. We do not know whether she is presented as ideal or as leaning too much in the direction of Lady Macbeth; but the presentation of Virgilia as an ideal type (and we must note the touching genuineness of her husband's affection for her) tells us how we must ultimately judge the hero's mother.

At the moment, however, we do not know that our feelings will eventually be so directed, and toward both Volumnia and her son they remain ambivalent, as they will through much of this movement of the play. As he has done so often, Shakespeare forces us once again to see a crucial characterization according to opposing systems of value. We simultaneously admire and are horrified by Volumnia and her vision. And so it is with war and soldiery. Marcius has already aroused in us one possible attitude toward war, our sense of its brutality, its meaninglessness, its ability to degrade the men who pursue it. But in the next scene we find corroboration for the gallant and inspiring picture of war suggested earlier by Volumnia's first speeches, as Marcius and his fellow general Titus Lartius, camped before Corioles, show us what friendship among men of war can be: hearty, unaffected, cheerful, laconic, and mutually respectful. This sense of Marcius' military life and of war becomes more pleasant as, his tone reminiscent of Henry V, he urges his men enthusiastically to battle; but it collapses immediately as, his soldiers beaten back, Marcius storms on stage ranting at his men:

> All the contagion of the south light on you,
> You shames of Rome! you herd of——Boils and plagues
> Plaster you o'er, that you may be abhorr'd
> Further than seen and one infect another
> Against the wind a mile!
>
> (I. iv. 30–34)

Through all the military scenes of the first act we are held poised between our sense of the gallantry of war and our feeling of its hideousness. Let me cite one example of the subtle efficiency with which Shakespeare thus suspends our judgments. The Romans have virtually been defeated; against impossible odds Marcius fights his way back to Cominius' camp, and the two generals select soldiers to accompany Marcius back into the battle he insists on fighting despite his wounds. Cominius asks Marcius to take his choice of the men who will be most useful to him, and Marcius answers:

> Those are they
> That most are willing. If any such be here—
> As it were sin to doubt—that love this painting
> Wherein you see me smear'd; if any fear
> Lesser his person than an ill report;
> If any think brave death outweighs bad life
> And that his country's dearer than himself;
> Let him alone, or so many so minded,
> Wave thus, to express his disposition,
> And follow Marcius.
>
> (I. vi. 66–75)

Again shades of Henry V at Agincourt. But notice that the love of bloody painting comes first, the love of country last. The opposition Shakespeare has so carefully established between two aspects of the warlike personality reveals the doubleness of our own attitudes toward war, and more particularly the composite nature of that personality. The gallantry is inseparable from the bloodiness; it is not the gentle Cominius but the savage Marcius who has the force to lead his broken troops into victory. But Shakespeare is not, like a sociologist, simply reporting his observations, but rather challenging our moral sensibility. If the character of the soldier is as we see it here, what is its moral status? As the play is set up so far, this is a disturbing and unanswerable question.

I. ix enlarges and changes this question. A crucial scene, it introduces what from the hero's point of view will be the most important question of the play. What we have been asking so far, as we have tried to come to a simple attitude toward Volumnia and her son, is what judgment we are to pass on that classical Rome we recognize in the play. What is Rome, a world of bloody passion and the love of death, or a theater for exemplary heroism? But the question I. ix presents Marcius is rather, "What is honor?"

Again it is structure—the juxtaposition of scenes—that makes us know what questions Shakespeare wants us to ask. Increas-

ingly through this act Marcius has grown in our esteem as his
prowess and manliness have met all tests. In the minuscule eighth
scene, which lasts scarcely a minute, we have watched his climactic defeat of Aufidius, which both ends the battle and, equally
importantly, reminds us of the opposition between the dishonorable leader of the Volscians and the upright Roman general. And
now in scene ix we find Marcius' superior Cominius offering him
the honors he has earned. With the economy characteristic of his
maturest plays, Shakespeare simultaneously presents in the terse
opening dialogue of this scene a brilliant bit of drama, a tense
exchange between two complicated human beings, and an almost
abstract argument.

Cominius praises Rome's noblest soldier; Marcius objects
mildly but firmly to the praise, which embarrasses him no matter
who gives it.[28] His reasoning is appropriately modest and his manner gracious:

> I have done
> As you have done; that's what I can; induced
> As you have been; that's for my country:
> He that has but effected his good will
> Hath overta'en mine act.
>
> (15–19)

But Cominius can answer Marcius on his own grounds: If it is
Rome he is interested in, it is for Rome's benefit that Marcius
must accept praise:

> You shall not be
> The grave of your deserving; Rome must know
> The value of her own: 'twere a concealment
> Worse than a theft, no less than a traducement,
> To hide your doings . . .
>
> (I. ix. 19–23)

Marcius does not attempt to answer this argument, remarking only that his wounds hurt when they are talked about;
Cominius replies that they would hurt worse if ingratitude were
their reward, and signals his estimation of Marcius' services' worth
by offering him the tenth part of the spoils taken, and at this

point the action erupts. "I thank you, general," the hero says, "But cannot make my heart consent to take/ A bribe to pay my sword." A flourish sounds, the army cheers, "Marcius, Marcius," and throws up caps and lances—and Marcius denounces the entire gathering as flatterers and hypocrites.

> You shout me forth
> In acclamations hyperbolical;
> As if I loved my little should be dieted
> In praises sauced with lies.
>
> (I. ix. 50–53)

This is a peculiar performance. Modesty and self-respecting dignity are one thing, but the gratuitous insulting of his friend and benefactor as a briber and of the army he has led to victory as a pack of liars is another. What is most peculiar is what Cominius observes in calmly ignoring the insult and answering his difficult protégé: In rejecting the offered honors Marcius is damaging the good report that he has earned.

And now, at this crucial impasse, Shakespeare gives us the most dramatic example of a device he has used elsewhere: He makes an issue of his hero's name in order to make us think about the problem of the hero's identity. Just so in *Troilus and Cressida*, as we have seen, the questions are explicitly and repeatedly asked: What is Cressid? Who is Troilus? And in *Antony and Cleopatra*, troubled by the two possible judgments between which we are suspended, we hear constantly: "Antony will be himself"; "Sometimes, when he is not Antony"; "Name Cleopatra as she is called in Rome"; "Had our general been what he knew himself, it had gone well"; "Observe how Antony becomes his flaw"; "I am Antony yet"; "What's her name/ Since she was called Cleopatra?"; "But since my lord is Antony again, I will be Cleopatra." But here history allows Shakespeare to do what he could not do elsewhere, actually to change the name of his character on the stage. From now on, since Marcius will accept no other rewards, Cominius announces he will be called Coriolanus, the conqueror of Corioles. Marcius accepts without protest; his new identity is defined—like the identity of all Shakespearean heroes, we might note—by his achievement.

But the meaning of the name is ambiguous, and does not solve the debate which underlies the quarrel between Marcius and Cominius. For there is a real issue there, making sense of what otherwise would be quirky perversity in the hero. For Cominius, and for the army so eager that their hero accept their gifts, honor is something that comes to one for one's achievement in the world; it is conferred by society, involved in good name and reputation, public praise and office; the unrewarded deed is the grave of its deserving. For Caius Marcius, however, the deed is its own reward, honorable or dishonorable regardless of what people think of it; honor is a quality of action, not of action's effects; honest praise is flattery and lies because all words that describe what is ultimately personal and subjective must miss the point. As we shall discover later, Marcius feels special justification in his position because he feels those who would "honor" him to be so unworthy, but he rejects accolades even from the worthy Cominius; the argument is philosophical.

As he had done in *Henry IV*, Shakespeare is exploring the double implications of a word on which are built some of our most important ethical and social structures.[29] Shakespeare did not invent the problem, nor did it end with his plays. E. R. Dodds and Bruno Snell, among others, have demonstrated in their brilliant studies of the development of Greek religious concepts that Greek thought fluctuated from prephilosophical times between the Homeric assumption that virtue is defined by and consists in a certain kind of social approval and the later idea of an internalized virtue responsible only to absolutes that lie beyond social jurisdiction.[30] An interesting history of the west might be written from the point of view of our culture's inability to determine finally whether it is what anthropologists call a shame culture, based on an intense sensitivity to communal standards, or a guilt culture, in which individual conscience and consciousness are the only standards the virtuous man can respect. It is not surprising that the Renaissance, that age in which the syncretism of western culture was felt most urgently and in which much that is important in philosophy, statecraft, and the arts was the result of an often conscious tension between Hebrew-Christian and classical elements, should have produced so many literary works in which the idea of honor in its opposed meanings is crucial. The ambiguity of the idea, classically developed in the implicit debate between Hotspur and Falstaff, is crucial as well in numerous plays by Shakespeare's contemporaries, and by the mid-seventeenth century has become one of the few subjects left to tragedy. Nor does it fail to trouble subsequent ages. I have argued elsewhere that the meaning of Richardson's *Clarissa* is its author's understanding of the process by which the shame-culture idea of honor, the idea that virtue and social approval are identical, has itself become internalized in his heroine so that it has the force of the guilt-culture idea. For the middle-class eighteenth-century heroine social propriety and convention are sacred virtues; her " 'character' "—a word ambiguous precisely as "honor" is ambiguous—is " 'more valuable . . . than my life.' "[31] The problem still occupies us; statesmen find themselves caught in the trap of our "national honor," unable to determine whether by it they mean our commitment to certain inviolable political ideals or what other nations think of us; and an interesting bit of material for the cultural history of our time is the formula of firms admonishing clients for whom they have opened charge accounts, "Your credit rating is a sacred trust." In *Coriolanus* Shakespeare comes most to grips with the problem that has troubled his treatment of politics from the beginning: the problem of honor.

In accepting the name Coriolanus, Marcius accepts public recognition for what he has done, and necessarily compromises himself. Like Lear, Macbeth, Brutus, and Hamlet, Coriolanus makes us realize here how much the hero is created by what he has accomplished, defined by the events through which he has passed. And perhaps in accepting his new name Coriolanus realizes, as certainly those do who give him the name and we do who watch the ceremony, that the world is not quite so subjective as Marcius had thought. Most of the events in which we are involved include other people; Coriolanus' name memorializes a public battle and, like all names, is given *to* him; the achievement recorded by the new name is an achievement whose meaning derives from the fact that it was performed for Rome. Coriolanus cannot both insist on the privateness of his action and act as a public leader in a public cause. The moral problem suggested by the ambiguity of "honor" here seems already to be resolved; yet we will find it becoming more acute as the play continues.

Coriolanus has acted somewhat churlishly in this scene; whatever the principle according to which he justifies his action, his manner to Cominius and the rest is unwarrantedly unpleasant, and one suspects at its root a social awkwardness of which we shall see a good deal later. At the end of the scene we are left primarily with a sense of ineptness. Coriolanus gallantly asks that a poor man who gave him quarters and assistance be given his freedom, then realizes he doesn't remember the man's name and can't return his kindness. But whatever we hold against the Coriolanus we have come to know in the first act, our meeting with Aufidius in the tenth and last scene of the act reminds us of Coriolanus' unique virtues: Aufidius too is concerned with honor, but only as an impulse to put out of the way in order to get what he wants, and he self-consciously disavows the course of honor, boasting to his cronies that if wrath will not destroy Marcius then craft will.

I have gone through the first act serially because in it Shakespeare so carefully establishes the problem that will generate the entire play. The world of the tragedy is set in motion at the moment Marcius becomes Coriolanus and Aufidius declares his true colors to us, and immediately the problems we have merely sensed underlying the earlier action burst into crisis. Returned to peace, Coriolanus is summoned to the Capitol, where, to the surprise of no one, the Senate offers him the consulship. Only one formality must be observed: To mark ceremonially the role of the people in the choice of their leader, Coriolanus must go through the motions of a popular campaign, showing the citizens his wounds, wearing the gown of humility. And so a group of citizens gathers at the Forum to put their hero through his performance. Though somewhat uneasy because of his former contempt for them, they are comically smug and benevolent as they make preparations to grant the great man their largesse.

Here he comes, and in the gown of humility: mark his behaviour. We are not to stay all together, but to come by

> him where he stands, by ones, by twos, and by threes. He's to
> make his requests by particulars; wherein everyone of us has
> a single honour, in giving him our own voices with our own
> tongues: therefore follow me, and I'll direct you how you
> shall go by him.
>
> (II. iii. 44–51)

In the situation Shakespeare has taken from Plutarch he
finds a vehicle for a political question as relevant to our demo-
cratic society as to Roman democracy, the question in fact that
John F. Kennedy asked in *Profiles in Courage*: What is the role
of the man of principle in politics? Can he act, involve himself
in the world, and retain his honor? Can he uncompromisingly
stand by his principles and yet be a force in the world? Or, if
he must compromise his principles in order to gain the popular
support he needs to give him force, can those principles remain
operative? The passage just cited ironically suggests Coriolanus'
grounds for refusing to concede anything to popular will. Each
of the citizens has a single honor to confer; honor is what comes
to the man who deserves it; it is given by voices; it is thus at least
as much the reflection of those who confer it as of him who receives it. We already know what Coriolanus would say to such
a definition of honor, and he does not disappoint us. His tone
at first is one of bitter mockery as he realizes how neatly the
situation sets his required role against his political philosophy:

> What must I say?
> "I pray, sir,"—Plague upon't! I cannot bring
> My tongue to such a pace:—"Look, sir, my wounds!
> I got them in my country's service, when
> Some certain of your brethren roar'd and ran
> From the noise of our own drums."
>
> (II. iii. 55–60)

Disregarding Menenius' cagy advice to avoid mentioning his con-
stituents' cowardice, Coriolanus continues to mock them, and
finally performs his assignment only by casting his requests in an
ironic mold which the citizens, though it makes them nervous,
are unable to understand and reject. All that the candidate asks
is all that he thinks them capable of giving him: their *voices*.

The word, which occurs an astonishing forty-one times in the play, is sounded no less than twenty-four times in this scene, until we come around to the hero's point of view in which the people *are* merely *voices*. Like Menenius' fable of the belly, Coriolanus' image for the citizens denies them the power of reason, reducing them to the willful expression of worthless opinions. Uneasily awed by his haughtiness, the populace assents to the election of its new consul.[32]

Thus, searching for a way to accept public office in a democracy without compromising his honor, Coriolanus has chosen the way of absolute allegiance to his ideals. If Shakespeare wants us to think that the hero has made the right choice, he nevertheless makes us see the disastrous results of that choice. In the first place, the unscrupulous tribunes have no trouble in capitalizing on the people's vague sense that their consul-elect does not like them, and soon they have whipped the rabble up to a rebellion. The only solution is that Coriolanus must once again go hat in hand to his electors, and this time show the wounds he has received in their behalf. Driven on by the pleas of Menenius and Volumnia and by arguments that he must serve the common good, Coriolanus agrees to perform, but knowing their man the tribunes easily goad him to public display of such fury that in one moment he ends his political career in Rome. This turn of events is as much Coriolanus' choice as it is that of his opponents. It is not merely that he is unwilling to compromise, but that the society for which he would have to compromise is not worth serving. Thus Rome banishes him; but from his own point of view Coriolanus banishes the city (III. iii. 123). "My birth-place hate I," he will say shortly at the gates of Aufidius' home, "and my love's upon/ This enemy town" (IV. iv. 23–24).

Rome is an idea for Coriolanus, the idea of honor, and paradoxically that idea has led him to reject the state which had been its avatar. With increasing painfulness for the audience, Shakespeare explores the implications of this paradox as the play moves toward its bitter end. His honor drives the only honorable man in Rome to treachery, to the betrayal of the state with whom not only his fortunes but also his values are inextricably associated. The process means the destruction of the man. Having accepted his identity and his name as Rome's defender, he must now reject that identity until nothing is left but his ever more intense sense of personal honor and a consuming hatred for what he takes to be the source of his humiliation. "Coriolanus/ He would not answer to," reports Cominius after an unsuccessful embassy to his old friend;

> forbade all names;
> He was a kind of nothing, titleless,
> Till he had forged himself a name o' the fire
> Of burning Rome.
>
> (V. i. 11–14)

And the hero cannot reach his final destruction without learning from the mother who has instilled his virtue and his passion in him the meaning of his action.

> Thou know'st, great son,
> The end of war's uncertain, but this certain,
> That, if thou conquer Rome, the benefit
> Which thou shalt thereby reap is such a name,
> Whose repetition will be dogg'd with curses;
> Whose chronicle thus writ: "The man was noble,
> But with his last attempt he wiped it out;
> Destroy'd his country, and his name remains
> To the ensuing age abhorr'd." Speak to me, son:
> Thou hast affected the fine strains of honour,
> To imitate the graces of the gods.
>
> (V. iii. 140–150)

Defining his entire life in terms of his inner principle of integrity, Caius Marcius Coriolanus has destroyed his very identity.

The hero's choice, then, whatever its merits, does not work in the world of the play. But what is the alternative to it? Almost schematically, Shakespeare offers a range of possibilities—and none of them is any better. In the first place there is the way taken by Aufidius and the tribunes, a callous and utterly unprincipled opportunism. Sicinius and Brutus regard the events of the world only in terms of what they will bring; spokesmen of the people, they hate those they represent as much as Coriolanus does, yet hypocritically pretend class loyalty in order to acquire personal power. Aufidius' behavior is somewhat more respectable because at least it is based on a kind of principle, the belief that principles have no force in the world. Thus, shrewdly analyzing Coriolanus' political failure—like the citizen at the beginning of the play, he offers a number of psychological and moral causes for the hero's behavior—Aufidius enunciates his own credo:

> So our virtues
> Lie in the interpretation of the time;
> And power, unto itself most commendable,
> Hath not a tomb so evident as a chair
> To extol what it hath done.
> One fire drives out one fire; one nail, one nail;
> Rights by rights falter, strengths by strengths do fail.
>
> (IV. vii. 49–55)

Shakespeare does not ask us to decide on the basis of abstract principles that Aufidian *Realpolitik* is wrong; rather, he destroys any sympathy with Aufidius we may have by letting us watch the Volscian cruelly betray Coriolanus while pretending the most intense friendship for him.

But other alternatives seem more attractive. "All's well," says Menenius to the tribunes after the banishment, "and might have been much better, if/ He could have temporized" (IV. vi. 16–17). Does Shakespeare suggest compromise, paying the world its due, as a rational course of behavior in contrast to that taken by Coriolanus? Ultimately, we must note, it is Coriolanus' decision to compromise that destroys him. Three likable characters are temporizers: Cominius, Menenius, and Volumnia. None of them will do. Cominius is gracious, noble, civilized, and generous, but he needs Marcius to win his battles for him. In times of crisis societies respond only to the leadership of the passionately committed; Cominius has insufficient vision to take Rome to greatness. Menenius is amiable enough. His notion of social responsibility entails taking all reasonable precautions to insure that he and his fellows will not be driven from the club where they drink their after-dinner port and speak with disarming deprecation of themselves. To charge that his only principle is that one should not rock the boat is to do him an injustice, for Menenius bases

his justification of society on a sense of the value of civilization
and comfort so pervading that he never feels the need to formulate
it. But Menenius' comfortable dream, though it seems in the hour
of security and stability to embody vast political power, is insub-
stantial; it is parasitic, living off the wealth of an established state.
Perhaps it is significant that Menenius' thoughts turn constantly
to eating, that he can interpret Coriolanus' behavior only by
speculating that Coriolanus is hungry. Even the Coriolanuses of
the world are glad that it has room for such men as Menenius,
and the genuine friendship between the two patricians is touching;
but Menenius is a by-product, not an end, and his way of life is
no answer to the problems built into the ethical structure of the
universe of *Coriolanus*. And finally there is Volumnia. For the
Roman matriarch Rome comes first, and she has raised her son
as an offering to it. But Rome for Volumnia is not, as it is for
Marcius, an abstract ethical idea, but a city, a people, a state, a
history. For Rome anything can be sacrificed, and always in honor:

> I would dissemble with my nature where
> My fortunes and my friends at stake required
> I should do so in honour . . .
> (III. ii. 62–64)

Honor is her theme as it is her son's. But we have seen from the
beginning that for Volumnia honor is the glory that Rome can
confer on its loyal servants, and that honor can therefore employ
policy, political expediency. Her notion of honor is the most tempting alternative to Marcius' idea, but finally it, too, is unsatisfactory.
Volumnia's honor requires that Coriolanus violate his sworn word
to the Volscians in order to give up the battle against Rome. It
demands that Coriolanus see his virtue not in terms of what he
has accomplished, but in terms of what it can get him. It concedes that value is dictated not by the nature of the object but
by the tastes of the valuer, so that Coriolanus is honorable not
so much when he rescues Rome as when he receives the accolades
of its worthless citizens.[33]

In fact, the play allows no alternative to Coriolanus' understanding of glory. What does it mean to strive for the recognition
of those whose recognition is meaningless—fickle, corruptible,

emotional, selfish people held in contempt even by their own tribunes? From the beginning to the end of this somber story the populace is concerned only with what it gets for itself. If, as the tribunes argue, the city is no more than the people, it is scarcely worth the efforts of a Coriolanus. The only leader they will accept is one who is willing and able to tailor himself to fit their need for a leader with the proper image, with the wounds he has earned for them still bleeding and scarcely covered by a tattered garment. The citizens know it is a game they are asking Coriolanus to play, but his willingness to play the game would tell them that he is their man. Do we really want Coriolanus to play the game? In our own world we are all too familiar with the nightmare situation in which the leaders and the led willingly agree on the self-flattery and the self-deception involved in the myth of the state in which they live, and which will collapse the moment it is put to the test because image must ultimately yield to reality. There is a good deal to be said for the man of vision who will not compromise because he recognizes that in the act of compromise itself one can destroy the very object one wants to save.

Nevertheless, Coriolanus' refusal is every bit as destructive. Shakespeare offers us two alternatives, the idea of the state as unbending moral imperative and the idea of the state as a community organized for the benefit of its members—on the one hand, the state as worthy of allegiance only when it represents the highest moral ideals; on the other, "my country right or wrong." And he seems to be telling us hopelessly that neither of these notions of the state will work. The problem is not just that of democracy (which could not in itself have been a burning issue to Shakespeare in 1608), but of the ethical status of the body politic itself.[34]

The question of the radically opposed senses of the word "honor" recurs increasingly in the drama of the early seventeenth century until by the time of the outbreak of civil war in 1642 it has become the main theme of almost all serious plays. This is not surprising in an age in which, as in ours, all is called into question. But Shakespeare is concerned with more than an abstract moral issue; or rather, he recognizes that abstract moral issues are crucial in life because they touch our inner lives, and those inner lives are not computers into which propositions are fed at one end so that syllogistic conclusions can come out at the other. Rather as imaginative literature in general and Shakespeare in particular constantly teach us, we are enormously complicated creatures, and our ideas, whatever their validity and truth, are the product of the most tortuous complex of psychological drives, inexplicable impulses, desires, tastes, and quirks. Often in my account of the hero's behavior I have simplified events by describing them in terms of his rationale, implying that Coriolanus has consciously and coolly chosen the way of honor and that he acts according to a code. In a very important sense this is true, but it is far from being the whole story. As the citizens' descriptions suggested at the beginning of the play, Coriolanus' behavior has a number of causes. He believes in honor as a principle, but perhaps he does so because he has to. Least important, but unmistakable among the forces that shape his behavior, is Marcius' social ineptness. He does not know how to accept praise or to demonstrate gratitude. The only times at which we see him fully at ease and unself-conscious are a few fleeting moments between battles when he is a man among men he trusts, or with his family. Otherwise he can all too easily insult his friends and infuriate his enemies when he has no intention of doing so; a man more socially adept might understand and detachedly put up with the rituals through which society functions, while Coriolanus, unable to perform them gracefully, rejects them furiously. Of this gaucherie Marcius makes a principle too, priding himself on his rocky harshness, his freedom from corrupting social smoothness; but the behavior seems rooted more deeply than the attitude toward it. The second element in the complex of Coriolanus' character is his pride. One character after another, friend or enemy, points out how godlike the man's aspirations and self-image are. In this Coriolanus is not unlike certain intractable political figures of our own day, whose dignity brooks no contradiction, in whom magnificence is as much a matter of personality as it is of principle. Third is his brutality, the quality that makes Marcius a born warrior: "Death, that dark spirit, in's nervy arm doth lie;/ Which, being advanced, declines, and then men die" (II. i. 177–178). As we have already seen, the attitude which

Shakespeare determines in us toward this quality is as ambivalent as our attitude toward his idea of honor. We admire it as the only possible nature for a man called on to accomplish what he must, but fear it as inimical to civilization.

Finally, and most painfully, we recognize the part played in Coriolanus' life by his relation to his mother. She is unmistakably the source of his values, though paradoxically he has learned to love honor and Rome with a totally different understanding from hers of what they mean. (Shakespeare is always skeptical of the success of plans: You may bring up your son to exemplify all that you believe in only to discover that you have succeeded in creating an opponent to your values.) Twice in the play Coriolanus is forced to realize that his passion for honor is merely a lesson badly learned from Volumnia. To see it only as such would be more cynical than Shakespeare teaches us to be; the duality of Coriolanus' motivation in character and principle does not vitiate the principles in which the hero genuinely believes; all men have reasons for believing what they believe. But to Marcius himself it is a shock to realize that he has betrayed the Roman faith of his mother which he had thought he was emulating and gratifying; and once he makes the concession (which Volumnia maneuvers with great subtlety and skill), he recognizes the ambiguity of his position. Each time, he yields to Volumnia: first to agree to submit himself once more to popular judgment, second to betray his new Volscian allies. Each time he gives up his own principle for Volumnia, and each time the result is disaster. Perhaps nothing in Shakespeare is more mortifying than Coriolanus' collapse before his mother's will:

> O my mother, mother! O!
> You have won a happy victory to Rome;
> But, for your son,—believe it, O, believe it,
> Most dangerously you have with him prevail'd,
> If not most mortal to him. But, let it come.
> Aufidius, though I cannot make true wars,
> I'll frame convenient peace. Now, good Aufidius,
> Were you in my stead, would you have heard
> A mother less? Or granted less, Aufidius?
>   (V. iii. 185–193)

What makes Volumnia twice successful in shifting Coriolanus' course when Cominius, Menenius, and the rest consistently fail is her ability to make her son doubt the integrity of his own faith. If she taught it to him, and if from her point of view he has not got it right, then he cannot have that godlike sense of his own power and independence; in granting Volumnia a favor he is broken as banishment from Rome and military defeat could never have broken him. He would rather not know that the source of his behavior lies in character rather than rational principle.[35]

It is Shakespeare's demonstration of the dominance of character over what we would like to be, of the priority of personality over principle in the motivation of human action, that brings this play as close to being a depressing experience as any tragedy of Shakespeare ever gets. Fighting against the Volscians, haranguing the plebians, justifying his life on philosophical grounds, Coriolanus impresses us as a rare man of principle. But when we see him listening to his mother's reminder that he is the best of her flesh; when we see him struggling hopelessly against the impulses of a loving son; and when we watch him, as he holds Volumnia's hand, surrendering to her all that he has been defending, we realize what power a personal bond possesses, how little one really knows of one's own motivations. And it may occur to us that much of what we have ascribed to Marcius' high principles—his intense idealism, his quick temper, his passionate self-righteousness, his refusal to make accommodating concessions, his lack of concern with physical comfort—may just as well be a function of the fact that he is still hardly more than a boy.[36] Having dismayed us with the suggestion that principle—the only way to live admirably—must lead to ruin, Shakespeare will not allow us to find consolation in the thought that defeated principle at least has its integrity, but rather makes us wonder if we can properly admire what is itself a conditioned result rather than a freely chosen cause.

The inevitability of Coriolanus' fate may not be any more striking than that of other Shakespearean heroes, but because it is based on unmistakable and insuperable qualities of character rather than on such an atmosphere of universal fatality as permeates *King Lear* or *Hamlet*, it seems more ineluctable, more immediately confining. Not just Coriolanus, but Menenius and Volumnia, Aufidius and Sicinius and Brutus seem immutable, determined by social and psychological forces over which they have no control. In no other tragedy of Shakespeare is there so little growth and change in character. The sense that man is determined by what is given to him, that little or no room is left for the always elusive but clearly discernible freedom of the other tragic heroes, may be Shakespeare's response to a growing strain in contemporary ethical and psychological speculation. It is not a permanent attitude, at any rate. In *Antony and Cleopatra* the implication is strong that Antony chooses his own destiny: He decides to fight at sea, to follow Cleopatra at Actium, to identify himself with Egypt rather than Rome; and in giving us the impression that he is a free agent, accountable for his actions, Antony reveals his kinship with other tragic heroes in Shakespeare. Not so with Coriolanus.

But in a larger sense *Coriolanus* typifies and carries to an extreme the familiar pattern of Shakespearean tragedy. The hero's virtue—his passionate sense of honor and allegiance to principles —is also his vice. It makes him incomparably better than anyone else in the play and paradoxically worse by the end than all the others. He is the only man whose principles are presented as worthy of respect; he is also, out of love for the idea of Rome, the man who, as Volumnia points out (V. iii. 114ff.), must either be led through the streets of his Rome as a foreign traitor or "bear the palm for having bravely shed/ Thy wife and children's blood." Because of the abstraction with which the ideas are often presented, the paradoxes of the tragic hero and of Shakespeare's dismayed awareness of the nature and role and fate of moral goodness in the world seem more acute here than anywhere else. Coriolanus carries virtue and vice as far as they can go, and almost parodies the Shakespearean identification of the one with the other. In Brutus and Hotspur honor has led the honorable man to dishonor, but nowhere does the dishonor seem so great as at the end of *Coriolanus*, when even the expected reconstruction of the tragic hero in the play's final speeches turns into bitterness and mockery. By the end we know that rational and humane order cannot really be restored because it cannot exist in society. There are no more heroic virtues to learn. Shakespeare has embarked on a new kind of tragedy. Unlike Hamlet, Coriolanus brings down with him all hope of a society that embodies his vision; no catharsis is possible.

If *Coriolanus* thus reaches the limits of Shakespeare's tragic universe, it similarly provides a fit conclusion to his career as composer of plays about history. For here, focusing on the essential problems that sometimes seem to get lost amid the richness and bustle of the earlier history plays, he makes us understand most fully the tragic complementarity of all solutions to the political world he sees. In *Coriolanus* both idealism and grubby reality are subjected to their most searching examination, and the result, perhaps the grimmest play in the canon, brings us to the full understanding of the world of Shakespeare's politics.

NOTES

1. Jan Kott, *Shakespeare, Our Contemporary,* tr. Boleslaw Taborski (London, 1964), p. 7.

2. E. W. Talbert, *The Problem of Order: Elizabethan Political Commonplaces and an Example of Shakespeare's Art* (Chapel Hill, 1962), p. 200. Talbert provides a useful survey of historiographical and other background materials to support the contention that Shakespeare's treatment of English political history might be expected to be ambivalent. A great quantity of useful criticism of the histories has appeared in recent years, with much of which the present essay frequently agrees, though I have reached my own conclusions independently. Particularly relevant are Derek Traversi, *Shakespeare from Richard II to Henry V* (Stanford, 1957); A. P. Rossiter, *Angel with Horns and Other Shakespeare Lectures,* ed. Graham Storey (New York, 1961), especially the title essay on *Richard III,* "Ambivalence: the Dialectic of the Histories," and "*Richard II*"; J. A. Bryant, Jr., "The Linked Analogies of *Richard II,*" *Sewanee Review,* LXV (1957), 420–433; Michael Quinn, " 'The King Is Not Himself'; the Personal Tragedy of *Richard II,*" *SP,* LVI (1959), 169–186; W. H. Auden, "The Prince's Dog," *The Dyer's Hand and other Essays* (New York, 1962), pp. 182–208. Since any attempt to conduct a running dialogue with these studies would make the present study unwieldy, I simply recommend them here to the interested reader.

3. Virtually the only generalization one may make about Shakespeare's use of soliloquies arises from the truism that in all Elizabethan plays and par-

ticularly in Shakespeare the soliloquy is consistently the vehicle of true statement. Shakespeare uses the device when he wants us to know a character in a particular way. In *Macbeth* the soliloquy serves to counter our moral judgment of the protagonist, which tends to equate itself with that made on him by his victims and their survivors, with a complementary sense of Macbeth's selfhood as experienced from within. Iago's soliloquies, on the other hand, serve not to attract our sympathy but to make clear his villainy and, because of the welter of conflicting motivations he confesses, to give him the aura of mystery that his metaphysical role demands. The absence of soliloquies is not always significant; Hotspur's character, for example, is conveyed so fully in his interactions with other characters that soliloquy would be supererogatory, and this is true of a good many persons in the plays. In the characterization of crucial figures like Bolingbroke and Caesar, whose motivation at certain critical points is a question that we must answer in order to judge their actions, the absence of soliloquy is a striking device.

4. See Geoffrey Bullough, *Narrative and Dramatic Sources of Shakespeare*, III (London, 1960), pp. 394–397. In the chronicle there is no doubt that Bolingbroke is returning to England to capture the crown, but Shakespeare does not give us clear evidence that this is his mission.

5. To some extent he does develop these capacities in the *Henry IV* plays, where time and circumstance force him to take account of himself and to reflect on his ascent; but in these plays he is no longer a success.

6. W. B. Yeats, "At Stratford-on-Avon," *The Collected Works in Verse and Prose of William Butler Yeats*, VI (London, 1908), p. 124. The essay was written in 1901.

7. Oppenheimer, *Science and the Common Understanding*, p. 40.

8. The most familiar example is E. M. W. Tillyard, *Shakespeare's History Plays* (London, 1944), pp. 304–314.

9. *Johnson on Shakespeare*, ed. Walter Raleigh (Oxford, 1925), p. 132.

10. C. L. Barber, *Shakespeare's Festive Comedy* (Princeton, 1959), p. 13; Jonas A. Barish, "The Turning Away of Prince Hal," *Shakespeare Studies*, I (1965), 9–17.

11. Ernest Schanzer, *The Problem Plays of Shakespeare* (London, 1963), p. 100.

12. D. A. Traversi, *An Approach to Shakespeare* (New York, 1956), p. 107.

13. E. g., Ernest Schanzer, "The Tragedy of Shakespeare's Brutus," *ELH*, XXII (1955), 1–15; Brents Stirling, *Unity in Shakespearean Tragedy: The Interplay of Theme and Character* (New York, 1956), p. 41 *et passim*.

14. *Prefaces to Shakespeare* (Princeton, 1947), II, p. 386.

15. Shakespeare has moved this moment from its original place in the narrative just after the assassination to the present scene on the eve.

16. The change in tone is unmistakable. It puzzled Hazlitt, who remarked in a note that "we do not much admire the representation here given of Julius Caesar, nor do we think it answers the portrait given of him in his *Commentaries*" (New Variorum Edition of *Julius Caesar*, ed. H. H. Furness, Jr., second

edition [Philadelphia, 1913], p. 118). On the discrepancies in Caesar's behavior in this scene, see John Palmer, *Political Characters of Shakespeare* (London, 1945), pp. 38–39.

17. On the ambiguity of Brutus' moral standards here, see Palmer, *op. cit.*, p. 50.

18. Ernest Schanzer, "The Problem of *Julius Caesar*," *SQ*, VI (1955), p. 307. Though to my knowledge it has formed the basis of no previous interpretation of the play, the resemblance between Brutus and Caesar has not gone unnoticed. M. W. MacCallum, *Shakespeare's Roman Plays and Their Background* (London, 1910) observed how "their different ideals dominate and impel both men in an almost equal degree. And in each case this leads to a kind of pose" (cited in the New Variorum edition, p. 419). Adrien Bonjour, *The Structure of Julius Caesar* (Liverpool, 1958), discusses convincingly, though without coming to my conclusions, the "ambivalence" of Brutus and Caesar and their complementary roles. Judah L. Stampfer, "Ideas of Order in Shakespeare's Histories and Tragedies," unpub. diss. (Harvard, 1959), whose discussion of *Julius Caesar* has been seminal in the formulation of my own interpretation, notes significant similarities between the two figures, though again reaching different conclusions. More recently Professor Irving Ribner has observed that "there are . . . two tragic heroes in *Julius Caesar*, Brutus and Caesar, although the one is treated more fully than the other. Each brings about his own destruction, and together they bring chaos to Rome. Each is among the greatest men the world has ever known, but each makes a wrong moral choice" (*Patterns in Shakespearian Tragedy* [London, 1960], p. 56). The assessment of both characters has been and remains a controversial matter. Opinions of Caesar range between MacCallum's sensitive account of his greatness (*Shakespeare's Roman Plays*, pp. 226ff.) and Dover Wilson's picture of Caesar and what he represents as "a secular threat to the human spirit" (*Julius Caesar*, ed. John Dover Wilson [Cambridge, 1949], p. xxii). Ernest Schanzer, "The Problem of *Julius Caesar*," *SQ*, VI (1955), 297–308, describes the contradictory source materials available to Shakespeare in the creation of his Caesar. Palmer, *op. cit.*, p. 36, suggests that Shakespeare assumes Caesar's greatness so thoroughly that he can afford to present the dictator's weaknesses. "This method of presentation," he suggests, ". . . gives reality to Caesar, the man; it suggests that Caesar's spirit is mightier than his person, a suggestion which is essential to the unity of the play; it enables the dramatist to present him in flesh and blood without reducing in stature the men who murder him; finally, it permits the audience to sympathize with Brutus just sufficiently to give poignancy to the disaster which overtakes him." Palmer does not recognize, however, the similarity between Caesar's faults and those of Brutus, and therefore does not see the supreme value of the ambiguity in Caesar's characterization. Brutus, of course, has been a center of even greater controversy than Caesar. For an interesting record of an early eighteenth-century letter which, uncomfortable with both characters, suggests that (in the words of its modern editor) "Brutus is not 'good' enough; Caesar is not 'bad' enough," see G. Blakemore Evans, "The

Problem of Brutus: An Eighteenth-Century Solution," in D. C. Allen, ed., *Studies in Honor of T. W. Baldwin* (Urbana, 1958), p. 235.

19. "The Problem of *Julius Caesar*," pp. 307–308.

20. For a discussion of the nature of the hero-villain in revenge tragedy, see Fredson Bowers, *Elizabethan Revenge Tragedy, 1587–1642* (Princeton, 1940). Curiously, Professor Bowers does not mention *Julius Caesar* in his book, and except for unconvincing disintegrationist claims by Fleay and J. M. Robertson—refuted by Kittredge in his 1939 edition of *Julius Caesar* (pp. xii–xiii)—that the second half of the play is a reworking of a *Revenge for Caesar*, critics have been rather surprisingly reluctant to assert in print that the play is a revenge play. Leo Kirschbaum, "Shakespeare's Stage Blood and Its Critical Significance," *PMLA*, LXIV (1949), 517–529, explores the various functions of blood in *Julius Caesar* and elsewhere but does not speak of it as a convention of revenge tragedy. Maurice Charney, *Shakespeare's Roman Plays: The Function of Imagery in the Drama* (Cambridge, Mass., 1961), p. 48, asserts that "the central issue about the meaning of *Julius Caesar* is raised most forcefully and vividly by the imagery of blood," but in the twelve pages (48–59) devoted to a useful discussion of the blood imagery he does not refer to the significance of blood in revenge plays. Professor Schanzer himself, it should be noted, has argued that the anonymous *Caesar's Revenge* is a source for Shakespeare's play ("A Neglected Source of *Julius Caesar*," *N&Q*, CXCIX [1954], 196–197), and suggests that one of the play's "three tragedies" is a revenge tragedy, though that tragedy is "merely rudimentary." In "The Tragedy of Shakespeare's Brutus," p. 14, he again speaks suggestively of revenge elements in the last two acts, but does not develop the argument.

21. Approaching the play from a different direction, Schanzer argues that its irony arises from Brutus' self-deception, which causes him to kill Caesar unwarrantedly out of a love for *res publica*, only to bring his country to a much worse condition ("The Tragedy of Shakespeare's Brutus"); and Palmer speaks of Brutus' entangling himself in "unforeseen consequences with which he was unable to cope" (p. 1). For a perceptive account of Brutus' ability to turn moral problems into abstract speculation, blinding himself to moral realities, and for the interesting suggestion that such a view of Brutus was available to Shakespeare and his audience, see Robert Ornstein, "Seneca and the Political Drama of *Julius Caesar*," *JEGP*, LVII (1958), 51–56. Another useful view of Brutus' difficulty is offered by L. C. Knights, who, in "Shakespeare and Political Wisdom: A Note on the Personalism of *Julius Caesar* and *Coriolanus*," *Sewanee Review*, LXI (1953), 53, sees Brutus as failing to perceive that "human actuality is more important than *any* political abstraction, though more difficult to bear." Such a view resembles Palmer's characterization of Brutus (p. 7) as "the reflective idealist, living in imagination, . . . more impressed by the idea or symbol of power than by the thing itself."

22. Bonjour (p. 15) discusses the ghost as a means of portraying Nemesis, though he does not treat *Julius Caesar* as a revenge play.

23. Though some critics, typified by Dover Wilson (p. xxxi), see Shake-

speare's Caesar as overreacher and Brutus as correct in his assessment, or at least, in Dover Wilson's terms, correctly apprehensive as to what absolute power would do to Caesar if he were granted a crown, Shakespeare offers us little evidence to damn the dictator. Significantly the offer and rejection of the crown take place off stage, and are presented to us in the not disinterested accounts of Casca and Mark Antony. Caesar never mentions any interest in becoming king—only the most suspicious of men could find cause for blame in his desire to bring fertility to Calpurnia—and Decius' report that the Senate is planning to offer Caesar the crown on the Ides, in a speech which persuades the dictator to go to the Capitol, is only one argument early in the speech, and reinforced by numerous shrewd appeals to Caesar's less pernicious vanity and his sense of dignity. Thus Professor Ribner's assertion (p. 59) that "Caesar's wrong moral choice is his decision to go to the Senate to accept a crown to which he has no lawful claim" needs qualification. To the statement about the offer of the crown Caesar offers no reply. His ambition, here as not in Plutarch, is at the worst ambiguous. If Shakespeare wanted to justify the assassination on the grounds that Caesar would be king, one might expect stronger indication that such indeed is the case.

24. Dover Wilson (pp. xxx–xxxi) summarizes the extent to which Brutus' logic "has puzzled all the critics, including Coleridge and Granville-Barker." For intelligent analyses of the speech, see Schanzer, "The Tragedy of Shakespeare's Brutus," p. 9, and Ornstein, pp. 52–53.

25. A. A. Smirnov, *Shakespeare: A Marxist Interpretation*, tr. Sonia Volochova *et al.* (New York, 1936), p. 78. The citizens' gravest flaw, according to Smirnov, is their innocent trust in the aristocratic and therefore evil Coriolanus.

26. Traversi, *An Approach to Shakespeare*, p. 219. My approach to the military aspects of Coriolanus, to the presentation of war, and to the hero's commitment to honor owes a good deal to Traversi's pioneering essay. Except for a few penetrating remarks, however, Traversi does not devote much attention to the politics of the play. The same can be said of the lengthier essay in his recent *Shakespeare's Roman Plays* (London, 1963).

27. *An Approach to Shakespeare*, pp. 225–226.

28. A. C. Bradley's analysis of the combination of arrogance and true modesty in Coriolanus is among his most acute studies. See "*Coriolanus*," the second Annual Shakespeare Lecture of the British Academy, reprinted in *Studies in Shakespeare*, ed. Peter Alexander (Oxford, 1964), pp. 219–237.

29. The closest view of "honor" in *Coriolanus* to the one I have taken is D. J. Gordon, "Name and Fame: Shakespeare's *Coriolanus*," *Papers Mainly Shakespearian*, ed. G. I. Duthie, University of Aberdeen Studies 147 (Edinburgh, 1964), 40–57. Published after I had completed the present study of *Coriolanus*, Gordon's article brilliantly explores the history of the concept of honor as fame, and suggests the opposition of that notion in the play to an internalized honor; the bibliography in the notes of the article is invaluable. Like me, Gordon sees great significance in Marcius' change of name. In *Shakespeare and the Renaissance Concept of Honor* (Princeton, 1960), C. B. Watson deals with the same dual understanding of honor, but his study is limited

in value both because Watson postulates too schematic a distinction between "pagan-humanist" and Christian values and because he sees Shakespeare rather as caught between and confused by the conflicting values of his age than as aware of the conflict and able to make dramatic capital of it. See, for example, Watson's discussion of *Hamlet* on p. 282. Nevertheless, Watson's view bears some similarity to mine.

30. E. R. Dodds, *The Greeks and the Irrational* (Boston, 1957), pp. 17ff., 28–63; Bruno Snell, *The Discovery of the Mind* (Oxford, 1953).

31. "*Clarissa:* A Study in the Nature of Convention," *ELH*, XXIII (1956), 207.

32. On the significance of the "voices," see also Gordon's essay cited above. Leonard Dean, "Voice and Deed in *Coriolanus*," *University of Kansas City Review*, XXI (1955), 177–184, locates the reason for much of the play's emphasis on voices in the sustained contrast between words and deeds, which constitutes a moral judgment on the universe of the play. Maurice Charney, *Shakespeare's Roman Plays*, pp. 66–78, points usefully at theatrical images in the play which suggest the tension between words and action in its world.

33. Insofar as the play's ambivalence points at the question of the objectivity of value, *Coriolanus* resembles *Troilus and Cressida*; cf. pp. 34–53, above.

34. W. Gordon Zeeveld, "*Coriolanus* and Jacobean Politics," *MLR*, LVII (1962), 321–334, discusses the play as a study of the "dismemberment of commonwealth" with close reference to the problems of early-seventeenth-century English politics. Another recent study of the politics of *Coriolanus*, which, like many current analyses of the play, sees it in terms of what Coleridge called "the wonderfully philosophic impartiality of Shakespeare's politics," is Kenneth Muir, "Shakespeare and Politics," *Shakespeare in a Changing World*, ed. Arnold Kettle (London, 1964), pp. 65–83. Like me, Muir locates the political problem of the tragedy in the relation between private virtue and public life. Perhaps the most suggestive, though certainly not the most carefully worked out, reading of *Coriolanus* in terms of the conflict between the hero's constancy and a political world in which such constancy is irrelevant is A. P. Rossiter, "*Coriolanus*," in *Angel with Horns*, pp. 235–252.

35. Two fascinating illustrations of the richness of Shakespeare's characterization of his hero and the degree to which the character may be understood in psychological terms are David B. Barron, "*Coriolanus:* Portrait of the Artist as Infant," *American Imago*, XIX (1962), 171–193, and Charles K. Hofling, "An Interpretation of Shakespeare's *Coriolanus*," *ibid.*, XIV (1957), 407–435. For further psychoanalytic interpretations of *Coriolanus* and of other works by Shakespeare, see Professor Norman N. Holland's extraordinarily judicious and useful *Psychoanalysis and Shakespeare* (New York, 1966).

36. See F. H. Rouda, "*Coriolanus*—A Tragedy of Youth," *SQ*, XII (1961), 103–106. Characteristically, Bradley anticipates the modern critic, remarking of Coriolanus in 1912 that "often he reminds us of a huge boy" (p. 228).

Eros and Death

ON ONE MATTER ALL THE PLAYS ABOUT LOVE AGREE: IT IS IRRE-
ducibly problematic. As a major and troublesome fact of human
experience love could scarcely have escaped the complementary
view with which Shakespeare regards other experience. As the
most intense expression of the pleasure principle, which itself
as we have seen in our reading of the history plays is a focus of
ambivalent attitudes, it almost inevitably provokes opposed valuations in Shakespeare. And as a force which at the moment of
dominating human personality involves the lover in problems of
value, faith, and choice based on irrational considerations, love
provides a basis for plots that explore the areas of life Shakespeare found—and his audience finds—most perplexing. The
treatments of love in the plays are, in fact, so quintessentially
Shakespearean, so deeply related to the playwright's other basic
concerns, that it might seem scarcely necessary to isolate a group
of works in order to discuss love as a discrete phenomenon.

But this is not so. In dealing with the political plays we saw
confirmation of a thesis on which I have insisted from the outset:

The complementary vision is never an end in itself, but rather a mode of perception and communication. Focused on the polity, that vision reveals much in the nature of political problems that without it might never have been seen. It is politics, not complementarity, that the history plays are about. So it is with the plays about love. We have treated some plays primarily concerned with other matters—*Troilus and Cressida*, for example, where the thematic focus is not love but value, and *Othello*, where it is love as a form of faith—in which we are made to view love complementarily, recognizing its ennobling and its degrading aspects. But only in those few plays where love is the thing itself, the center of our emotional and contemplative response, do we see fully worked out the dramatization of that particular quality of love which demands that our final view be complementary. In the three works most clearly devoted to the mimesis of love Shakespeare subsumes and transcends what he has to say about love elsewhere, adding to what we learn from *A Midsummer Night's Dream*, *Troilus and Cressida*, *Twelfth Night*, and *Othello* a perception that looks backward to the greatest of medieval romances and forward to Wagner and Freud. In *Venus and Adonis*, *Romeo and Juliet*, and *Antony and Cleopatra* Shakespeare tells us that love, the most intense manifestation of the urge to life, is ineluctably linked with the self-destructive yearning for annihilation that we recognize as the death wish.

The place to begin is where Shakespeare begins, with *Venus and Adonis*. Not only his first full treatment of love, Shakespeare's epyllion is also his unique excursion into the fashionable genre of allegorized mythological romance. It is no less than an ambitious attempt to create a myth which, in portraying the genesis of love, explains its tragicomic complementarity in the fallen world in which we live.

Critics have not always known what to make of *Venus and Adonis*. Participants in the old debate could agree on the one side that the poem is correct, salable, meaningless poetry written to please the palate of a jaded earl, on the other that it is a glowing fragment of the sunrise landscape of the Renaissance, a verbal counterpart to Botticelli's *Venus* and Piero di Cosimo's *Cephalus and Procris*. But that debate has died, because the view of poetry that underlay it is gone; for or against Venus and Adonis, modern critics all assume, as did neither Robertson in attacking it nor Wyndham in defending it, that a poem by Shakespeare is likely to be a coherent and significant structure. The estimation of its value perhaps remains the critic's goal, but the way to that goal is through the process of understanding. And here the trouble starts all over again, for the disagreements are as sharp among the critics who think they know what the poem means as they once were among critics who thought they knew its worth. To Dover Wilson Venus and Adonis is a supreme example of the " 'fleshly school of poetry,' " whose theme is "a frank acceptance of what Rossetti called 'the passionate and just delights of the body.' " To Geoffrey Bush, on the other hand, "the theme [of the poem] is the phrase from one of the sonnets, 'Desire is death,' " and to Hereward T. Price it is a bitter rejection of physical passion: Venus as the embodiment of the principle of lust is a primal force of destruction; the boar that kills the beautiful and innocent Adonis is "Venus in her most horrible symbol." In another view, Adonis is neither beauty incarnate nor an epicurean feast for the senses, but rather "an adolescent lout . . . from the country and very conscious that he hasn't been around"; not "a creature of a world of myth, but . . . a young fellow from Stratford ill at ease in the presence of a court lady."[1]

Critical conflicts as serious as this need reduce us neither to skepticism about the ultimate validity of criticism nor to mistrust of the poem in question. They may indicate only that the critics have not learned what kinds of questions to ask. Approaching Venus and Adonis, critics have behaved often like travelers from an immaterial universe alighting on the earth, unable yet to interpret the signals that should tell them what are mountains and what valleys. Thus for one scholar the fact that Venus and Adonis is a version of myth is paramount; for another, the fact that it is rich in decorative embellishment; for a third, the episode of the horses; for a fourth, the symbolism of white and red; and for a fifth, the reflection of Florentine neoplatonism. All of these views are presented as if they were as mutually exclusive as once were the views of Hamlet which have filled our libraries. And here lies the clue as to how to read the poem, and how to account for the divergences of critical treatments of it. As we have repeatedly seen in examining the plays, critical disagreement often leads us directly to the center of interest and to the meaning of a work.

The critical problem of *Venus and Adonis* is compounded, however, by the fact that it is a poem rather than a play, and therefore not obviously typical of its author. It might be wise, then, before embarking on interpretation, simply to remind ourselves of certain undeniable facts: the qualities of the poem. With the entire landscape in view we are less likely to mistake a bush for a bear. The first thing we have to notice is that this romance is funny. Whatever one wants to make of the famous horse episode, for example, in which "Adonis' trampling courser" carries on with "a breeding jennet, lusty, young and proud" (260–261) to the delight of Venus and the dismay of Adonis, who refuses to accept the example as useful instruction, one begins by laughing:

'Give me my hand,' saith he, 'why dost thou feel it?'
'Give me my heart,' saith she, 'and thou shalt have it;
O, give it me, lest thy hard heart do steel it,
And being steel'd, soft sighs can never grave it:
　　Then love's deep groans I never shall regard,
　　Because Adonis' heart hath made mine hard.'

'For shame,' he cries, 'let go, and let me go;
My day's delight is past, my horse is gone,
And 'tis your fault I am bereft him so:
I pray you hence, and leave me here alone;
　　For all my mind, my thought, my busy care,
　　Is how to get my palfrey from the mare.'
　　　　　　　　　　　　　　(373–384)

One laughs at the high comedy of the overbearing, lustful Venus and the boy too young and too uninterested to respond; at sudden changes in tone and unexpected disruptions of the placid atmosphere:

'I know not love,' quoth he, 'nor will not know it,
Unless it be a boar, and then I chase it;
'Tis much to borrow, and I will not owe it;
My love to love is love but to disgrace it;
　　For I have heard it is a life in death,
　　That laughs and weeps, and all but with a breath.

'Who· wears a garment shapeless and unfinish'd?
Who plucks the bud before one leaf put forth?
If springing things be any jot diminish'd,
They wither in their prime, prove nothing worth:
   The colt that's back'd and burden'd being young
   Loseth his pride and never waxeth strong.

'You hurt my hand with wringing; let us part,
And leave this idle theme, this bootless chat:
Remove your siege from my unyielding heart;
To love's alarms it will not ope the gate:
   Dismiss your vows, your feigned tears, your flattery;
   For where a heart is hard they make no battery?'
'What! canst thou talk?' quoth she, 'hast thou a tongue?'
                                          (409–427)

The outcome of *Venus and Adonis* and the issues it raises are serious, but the vehicle is seldom far from comedy.

Moreover, the poem is vivid and sensuously immediate; it is
realized. Even a first reading leaves indelible memories of the
horses and the boar and poor Wat, the dew-bedabbled hare, of
Venus' fainting, of Adonis at the mercy of his enormous and un-
inviting lady-love:

   The studded bridle on a ragged bough
   Nimbly she fastens:—O, how quick is love!—
   The steed is stalled up, and even now
   To tie the rider she begins to prove:
      Backward she push'd him, as she would be thrust,
      And govern'd him in strength, though not in lust.

   So soon was she along as he was down,
   Each leaning on their elbows and their hips:
   Now doth she stroke his cheek, now doth he frown,
   And 'gins to chide, but soon she stops his lips;
      And kissing speaks, with lustful language broken,
      'If thou wilt chide, thy lips shall never open."
                                          (37–48)

In good part the poem's vividness is the illusion created by
its characters: the illusion, that is, that they *are* characters. Much
of the critics' trouble stems, in fact, from being deceived into

seeing the entire poem in terms of its characters alone and finding
on closer examination that the illusion is undercut by the quality
of the language used to create it (thus C. S. Lewis); yet other
trouble, most notably that of Professor Price, stems from attempting to deal with *Venus and Adonis* as if it had no characters in it.

Another immediate impression, apparent even in what I have
been describing: Shakespeare maintains a remarkable control over
the responses of his reader. Theories about what the whole poem
adds up to may turn small matters into great, and vice versa, but
no reader fails to note the incongruity of the horse episode and
Venus' and Adonis' reactions to it, or the delicate shifts in tone
from sympathy to laughter as the poet regards the paradox of the
wooing mistress:

> Sometimes she shakes her head and then his hand,
> Now gazeth she on him, now on the ground;
> Sometimes her arms infold him like a band:
> She would, he will not in her arms be bound;
> > And when from thence he struggles to be gone,
> > She locks her lily fingers one in one.
>
> 'Fondling,' she saith, 'since I have hemm'd thee here
> Within the circuit of this ivory pale,
> I'll be a park, and thou shalt be my deer;
> Feed where thou wilt, on mountain or in dale:
> > Graze on my lips; and if those hills be dry,
> > Stray lower, where the pleasant fountains lie.
>
> 'Within this limit is relief enough,
> Sweet bottom-grass, and high delightful plain,
> Round rising hillocks, brakes obscure and rough,
> To shelter thee from tempest and from rain:
> > Then be my deer, since I am such a park;
> > No dog shall rouse thee, though a thousand bark.'
> > > > (223–240)

The last major element which the critic ignores only at his
own peril is the imagery which for some has seemed to *be* the
poem. The famous arias about the horses and the hare and the
boar are imbedded in a recitative in which motifs recur and are
continually varied; a central element in one's experience of *Venus*

and Adonis is the strong sense of clearly defined groups of images bridging and unifying the poem.

What can such a catalogue of the poem's most obvious qualities tell us? Listen to the most brilliant critic who has ever written about this work:

> *Venus and Adonis* seem[s] at once the characters themselves, and the whole representation of those characters by the most consummate actors. You seem to be *told* nothing, but to see and hear everything. Hence it is, that from the perpetual activity of attention required on the part of the reader; from the rapid flow, the quick change, and the playful nature of the thoughts and images; and above all from the alienation, and, if I may hazard such an expression, the utter *aloofness* of the poet's own feelings, from those of which he is at once the painter and the analyst; that though the very subject cannot but detract from the pleasure of a delicate mind, yet never was poem less dangerous on a moral account. . . . Shakspeare has here represented the animal impulse itself, so as to preclude all sympathy with it, by dissipating the reader's notice among the thousand outward images, and now beautiful, now fanciful circumstances, which form its dresses and its scenery.[2]

Coleridge is telling us that the poem is best read as one reads a Shakespearean play. Professor Price attempts "to show that *Venus and Adonis* is much greater than Coleridge knew or, at any rate, implied."[3] But if he really understood what Coleridge tells us, he could not make such a statement; and he could not reduce the poem so deftly to precisely half of its statement. To know that we can approach this poem as we have been approaching the plays is to know a good deal about it. We need not—should not—hinge our interpretation on the meaning of one image; we do not have to turn into iconologists or historians of philosophy and hunt for analogues and obscure sources, though all of these will help us to refine what we understand about the poem. If it shares, as Coleridge implies it does, some of the more important qualities of the plays, it is an aesthetic object which our experience with the plays has already well equipped us to understand.

One way in which the plays may be useful is in suggesting to us the kind of theme Shakespeare might conceive. "*Othello* and *Romeo and Juliet* and *Venus and Adonis*," says Professor Price, "are all about the same thing—that is to say, the destruction of something good by a force that is not only vile, but also so blind that it does not even know what it is destroying."[4] The sense of relationship among these works is as convincing as the interpretation is wrong. We might recall what we have learned of Shakespeare's attitude toward the subject of *Venus and Adonis* from the plays: Love must always be judged from contradictory points of view.

We have seen the doubleness of love's image in several plays; let us consider it briefly in several more. In *A Midsummer Night's Dream* love is both absurd and magnificent because, like art and other engagements of the imagination, it is willful, passionate, happily deceived and deceiving, unconditioned by and virtually irrelevant to reason. In *Twelfth Night* love is presented constantly as madness, yet as the source of festive and liberating joy. In *Much Ado About Nothing* Claudio is wrong when he believes what his eyes tell him about Hero, right when he ultimately agrees to marry her "cousin" about whom he knows absolutely nothing and in whom he agrees to believe faithfully. Beatrice and Benedick are comically wrong when they protect themselves, on rational grounds, against the irrationality of love, right when they forswear the life of wit in order to trust one another and their own feelings. Here Shakespeare seems to identify wit with sterile egotism; yet in his subplot lovers he presents the wit against which the play implies strong criticism as so attractive that the play lived for generations as "Beatrice and Benedick."[5] In such comedies as *A Midsummer Night's Dream* and *Much Ado* the irrational faith on which love is based is justified by the comic providence which guides and rewards the lovers, but Shakespeare is not always so sanguine, and the dualism of his vision of love produces a variety of somber themes. The very qualities that make Troilus' love admirable, and make it resemble the reformed Claudio's—its basis in commitment and faith—make him ultimately the satirized embodiment of values that a play which suggests no supporting providential order presents as dangerous and irresponsible; yet in *Othello*, as we saw, Shakespeare dramatizes a

tragic version of the theme of *Much Ado,* in which the faith of
the lover is the only valid criterion of love's worth. In exploring
the implications of the various relationships between the value of
love and the value of its object, the knowledge of the mind and
the knowledge of the heart, Shakespeare presents love as hopelessly paradoxical, based on tragic antinomies in the human spirit
and the world in which that spirit resides; always in Shakespeare
love is the noblest of passions for precisely the same reasons that
it is ridiculous.

What then of *Venus and Adonis?* The poem begins with a
contrast—ironic since Venus will throughout identify herself with
the body's cause, Adonis with spiritual longings—between "rose-
cheek'd Adonis" and "sick-thoughted Venus"; it describes Nature
in the second stanza as "with herself at strife"; its plot consists
of the unsuccessful wooing of Adonis, with his notion of what
love is all about, by Venus, who has another; it leads to the reconciliation in death of the opposition between principles that
makes the tragic ending inevitable; and it ends in Venus' prophecy
that "sorrow on love hereafter shall attend" (1136): Love will be
a torturesome mixture of paradoxical qualities, "raging-mad and
silly-mild . . . cause of war and dire events," "subject and servile
to all discontents" (1151, 1159, 1161); yet, while plucking down
the rich, it shall "enrich the poor with treasures" (1150). In brief,
by reinterpreting the myth of Venus and Adonis, Shakespeare is
half-playfully projecting the genesis of all the paradoxical qualities
of love he so frequently teaches us in his plays to observe.

The charms that lead one school of critics to see the poem as
an encomium to the life of the senses are demonstrably present.
Venus is the apologist for those charms, and in the poem's prelap-
sarian world we sense unmistakably a nature that is radiantly
fresh and appealing, populated by idyllic animals and flowers of
brilliant hue and infused with the magical force of generation.
Part of that same world is Adonis, most beautiful of all its creatures; and there's the rub. For, like the world not yet fallen in
Paradise Lost, the garden of *Venus and Adonis* carries the seeds
of its own destruction, and Adonis feels himself cut off by the
purity of his ideals from the ability to participate in its life:

'What have you urged that I can not reprove?
The path is smooth that leadeth on to danger:
I hate not love, but your device in love,
That lends embracements unto every stranger.
    You do it for increase: O, strange excuse,
    When reason is the bawd to lust's abuse!

'Call it not love, for Love to heaven is fled,
Since sweating Lust on earth usurp'd his name;
Under whose simple semblance he hath fed
Upon fresh beauty, blotting it with blame;
    Which the hot tyrant stains and soon bereaves,
    As caterpillars do the tender leaves.
                              (787–798)

If Venus sees love as the delights and fulfillment of the senses, with all the passion and transitoriness that this implies, Adonis sees it as precisely the opposite: immutable, not subject to time, passionless, incapable of being surfeited (while lust "like a glutton dies" [803]). The two argue their opposed positions magnificently, and the end is ruin. What Shakespeare has done is to present simply, embodied in two characters as two separate principles, the two aspects of love that the neoplatonic Renaissance delighted in seeing paradoxically fused. Venus argues for the steps of the ladder with no vision of its uppermost rung; Adonis longs for the spiritual consummation to which sensual love, as Castiglione and the like saw it, claimed to aspire, but hates the way to that consummation. Thus Shakespeare idealizes two incompatible views; and thus simplistic criticism can be led to glorify one at the expense of the other.[6]

The Shakespearean play is the climactic example of the ways in which art explores reality by imitating its complexity. Reading *Venus and Adonis* with the expectations given us by the plays, we find there the same sort of complexity. For its protagonists not only oppose each other; the poem's theme is the self-contradiction implicit in a central human activity, and, because they are imitations of human beings, Venus and Adonis, each clinging desperately to his own passionately held but partial view of experience, make clear in their own behavior the inadequacy as well as the magnificence of their views. Just so do Antony, Othello, Troilus,

Lysander, Romeo, and Benedick exemplify the paradoxes of love.

The trouble with love as Venus sees and embodies it is that it is bound to all that is least noble in life: animality, mortality, lust, egotism. At the beginning of the poem we find no criticism of Adonis, we hear only Venus; yet we know just what her limitations are. Time and again her eloquent arguments end in grotesque and risible detail. " 'Look in mine eye-balls, there thy beauty lies;/ Then why not lips on lips, since eyes in eyes?' " (119–120). In Venus' speech even the Petrarchan cliché about beauty finding its mirror in the beloved's eyes becomes an uncomfortably untranscendent statement. It is to the magic beauty of Adonis that she responds, but her response is flesh-bound. How often her rhetoric carries us only to this sort of awkwardness:

> 'Here come and sit, where never serpent hisses,
> And being set, I'll smother thee with kisses,
> 'And yet not cloy thy lips with loathed satiety,
> But rather famish them amid their plenty,
> Making them red and pale with fresh variety,
> Ten kisses short as one, one long as twenty:
> A summer's day will seem an hour but short,
> Being wasted in such time-beguiling sport.'
> With this she seizeth on his sweating palm,
> The precedent of pith and livelihood,
> And trembling in her passion, calls it balm,
> Earth's sovereign salve to do a goddess good:
> Being so enrag'd, desire doth lend her force
> Courageously to pluck him from his horse.
> (17–30)

When she argues that "Love is a spirit all compact of fire,/ Not gross to sink, but light, and will aspire" (149–150), Venus is almost convincing; when she becomes Venus Genetrix and argues, along with a number of the sonnets, that love is necessary to procreation, she sounds like Shakespeare himself:

> 'Upon the earth's increase why shouldst thou feed,
> Unless the earth with thy increase be fed?
> By law of nature thou art bound to breed,

That thine may live when thou thyself art dead;
And so, in spite of death, thou doest survive,
In that thy likeness still is left alive.

(169–174)

But the next line topples the whole argument: "By this the love-sick queen began to sweat." Undercutting the simple glorification of physical love as Spenser was doing in his contemporary *Hymn to Love*, Shakespeare makes his Venus catalogue the woes of love: the ugliness of age, of which she and Adonis are ironically free at this moment; "disturbing jealousy"; and the threat of mortality; and we know that her view of the world is tragically limited.[7] Likewise her appeal to the example of the horses works against itself: No matter how magnificent, they are after all only animals (not even Houyhnhnms), and, as R. P. Miller points out, Shakespeare emphasizes their inappropriateness to Venus' policy by calling them, three times out of seven, mere "breeders."[8] Venus then embodies the glorification of the senses without the rationale that justifies that glorification in the familiar Renaissance scheme.

The implicit criticism of Adonis is as easy to perceive. Many readers have found in the character of the boy too young to respond to Venus' aggressive wooing a figure of fun; and as soon as Adonis appears comic, it becomes difficult to maintain the view that he simply represents beauty. But the effect of the comedy at his expense is to lead us to an understanding of what is wrong with his position. If Venus unwittingly overemphasizes the animal element in love, Adonis conversely underestimates its importance, and the significance of his mistake becomes clear in some of the most famous images in the poem. Recall, for example, the stanza in which he is compared to "a wild bird being tamed with too much handling" and to "the fleet-foot roe that's tired with chasing" (560–561); such detail tells us more than that Venus is a huntress. It suggests also an aspect of Adonis that he never acknowledges. Throughout the poem he is associated with animals: The famous dive-dapper, like the bird tangled in the nest, is an analogy to Adonis, and the horse belongs to him. Furthermore, his hand sweats, despite his hatred for "sweating lust"; he pants; and he is described repeatedly in physical terms which belie the asceticism of his language and his action.

But even more important is the fact that the love Adonis yearns for, fled to heaven, is to be found not in life—that life which Venus so vigorously espouses and at the prospect of losing which poor Wat the hare so trembles—but only in death. Throughout the poem Adonis turns away from what Venus offers to seek the boar: " 'I know not love,' quoth he, 'nor will not know it./ Unless it be a boar, and then I chase it' " (409–410). As Adonis knows in his longing for that hunt, as Venus knows in her premonitory dream, and as the language demonstrates when the fatal encounter is consummated, the boar hunt is the pursuit of a kind of love, significantly parallel to Venus' pursuit of Adonis. As Don Cameron Allen observes, "the boar is death";[9] ironically, Adonis rejects the animal in himself only to be destroyed by the insentient beast he seeks. "And nuzzling in his flank, the loving swine/ Sheathed unaware the tusk in his soft groin" (1115–1116).

In this romance of the self-denying Adonis whose definition of love leads him in search of a purity attainable only in death, and of the earthbound Venus whose love never reaches beyond apotheosized animality, Shakespeare reflects the hopelessly opposed elements of love as he found it in Renaissance neoplatonism[10] and in the experience that his plays imitate; in the prophecy of Venus and the conclusion of the poem he reshapes a familiar myth, telling us how these elements were fused into the tragicomic hybrid that love is now. *Venus and Adonis* is not the merely decorative tapestry its enemies and some of its friends have taken it to be, but rather an immediate and sensuous presentation, in the narrative mode, of the issue that lies at the heart of some of Shakespeare's most intense plays. Like them it is a convincing and searching mirror of a view of life that makes great poetry because it cannot be reduced to a critical formula.

❧ II ❧

Venus and Adonis thus tells us something about eros that we have not learned from some of the plays that it calls to mind: that insofar as it is a yearning of the human spirit for stasis, completion, perfection, and freedom from the mortal flaws with which it is paradoxically implicated, it is a desire that can be fulfilled only by death. Shakespeare is not original in this. In fact, as Denis de Rougemont has brilliantly demonstrated in a book whose central thesis is scarcely vitiated by his unconvincing insistence on the origins of the phenomenon in the heresy of the Catharists, the theme that we have recognized in *Venus and Adonis* is the theme of the great twelfth-century *Tristan and Iseult* and its heirs.[11] Fed by the currents of Renaissance neoplatonism and the traditions of courtly love, deepened by the understanding of poets like Petrarch and Sidney that the eros of romantic love is a competing version of the love that finds its completion only in God, strengthened by a psychological tradition that extends from the Goethe of *Werther* through Nietzsche to Freud and Marcuse and N. O. Brown, the double vision of eros as the impulse to both life and death has remained one of the chief recurrences of western art, encompassing works as different from one another as *The Charterhouse of Parma*, Wagner's *Tristan and Isolde*, *War and Peace*, and *The Magic Mountain*. Among the dramatists of the Elizabethan theater only Shakespeare seems deeply rooted enough in the European experience fully to perceive it. Explored with characteristically original insight and force, the perception is the basis of his two great tragedies of romantic love.

It is an ironic fact that Shakespeare's early work would seem better to us if his later plays had not survived. The *Henry VI* plays rival all contemporary efforts in chronicle drama, *Titus Andronicus* is in many respects a better tragedy than any that Kyd or Marlowe produced, and the earliest comedies in the canon easily surpass Lyly, Peele, and Greene. By the standard of what Shakespeare was to do later, however, the work of his first half-decade tends—except when we are reading it—to seem slight. *Romeo and Juliet*, written as Shakespeare approached the brink of his mature abilities, is a clear example. Like *Venus and Adonis* it tends to be patronized. As with the epyllion, critics recognize the brilliance of its young author but feel it straining against a structure which the poet is not yet fully equipped to handle. Thus, in a stimulating and perceptive introduction, G. I. Duthie typically finds himself forced to conclude that "the impression that remains longest in our minds after witnessing or reading the play is not an impression depending on the tragic design that Shakespeare obviously intended to produce." H. B. Charlton argues, "While the play is in certain important respects a dramatic failure, it is a great poetic success."[12] I should like to suggest that if we block from our minds as much as we can the shadow of Shakespeare's mature achievements, if we imagine for a moment that *Romeo and Juliet* is the last play of a University Wit whose exact contemporaries had already reached the end of their careers in the theater, we may recognize that like *Venus and Adonis* it is a realized poetic creation which carries out a larger ambition than the patronizing critic has been ready to recognize. Alfred Harbage has rightly warned us of the new bardolatry which refuses to admit that Shakespeare ever made a mistake and which with a zeal he recognizes as religious manages to turn every mistake, every flaw in the plays, into a superhuman virtue.[13] The admonition should be re-read annually by every critic. But its corollary is equally important: If it is dangerously easy to find ingenious justifications for what our common sense tells us is wrong with a given play, it is equally easy and equally dangerous to dismiss as juvenile or not fully achieved what we have not yet come to understand. Such, as we have seen, has been the case with *Venus and Adonis*; so it is with *Romeo and Juliet*.

Two aspects of *Romeo and Juliet* most trouble critics who see it as deeply flawed: its structure as tragedy and its style. Numerous critics, even when enthusiastically praising the play, confess to what Duthie calls "some degree of failure on Shakespeare's part" in making clear what kind of tragedy he is attempting to write.[14] It is easy enough to locate the problem. The Prologue tells us that *Romeo and Juliet* is to be a tragedy of "star-crossed lovers," and Romeo on the verge of seeing Juliet for the first time discovers that his

> mind misgives
> Some consequences yet hanging in the stars,
> Shall bitterly begin his fearful date
> With this night's revels and expire the term
> Of a despised life closed in my breast
> By some vile forfeit of untimely death.
>
> (I. iv. 106–111)

Much in the play suggests that its tragedy is one of fate. But, as critics repeatedly observe, the sense of fatality is undercut by a series of accidents which remind us more of capricious fortune than of the nemesis of the Greeks: Capulet's impulsive decision to advance the date of the wedding, the detainment of Friar John, Romeo's chance meeting with Tybalt, Friar Laurence's failure to get to the tomb before Romeo. To Granville-Barker, one of the play's most sensitive critics, this suggests, not "a tragedy of fated disaster, but—for a more poignant if less highly heroic theme—of opportunity muddled away and marred by ill luck."[15] Moreover, tragedies in which fate is dominant generally move us by demonstrating that it operates at the center of character; yet, as Duthie puts it once again, the "defects" in Romeo and Juliet which "contribute directly and demonstrably to their doom"—their lack of "mature poise and balance," their impetuous youth, their tendency at moments to blubber and weep—are scarcely worthy of the dignity of tragedy and operate at cross-purposes with what the play would seem to be claiming as tragic, and with Friar Laurence's rather tedious rehearsal at the end of the accidents that have brought about the catastrophe. If *Hamlet* and *Othello* are tragedies whose force emanates from the fact that the heroes are brought down by faults of character which we have been led to understand as supreme virtues, then *Romeo and Juliet* does not immediately strike us as belonging to their company. And the burden of the action that frames the mishaps of the lovers, the suggestion that the protagonists have contributed their deaths as a sacrificial offering to heal the civil strife of Verona, has little to do with the central action.

The difficulties of the style are perhaps even more readily seen. Many passages belong to the body of Shakespeare's most successful poetry, and few readers would fail to agree that *Romeo and Juliet* is his first poetic masterpiece. Yet the style is uneven. As Granville-Barker has shown, one will find in *Romeo and Juliet* examples of Shakespeare's early, declamatory style, heavy on simile and merely decorative imagery, and of his mature style, in which metaphors more tersely embody complex ideas and no image seems extrinsic to the action; Wolfgang Clemen concludes that this stylistic unevenness, like other elements of the play, marks

Romeo and Juliet as a "play of transition."[16] Few mature plays of Shakespeare show such a variety of styles as are comprehended here. Consider side by side Paris' maundering over the Juliet he thinks dead—

> Beguiled, divorced, wronged, spited, slain!
> Most detestable death, by thee beguiled,
> By cruel, cruel thee quite overthrown!
> O love! O life! not life, but love in death!
> (IV. v. 55–58)

and Romeo's apostrophe a few scenes later:

> Ah, dear Juliet,
> Why art thou yet so fair? shall I believe
> That unsubstantial death is amorous,
> And that the lean abhorred monster keeps
> Thee here in dark to be his paramour?
> (V. iii. 101–105)

or, as expressions of love's grief,

> I am too sore enpierced with his shaft
> To soar with his light feathers, and so bound,
> I cannot bound a pitch above dull woe:
> Under love's heavy burden do I sink
> (I. iv. 19–22)

and

> Is it even so? then I defy you, stars!
> Thou know'st my lodging: get me ink and paper,
> And hire post-horses; I will hence to-night.
> (V. i. 24–26)

But to recognize the variety of styles is only to begin to consider the question of style in the play. Transitional or not—and, regarded in the light of the entire canon, which play is not transitional?—*Romeo and Juliet* manifests so much awareness of style on its author's part that it becomes impossible to accept such a judgment as Granville-Barker's:

> By all the rules, no doubt, there should be two Shakespeares
> at work here. But in such a ferment as we now find him
> (himself, in some sort, a young Romeo on the turn from a
> Rosaline of phrase-making to a deeper-welling love) he may
> well have been capable of working on Tuesday in one fash-
> ion, on Wednesday in another, capable of couplet, sonnet,
> word-juggling, straight sober verse, or hard-bitten prose, often
> as the popular story he was turning to account and the need
> of actors for the thing they and he were so apt at seemed to
> demand, at times out of the new strength breeding in him.[17]

This is praise, and it reveals the critic's love of Shakespeare; but
it is also patronizing, assuming that what we find troublesome will
be explained by the fact that the play—which a page earlier he calls
"Shakespeare's first unquestionable success, proof positive of his
unique quality"—is only an apprentice piece. Surely it is not
bardolatry to suggest that in a play whose every line reflects an
intense concern with language Shakespeare knew that he was
making Mercutio's language very different from Capulet's, and
the Nurse's from Paris', or that, as Clemen and most other critics
(including Granville-Barker) have been quick to perceive, Romeo
and Juliet themselves mature linguistically in most remarkable
fashion as the tragedy moves towards its catastrophe. Undeniably
there is a good deal of irregularity in the style; but the more one
studies the play the more reluctant one becomes to state cate-
gorically that any element of style is the result of Shakespeare's
failure to revise an early state of his manuscript or to take advantage everywhere in the play of the maturity that some of the
speeches and scenes immediately manifest. It might be valuable to
recall that the plays most probably contemporary with *Romeo
and Juliet* are *Richard II* and *A Midsummer Night's Dream*, and
that its immediate predecessor is *Love's Labour's Lost*. I suspect
that most readers, asked to identify the plays in which Shakespeare
most self-consciously experiments with style and relates the problem of style—what characters do with language—to their themes,
would choose these very plays.[18] Only by responding with sensitive
awareness to the variations in style, and to pondering what they
tell us, can we fully understand *Romeo and Juliet*.

Consider together two facts about *Romeo and Juliet*. First, the play is extraordinarily rich, even for Shakespeare, in poetic devices that call our attention to themselves. This is true not merely of the speeches critics are tempted to reject as immature, but of every part of the play. The speeches I cited as examples of Shakespeare's mature and unquestionably successful style are as full of rhetorical artifice as those to which I contrasted them, and the teacher who wants to demonstrate Shakespeare's indebtedness to the tropes which constituted sixteenth-century rhetorical theory finds *Romeo and Juliet* a virtual handbook; significantly, Sister Miriam Joseph in her useful study of Shakespeare's formal rhetoric catalogues as many tropical devices in the speeches that move us as in those that do not.[19] This is to say that the entire play is stylized. Second, and paradoxically, the play itself makes us respond to certain stylized speeches as too artificial and to others as genuine and powerfully effective poetry. Were *Romeo and Juliet* as homogeneous in tone as *Titus Andronicus*, we should regard as harmonious parts of a stylized whole those passages that strike us now as excessive. What makes us respond to certain speeches as if they were natural utterances, so that we are scarcely aware of "style" when we hear them, is the staginess of others. The inconsistency of style in *Romeo and Juliet* directs our intense response to its most powerful language, and that forces us to attend to its meaning.

Consider one scene, that in which Juliet's family circle discovers her apparent death (IV. v).

Enter Nurse

Nurse. Mistress! what, mistress! Juliet! fast, I warrant
    her, she:
Why, lamb! why, lady! fie, you slug-a-bed!
Why, love, I say! madam! sweetheart! why, bride!
What, not a word? You take your pennyworths now;
Sleep for a week; for the next night, I warrant,
The County Paris hath set up his rest,
That you shall rest but little. God forgive me,
Marry, and amen, how sound is she asleep!
I needs must wake her. Madam, madam, madam!
Ay, let the County take you in your bed;

He'll fright you up, i'faith. Will it not be?
> [*Undraws the curtains.*]

What, dress'd! and in your clothes! and down again!
I must needs wake you: Lady! lady! lady!
Alas, alas! Help, help! My lady's dead!
O well-a-day, that ever I was born!
Some aqua vitae, ho! my lord! my lady!

Enter Lady Capulet

Lady Capulet. What noise is here?
Nurse. O lamentable day!
Lady Capulet. What is the matter?
Nurse. Look, look! O heavy day!
Lady Capulet. O me, O me! My child, my only life,
Revive, look up, or I will die with thee!
Help, help! Call help.

Enter Capulet

Capulet. For shame, bring Juliet forth; her lord is come.
Nurse. She's dead, deceased, she's dead; alack the day!
Lady Capulet. Alack the day, she's dead, she's dead,
    she's dead!
Capulet. Ha! let me see her: out, alas! she's cold;
Her blood is settled, and her joints are stiff:
Life and these lips have long been separated:
Death lies on her like an untimely frost
Upon the sweetest flower of all the field.

Nurse. O lamentable day!
Lady Capulet. O woful time!
Capulet. Death, that hath ta'en her hence to make me
    wail,
Ties up my tongue, and will not let me speak.

Enter Friar Laurence and Paris, with Musicians

Friar. Come, is the bride ready to go to church?
Capulet. Ready to go, but never to return.
O son! the night before thy wedding-day
Hath Death lain with thy wife. There she lies,
Flower as she was, deflowered by him.
Death is my son-in-law, Death is my heir;
My daughter he hath wedded: I will die,
And leave him all; life, living, all is Death's.

Paris. Have I thought long to see this morning's face,

And doth it give me such a sight as this?
> *Lady Capulet.* Accursed, unhappy, wretched, hateful
> > day!
Most miserable hour that e'er time saw
In lasting labour of his pilgrimage!
But one, poor one, one poor and loving child,
But one thing to rejoice and solace in,
And cruel Death hath catch'd it from my sight!
> *Nurse.* O woe! O woful, woful, woful day!
Most lamentable day, most woful day
That ever, ever, I did yet behold!
O day! O day! O day! O hateful day!
Never was seen so black a day as this:
O woful day, O woful day!
> *Paris.* Beguiled, divorced, wronged, spited, slain!
Most detestable death, by thee beguiled,
By cruel cruel thee quite overthrown!
O love! O life! not life, but love in death!
> *Capulet.* Despised, distressed, hated, martyr'd, kill'd!
Uncomfortable time, why camest thou now
To murder, murder our solemnity?
O child! O child! my soul, and not my child!
Dead art thou! Alack! my child is dead,
And with my child my joys are buried.
> *Friar.* Peace, ho, for shame! confusion's cure lives not
In these confusions. Heaven and yourself
Had part in this fair maid; now heaven hath all,
And all the better is it for the maid:
Your part in her you could not keep from death,
But heaven keeps his part in eternal life.
The most you sought was her promotion;
For 'twas your heaven she should be advanced:
And weep ye now, seeing she is advanced
Above the clouds, as high as heaven itself?

> > > > (IV. v. 1–74)

Opening the scene with the Nurse's characteristic chatter, which disjointedly reflects her amusing and touching love of Juliet and her pleasure in bawdy, Shakespeare resumes the tone of earthy commonplace present whenever she or Mercutio is on stage. As she realizes why she cannot awaken Juliet, she responds

in a series of cries whose words hardly matter, and when Lady
Capulet answers her summons the Nurse cannot even find words
to tell her what has happened. Lady Capulet's first reaction is
equally direct:

> O me, O me! My child, my only life,
> Revive, look up, or I will die with thee!
> Help, help! Call help.

In the moment of her first shock Juliet's mother expresses with
the economy of a single outcry her full understanding of what
she has seen.

Upon entering her husband does the same; against the background of two lines of imageless blank verse spoken by Juliet's
mother and her Nurse, in which five beats out of ten fall on the
word "dead," a heretofore verbose Capulet reacts with a clinically
precise description of his drugged daughter, and then with something new, a poetic image which arises from the physical fact of
her coldness:

> Death lies on her like an untimely frost
> Upon the sweetest flower of all the field.

These lines operate with all the force that poetry is capable of:
They make us understand the poignant alacrity with which untimely death destroys what is delicate, beautiful, dear, and young.
In this brilliant and classical image Capulet would seem to have
said all that can be said, and as his wife and the Nurse continue
to wail in conventional phrases—using language as a simple outlet
for emotions they seem incapable of expressing, as Capulet has
done—he declares that he too has been made inarticulate by death.
But Shakespeare has not finished with our emotions, for now the
wedding party arrives. The staggered entrances enable us to watch
each character respond serially to the same shocking news, and
Capulet answers the Friar's ironic greeting with a poetic reflection
on the implications of the image he introduced a moment earlier.
The speech is as spare as those that follow it are prolix. It states
a series of simple and terrible truths, whose accuracy we fully
realize only by our response to the entire play. Death is Juliet's

groom; the young dead, there is no life for the old; if Juliet is a flower and has married Death, then death has deflowered her (how different this is from the innocent puns on coal-collier-choler-collar of the opening scene or the self-conscious quibbles in which Rosaline's lover indulged); if Juliet has married Death, Death is, as Capulet recognizes when again he begins to think about himself, his son-in-law, and as the possessor of an old man who has no more reason to live the heir of an inheritance that makes a mockery of lesser dowries. The end of Capulet's speech is a lyrical paradox which the alliteration of "leave" and "life" and "living" emphasizes, and its last phrase, "living, all is Death's" is in its context both a freshly stated reminder of what we know most painfully and an incisive summary of what the tragedy is insisting that we feel (even though, of course, Juliet is not really dead).

But now a new movement begins in the scene. As Paris, whose love for Juliet not only has failed to move us before, but has constituted a fatal obstacle to the hopes of the protagonists, demands that we sympathize with his woes too, we may recall that Juliet is not yet dead. Lady Capulet's next speech touchingly reveals that she has heard nothing but her own grief, for it takes off from her last line, "o woful time," spoken before Paris and the Friar arrived. It would be a cruel auditor who did not feel for Lady Capulet, yet her response is on the verge of self-pity:

> But one, poor one, one poor and loving child,
> But one thing to rejoice and solace in,
> And cruel death hath catch'd it from my sight!

The detachment that we may be beginning to feel from the grief of the characters on stage grows more marked now in the next four speeches, and it does so because Shakespeare wants it to do so. Like Lady Capulet, the Nurse picks up where she left off in "o lamentable day!"; but unlike Lady Capulet's speech, her own is thoroughly inadequate to communicate her grief, rather telling us that she is unhappy than compelling us to share her sorrow.

> O woe! O woful, woful day!
> Most lamentable day, most woful day,
> That ever, ever, I did yet behold!

> O day! O day! O day! O hateful day!
> Never was seen so black a day as this:
> O woful day, O woful day!

In its symmetry and artifice her speech reflects not a spontaneous outcry of grief, but an unsuccessful attempt—compared with what we have heard a moment earlier from Capulet—to find a rhetoric that will do justice to what she is feeling. It is followed by a speech which, out of context, I cited earlier as an example of the style that we do not admire in *Romeo and Juliet*. In context Paris' speech is even more distressing, for its manner, cataloguing and repetitious, is an awkward reprise of the Nurse's speech. Its last line, "O love! O life! Not life, but love in death!" jars in a new way, for it is a parody of one of the most frequently parodied lines in *The Spanish Tragedy*, "O life! no life, but lively form of death."[20] Paris' style is the style of Bottom's Pyramus recognizing the remains of his lady love. If we have any doubts about Shakespeare's intention here, we need only listen to the next and last speech in the strange litany as Capulet, beginning like Paris with a string of past participles, once again parodies Hieronymo: "O child! O child! my soul, and not my child!" Ironically it is Capulet, whose first speeches in this scene so moved us, who calls forth the Friar's reproach for futile and self-pitying lamentation.

Even the Friar, however, is not spared. We are grateful for his interruption of a series of speeches which are awakening in us more embarrassment than sympathy, but as he continues he falls into rhymed *sententiae*, cant formulae which we expect of his stock role but which no more satisfy us as adequately embodying what is happening on the stage than what they interrupt. A lesser dramatist might have used the speeches I have been running down to move his audience within a context whose style never admitted of the possibility of better things, as Kyd employed similar rhetoric to extort tears from his audience. But Shakespeare has established a context in which the norm represented by such speeches rings false.

Why does he do so? Because, though he wants us to feel the impact of the event on Juliet's parents, the tragedy is not theirs but Romeo's, and it is his response we must feel most deeply.

Thus the scene we have been examining is followed by a brief interlude in which the musicians banter with one another, so that grief will not be laid ineffectively on grief, and so that the illusion of passing time may be conveyed more easily, and then immediately the action moves to Mantua where Romeo hears Balthasar's report of the catastrophe:

Enter Romeo

Romeo. If I may trust the flattering truth of sleep,
My dreams presage some joyful news at hand:
My bosom's lord sits lightly in his throne;
And all this day an unaccustom'd spirit
Lifts me above the ground with cheerful thoughts.
I dreamt my lady came and found me dead—
Strange dream, that gives a dead man leave to think!—
And breathed such life with kisses in my lips,
That I revived, and was an emperor.
Ah me! how sweet is love itself possess'd,
When but love's shadows are so rich in joy!
                    Enter Balthasar, *booted*
News from Verona!—How now, Balthasar!
Dost thou not bring me letters from the friar?
How doth my lady? Is my father well?
How fares my Juliet? That I ask again;
For nothing can be ill, if she be well.

Balthasar. Then she is well, and nothing can be ill:
Her body sleeps in Capels' monument,
And her immortal part with angels lives.
I saw her laid low in her kindred's vault,
And presently took post to tell it you:
O, pardon me for bringing these ill news,
Since you did leave it for my office, sir.

Romeo. Is it even so? then I defy you, stars!
Thou know'st my lodging: get me ink and paper,
And hire post-horses; I will hence to-night.

Balthasar. I do beseech you, sir, have patience.
Your looks are pale and wild, and do import
Some misadventure.

Romeo.   Tush, thou art deceived:
Leave me, and do the thing I bid thee do.
Hast thou no letters to me from the friar?

Balthasar. No, my good lord.
Romeo.   No matter: get thee gone,
And hire those horses; I'll be with thee straight.
                    [*Exit* Balthasar
Well, Juliet, I will lie with thee to-night.
Let's see for means: O mischief, thou are swift
To enter in the thoughts of desperate men!
I do remember an apothecary,—
And hereabouts he dwells,—which late I noted
In tatter'd weeds, with overwhelming brows,
Culling of simples; meagre were his looks,
Sharp misery had worn him to the bones:
And in his needy shop a tortoise hung,
An alligator stuff'd, and other skins
Of ill-shaped fishes; and about his shelves
A beggarly account of empty boxes,
Green earthen pots, bladders and musty seeds,
Remnants of packthread and old cakes of roses,
Were thinly scatter'd, to make up a show.
Noting this penury, to myself I said
'An if a man did need a poison now,
Whose sale is present death in Mantua,
Here lives a caitiff wretch would sell it him.'
O, this same thought did but forerun my need;
And this same needy man must sell it me.
As I remember, this should be the house.
Being holiday, the beggar's shop is shut.
What, ho! apothecary!
                    (V. i. 1–57)

His ironic revery interrupted by the report that puts an end
to his joys, Romeo responds tersely. Now, tough-minded men do
not customarily address the stars, and presumably few lovers even
in Shakespeare's day would receive such news in Romeo's manner. But in the context established by the previous scene, his
language conveys the illusion that it is not poetry but rather the
direct utterance of the heart. He can deny Balthasar's worried
description of his "pale and wild" looks; he does not need to call
attention to a grief which is fully expressed in his immediate decision to die, couched in a laconic and powerful image that recalls
the irony of Capulet's picture of Death as Juliet's husband: "Well,

Juliet, I will lie with thee to-night." Like the Capulet of the preceding scene's opening, Romeo talks for the remainder of this speech in precise images evocative of a physical reality which tells us all we need to know to feel with him. His apothecary is as powerful an allegorization of death as Spenser ever achieved; yet it is simultaneously a disciplined and economical description of the world that our eyes see. Linked to an unblinking resolve really to die, it is more moving than all the protestations of Juliet's family circle that their lives are finished when in fact it is quite clear that their grief has not driven them to the death they apostrophize so repetitiously. Repeatedly Shakespeare has signaled to us that lamentations such as the Capulets' are inadequate: Capulet's resolve, soon broken, to say no more, the Friar's stern admonition to the grieving family, and Romeo's refusal to indulge in that ululation that Balthasar invites unmistakably ask us to contrast the styles we have witnessed.

Stylistic criticism such as this marks all of *Romeo and Juliet*. More trope-ridden than many of the nondramatic sonnets, the prologue employs alliteration, metonymy, paronomasia, antithesis, personification, and paradox, and the action opens with a punning match between servants. The play's rhetoric is continuously exuberant. Yet it is subject to almost constant reproach. Romeo first appears on the stage—having already been described in terms that present him as comically acting out the clichés of Petrarchan sonnets—spouting rhymed oxymora about love, and Benvolio promptly mocks him now as Mercutio will in subsequent scenes. The Nurse (I. iii) punctures Lady Capulet's elaborate conceit of Paris as a "book of love, this unbound lover" with the more prosaic (though witty and therefore still rhetorical) reminder that "women grow by men," opposing as Mercutio constantly does the realities of sexual love to verbal idealizations; the paradoxical realism of Mercutio's fantasy about Queen Mab—a classic exercise in the device of pseudomenos, precise in every whimsical detail—provides striking contrast to the loose verbosity of Romeo's laments. Friar Laurence, unable to understand the drift of Romeo's fanciful circumlocutions about his meeting with Juliet, urges him to "be plain, good son, and homely in thy drift;/ Riddling con-

fession finds but riddling shrift" (II. iii. 55–56). Juliet refuses
Romeo's invitation to blazon her love for him because

> Conceit, more rich in matter than in words,
> Brags of his substance, not of ornament:
> They are but beggars that can count their worth;
> But my true love is grown to such excess
> I cannot sum up sum of half my wealth.
>> (II. vi. 30–34)

Mercutio, insistent to his last breath on semantic accuracy, coun-
ters Romeo's consolation that his wound cannot hurt much with
a characteristic reminder, moving as a revelation of his steadfast-
ness to himself and significant for the play at large, that facts
matter more than formulations:

> No, 'tis not so deep as a well, nor so wide as a church
> door; but 'tis enough, 'twill serve.
>> (III. i. 99–100)

Not the least power of these words, followed by a pun on
"grave," is the fact that they recall another speech, of a very
different order, to which we have already responded as a similar
statement of fact that moves us and that reflects upon the entire
play, Juliet's avowal of love for Romeo:

> My bounty is as boundless as the sea,
> My love as deep; the more I give to thee,
> The more I have, for both are infinite.
>> (II. ii. 133–135)

And in contemplating these speeches, so far from one another,
yet so hauntingly linked by their metaphors of deepness, we may
begin to understand why Shakespeare has so made us concentrate
on the problem of style in *Romeo and Juliet*. I have already recalled the commonplace that Romeo matures in his speech as the
play develops. Of such speech as he utters in Mantua and after-
wards he is not capable in the early action of Verona:

Well, Juliet, I will lie with thee to-night.
                    Shall I believe
That unsubstantial death is amorous,
And that the lean abhorred monster keeps
Thee here in dark to be his paramour?
For fear of that, I still will stay with thee;
And never from this palace of dim night
Depart again: here, here will I remain
With worms that are thy chamber-maids; O, here
Will I set up my everlasting rest,
And shake the yoke of inauspicious stars
From this world-wearied flesh. Eyes, look your last!
Arms, take your last embrace! and lips, O you
The doors of breath, seal with a righteous kiss
A dateless bargain to engrossing death!
                    (V. iii. 102–115)

And before it was

Why, then, O brawling love! O loving hate!
O any thing, of nothing first create!
O heavy lightness! serious vanity!
Mis-shapen chaos of well-seeming forms!
Feather of lead, bright smoke, cold fire, sick health!
Still-waking sleep, that is not what it is!
This love feel I, that feel no love in this.
                    (I. i. 182–188)

and

Why, such is love's transgression.
Griefs of mine own lie heavy in my breast,
Which thou wilt propagate, to have it prest
With more of thine: this love that thou hast shown
Doth add more grief to too much of mine own.
Love is a smoke raised with the fume of sighs;
Being purged, a fire sparkling in lover's eyes;
Being vex'd, a sea nourish'd with lovers' tears:
What is it else? a madness most discreet,
A choking gall and a preserving sweet.
                    (I. i. 191–200)

The key to the speech of the early Romeo is that "What is it else?": Like a Renaissance schoolboy laying out a composition, he asks himself whether he has exhausted the copiousness of his subject, and finds a set of paradoxes to bring his oration to its period. In the strings of oxymora so carefully arranged we discover the self-conscious rhetorician exploring his subject, creating his argument through ingenuity and exuberant inventiveness. In the last speeches we perceive another kind of force, which we are compelled to recognize as heartfelt. Romeo does not search for verbal formulations, but finds them implicit in the situation. Clemen has shown us how in the scenes in which Romeo and Juliet fall in love their imagery becomes dramatic, so that the torches which Juliet teaches to burn bright are suggested by the torches illuminating the Capulets' party, and the image of Juliet as a "winged messenger of heaven" presented to "the white-up-turned wondering eyes/ Of mortals that fall back to gaze" (II. ii. 28–30) is again literally suggested by Romeo's posture on stage as he looks up to Juliet's room above. Just so, and as in Capulet's affecting account of Juliet the flower deflowered by her bride-groom Death, the imagery of Romeo's last speeches develops literally from his understanding of an actual situation; in context such poetry is not decorative, but rather the only satisfactory expression of things as they are and as they are felt. Jejune on Sunday, Romeo, according to his father,

> Away from light steals home . . .
> And private in his chamber pens himself,
> Shuts up his windows, locks fair daylight out
> And makes himself an artificial night;
> (I. i. 143–146)

mature on Wednesday, he shuts himself up in another dark chamber and resolves that he will "never from this palace of dim night/ Depart again" (V. iii. 107–108).

Yet in one crucial respect these two kinds of poetry are similar: They are founded on paradox. The paradoxes are not of the lovers' seeking, but tragically built into the experience to which they surrender themselves. Oxymoron is not simply a rhetorical

device; it is a definition of their lives. Like Romeo, Juliet knows
it from the start:

> My only love sprung from my only hate!
> Too early seen unknown, and known too late!
> Prodigious birth of love it is to me,
> That I must love a loathed enemy.
>
> (I. v. 140–143)

Love between the children of enemies is paradoxical; even more so
is a love that finds its marriage only in death. Such paradox emerges
not from the inventive mind of a sonnet-fed young man, turned
in upon himself and delighting in the ambiguities of emotions
simultaneously bitter and sweet, but from the actual confrontation of a reality that destroys in creating. We might consider
the paradoxes of *Romeo and Juliet* from yet another angle.
Throughout the first half of the play, as, among other critics,
Harry Levin has argued in his indispensable study, Romeo's idealization of romantic love is polarized against the naturalism of
Mercutio and the Nurse (Levin notes that the Nurse's role gains
force from her "natural" connection to Juliet as her wet-nurse).
It is equally significant that the Nurse's role is of a different order
in the second half, where it is her well-wishing advice to leave
bad enough alone and later her pathetic grief that are set in
counterpoint to Juliet's resolve; and that Mercutio, the voice of
earthy realism and common sense about love, is killed at the play's
center. In the first half of the tragedy Mercutio is opposed to a
lover fixed on a sterile and virginal affection for a mistress who
will have none of him; Romeo refuses to recognize the physical
fact of love on which his friend constantly insists. But in the
second half, Romeo is married and no longer needs Mercutio's
bawdy instruction in the full meaning of his love. By the time of
Mercutio's death Romeo has learned to salt his idealism with
Mercutio's awareness of the reality of the flesh. But he has learned
more than Mercutio knows, for he comes simultaneously to understand the full spirituality of his love for Juliet: He knows that it
can find its ultimate satisfaction not in the vigorous life that
Mercutio so poignantly embodies, but only in death. Having led
us to reject wanton Petrarchism, Shakespeare thus brings us to

affirm the existential antinomies from which Petrarch drew his true power.

Talking about style we have come back to character, and thus again to the problem of *Romeo and Juliet* as tragedy. The quality of Romeo's speech changes, as we have seen by examining it as speech, but the real change is that—except for some lapses— from the moment he falls in love with Juliet until he dies, Romeo's speech is bound to action. For Rosaline he "live[s] dead," he says (I. i. 230), and we do not believe him; for Juliet he dies. For Rosaline he turns the day into artificial night; but he can see Juliet only at night, when she "is the sun" (II. ii. 3); day brings about the event that drives him from her, and at the end he must lie with her in a dark vault which "her beauty makes . . . a feasting presence full of light" (V. iii. 85–86). Romeo and Juliet have given themselves over to passion. That passion is, as always in Shakespeare, thoughtless, impetuous, destructive, against all the advice of their elders to go "wisely and slow" because "they stumble that run fast" (II. iii. 94); and it is what makes them the emblem of love. We have heard constant warnings against the amorous and paradoxical world of words which the lovers inhabit, but come at last to admire their paradoxes as wiser than the words of caution. Similarly we watch them warned by the commonsensical Nurse and by Friar Laurence, even once by Juliet herself in urging Romeo not to swear oaths—

> this contract . . .
> . . . is too rash, too unadvised, too sudden;
> Too like the lightning, which doth cease to be
> Ere one can say 'It lightens.'
> (II. ii. 117–120)

—but we come to prize them as they prize each other, for the absoluteness of their passion. If Shakespeare has compressed a narrative which took months into a play which spans five days, if he has risked a growth in character that on reflection might seem to us to require more than even months, he has done so for a reason.

No critic's formulation could more accurately convey what I am talking about than Juliet's epithalamion, perhaps the most magnificent piece of poetry in the play, spoken at the center of the tragedy:

> Gallop apace, you fiery-footed steeds,
> Towards Phoebus' lodging: such a waggoner
> As Phaethon would whip you to the west,
> And bring in cloudy night immediately.
> Spread thy close curtain, love-performing night,
> That runaways' eyes may wing, and Romeo
> Leap to these arms, untalk'd of and unseen.
> Lovers can see to do their amorous rites
> By their own beauties; or, if love be blind,
> It best agrees with night. Come, civil night,
> Thou sober-suited matron, all in black,
> And learn me how to lose a winning match,
> Play'd for a pair of stainless maidenhoods:
> Hood my unmann'd blood, bating in my cheeks,
> With thy black mantle; till strange love, grown bold,
> Think true love acted simple modesty.
> Come, night; come, Romeo; come, thou day in night;
> For thou wilt lie upon the wings of night
> Whiter than new snow on a raven's back.
> Come, gentle night, come, loving, black-brow'd night,
> Give me my Romeo; and, when he shall die,
> Take him and cut him out in little stars,
> And he will make the face of heaven so fine
> That all the world will be in love with night
> And pay no worship to the garish sun.
> O, I have bought the mansion of a love,
> But not possess'd it, and, though I am sold,
> Not yet enjoy'd: so tedious is this day
> As is the night before some festival
> To an impatient child that hath new robes
> And may not wear them.
>
> (III. ii. 1–31)

As fanciful as any other passage in the play, it is nonetheless more precise than even Juliet knows. The night for which she longs is that long night in which she and Romeo will find that escape from a constantly interfering daylight world toward which they are rapidly being driven. Like the sonnet in which the lovers first woo one another, Juliet's invocation suggests her fealty to a religion of love, a religion set against that other represented by Friar Laurence, whose cautioning seems irrelevant and whose ministrations result only in killing the lovers. The generation of parents preaches moderation; Lady Capulet's advice to Juliet not to weep excessively (for Tybalt, she thinks) reminds us of Claudius' advice to his nephew. But here as in *Hamlet* Shakespeare teaches us that in the consuming fire of passion there is something more compelling than men of moderation ever imagine. Only annihilation can do full justice to such longings as Romeo and Juliet share. Theirs is not a love of propagation and domestic contentment, but rather a yearning for a transformation of the world that will correspond to their inner state. Anything but death would be a betrayal of that love.

Thus we feel at the end of *Romeo and Juliet* as we do at the end of every Shakespearean tragedy: We have watched not the process of nemesis, or of fortune, or of retribution, but rather the playing out of an awesome dialectic in which what is most worth prizing in the hero is set complementarily against the wisdom that the world for good reason advises. The play's expressed judgment is against impetuosity and irrationality as destructive, but the valuation it implies is a judgment in favor of precisely these qualities as the foundation and essence of a transcendent love. Juliet's wedding invocation to the friendly night and Romeo's love of night and blackness suggest their growing up, as we have seen, to a view of love which simultaneously incorporates and refutes Mercutio's; Romeo's rejection of a chaste interest in Rosaline for a love that is of the body as well as of the soul leads ironically to his fulfillment in a death which does not merely happen to him, but which he chooses, and which means a good deal more than it did in Brooke's tragedy of fortune that served Shakespeare as source. Were love simple—were it not, to recall the myth Shakespeare set out in *Venus and Adonis*, the cursed mingling of two unreconcilable worlds, two kinds of experience, two opposed drives—we could find Romeo and his bride either right or wrong. But in a universe whose values are always complementary there is no such simple judgment to be made. Even Friar Laurence understands that

Virtue itself turns vice, being misapplied;
And vice sometimes by action dignified.
(II. iii. 21–22)

From one point of view Romeo and Juliet lose all; from another they gain all that there is to be gained. Unlike the paradoxes the early Romeo seeks out, the antinomies of love are woven, as he learns, into the fabric of a universe which can be comprehended only by a complementary vision. The problem is eros; its form is Shakespearean.

⊸§ III §⊸

Romeo and Juliet is about youth and age. A young man's play, it stages the internal conflict in love as a tension between the consuming eros of adolescence, which so insists on the complete satisfaction of the ego that it must end in the annihilation of the self, and its polar opposite, that mature social love which insists on the sacrifice of the ego's fulfillment for another kind of good, a world that fosters rather than destroys. The lovers die for the one; recognizing their complicity in the tragedy, their survivors pledge to remake themselves so that they can survive for the other. To speak of both these forms of love is to beg the question as the very word "love" does.

To see love thus as a polarized value because of its generational aspect is to associate it with the problems of libido as *Henry IV* does, where Falstaff tragicomically insists on his perennial youth. But it is a young Hal who must reject the values of his old friend, and at such moments Shakespeare would have us understand that the problem is more than simply generational. More than a decade past *Romeo and Juliet* and within a very few years of his retirement from the theater, an older Shakespeare returns once more, in *Antony and Cleopatra*, to the theme of romantic love. The unanimity of critical applause, the absence of voices to tell us that elements of the play reflect levels of vision not fully liberated from a less mature point in the poet's development, and a plenitude controlled with more obvious success all point to the fullest realization of the theme with which Shakespeare had been concerned since *Venus and Adonis*. *Antony and*

Cleopatra does not negate what *Venus and Adonis* and *Romeo and Juliet* told us; but it separates the question of the role of eros from the problems of adolescence. In pitying Adonis and Romeo and Juliet for leaving life before they have had a chance to learn what it is that they are leaving, we find ourselves disappointed by a world that does not conform to the ideals of the young. But as we watch Antony and Cleopatra choosing between self-destruction for a similar love and all the power that the adult world has to offer, we confront a more disturbing challenge: The world as seen from the point of view of its own maximum achievements may not be worth the keeping. After Romeo and Juliet are gone, a purged and reconciled polity remains to profit by their instruction; with the deaths of Antony and Cleopatra, "the crown o' the earth doth melt. . . . And there is nothing left remarkable/ Beneath the visiting moon" (IV. xv. 63–68). As often happens in the later tragedies, the order restored makes a mockery of our aspirations to a good life that *Romeo and Juliet* could suggest to the end is possible.

This is not to suggest that *Antony and Cleopatra* is simpler or more monistic than the earlier works. If anything, it is more profoundly dualistic. So complementary is its vision that some critics continue to find in it a demonstration, depending on their particular sensibilities, either of the absolute transcendence or of the utter worthlessness of the love it presents, for both views are legitimately occasioned by aspects of the play.[21] Like *Hamlet*, *Antony and Cleopatra* has emerged in recent years from the clouds of partisan and partial interpretations into the light of an increasingly communal reading which makes one think in optimistic moments that literary study may be a progressive phenomenon, and that the insights of individual critics may be contributions to a body of enduring knowledge. Even to cite all the critics who have argued for a complementary reading of *Antony and Cleopatra* would be an enormous task; and those critics are to be thanked for the fact that about one of the most complex of Shakespeare's plays the least need be said.[22]

One point needs still to be stressed, however: As the last of Shakespeare's studies of romantic love, *Antony and Cleopatra* bases its complementarity as much on its author's late vision of

the political world and of tragedy as it does on his previous understanding of love. It may be helpful to recall that the play was
written most probably in the same year as *Coriolanus*,[23] Shakespeare's most pessimistic political play. In *Antony and Cleopatra*
—as not in *Romeo and Juliet*—the world which love throws away
is presented ambivalently. Thus Shakespeare gives us two pictures
of Rome. One is of the world that Antony loses in choosing
Cleopatra: a world in which honor is the watchword, military men
are giants who can survive superhuman trials, and fame is the
spur to noble men's ambition. But the other picture is of a vicious
political arena where honor is meaningless and comes only to
men who do not deserve it; a general atmosphere of treachery and
triviality makes Rome seem hardly worth the contemning. Seeing
Rome the first way we agree with Antony's friends that he has
thrown away a magnificent life in order to waste the lamps of
night in futile Alexandrian revelry; seeing Rome the second way
we realize that Antony alone among the men of Rome has found
a way to escape its pointless way of life and to fulfill himself.
Judging Antony's commitment to Cleopatra, we must take both
of these pictures into account. Implicated in each of these valuations of Rome is a corresponding valuation of the romantic
alliance; but even without reference to political grandeur the play
establishes a pair of polarized responses to the affair. Love is
ennobling and liberating as nothing else in life can be, yet only
at the expense of everything else we ordinarily prize in the world,
including honor, for it demands full payment of both Antony and
Cleopatra before it gives them what they seek. In other complementary terms present throughout the play love appears, in the
play that apotheosizes Shakespeare's vision of it, as preposterously
bound to aging flesh, and yet as so far beyond the merely physical
that to give it expression the whole world, life itself, must dissolve. As in *Romeo and Juliet*, so in *Antony and Cleopatra*: Love
is of the flesh, yet only the liberation from flesh and the finality
of death can express its full value.

    Romeo and Juliet divest themselves of the world as of a
thing of no value; from the moment in which their love is conceived their lives are a pilgrimage toward one inevitable and de-
sired end. But Antony and Cleopatra are more complicated people.

They have both the talent and the taste for power, and they fight to keep from surrendering it. True, Antony is willing to "let Rome in Tiber melt" (33) in the very first scene; he knows that to find the measure of his love one must "find out new heaven, new earth" (17). And Cleopatra seems to care at the moment of Antony's first departure for Rome only for the "eternity" that "was in our lips and eyes" (I. iii. 35). But not until they have been defeated by the world, not until Actium has put an end to Antony's last claim to Rome and Caesar to Cleopatra's sway over Egypt, not until life offers no alternative but death and, in the world's terms, complete failure are these world-weary lovers ready to commit themselves to that death so readily embraced by Romeo and Juliet. "My desolation does begin to make/ A better life," remarks Cleopatra (V. ii. 1–2). Having been forced to renounce the ambition to define themselves as pillars of the world —remember the play's insistence on the questions Who is Antony? and Who is Cleopatra?[24]—Antony and Cleopatra are finally free to pledge themselves as sacrifices to it. If they begin to give up their hold on life more reluctantly than Romeo and Juliet, they do so finally with more joyous abandon, more explicitly aware of what they are gaining than Shakespeare's first tragic lovers:

> 'Tis paltry to be Caesar;
> Not being Fortune, he's but Fortune's knave,
> A minister of her will: and it is great
> To do that thing that ends all other deeds;
> Which shackles accidents and bolts up change;
> Which sleeps, and never palates more the du[n]g,
> The beggar's nurse and Caesar's.
>
> (V. ii. 2–8)

> But I will be
> A bridegroom in my death, and run into't
> As to a lover's bed.
>
> (IV. xiv. 99–101)

> Give me my robe, put on my crown; I have
> Immortal longings in me: now no more
> The juice of Egypt's grape shall moist this lip:
>
> . . . .

husband, I come:
Now to that name my courage prove my title!
I am fire and air; my other elements
I give to baser life.

(V. ii. 282–293)

Of all of Shakespeare's characters, the lovers demand most
of life. Venus and Adonis, Romeo and Juliet, Antony and Cleopatra want, each in his own way, a satisfaction of the ego's desires
so complete that no obstruction remains to their commitment.
With the exception of Venus, who survives to will her unhappi-
ness to them, this means for all of them the final dissolution of
the ego itself: a definition of self gained by the loss of selfhood.
In his greatest tragedy of love Shakespeare makes most fully explicit the paradox of love which he recognized already in compos-
ing *Venus and Adonis*. Turning the complementary vision toward perhaps the most familiar cautionary legend against love in
his tradition, he finds in the myth of the archetypical lovers the
supreme model of the paradoxes of love. Cleopatra's defining
characteristic is her infinite variety. She embodies the sensuality
and spirituality, the intense egotism and the ultimate selflessness,
the love of life and the yearning to renounce it, that live side by
side in the western myth of romantic love. Attracted by all her
qualities, sharing her dichotomized longings, torn even more than
she by another notion of his selfhood that struggles for the repudi-
ation of what she represents, Antony is the most powerful image
between Gottfried's Tristan and Wagner's of the passion that we
regard alternately as the most noble and the most absurd of
human engagements. As a play about Rome and love, as the
vehicle of some of Shakespeare's most memorable poetry, and as
one of the last of his tragedies, *Antony and Cleopatra* is unique.
It is not, however, an aberration from his other work; rather, as
a simultaneously exultant and despairing dramatization of the
unresolvable dialectic between opposed values that claim us
equally and of the necessary tragedy of choice, it is a paradigm of
Shakespeare's art.

NOTES

1. Citations are from John Dover Wilson, *The Essential Shakespeare* (Cambridge, 1932), p. 55; Geoffrey Bush, *Shakespeare and the Natural Condition* (Cambridge, Mass., 1956), p. 25; H. T. Price, "Imagery in *Venus and Adonis*," *Papers of the Michigan Academy of Science, Arts, and Letters*, XXXI (1945), 277–278, 292; and Hallett Smith, *Elizabethan Poetry* (Cambridge, Mass., 1952), p. 86. For pre-1935 criticism of *Venus and Adonis*, see the New Variorum edition of *The Poems*, ed. Hyder E. Rollins (Philadelphia, 1938). The negative view is represented by Robertson, the laudatory by George Wyndham. For an extremely helpful summary of twentieth-century views of *Venus and Adonis*, see the survey by J. W. Lever in *Shakespeare Survey*, XV (1962), 19–22.

2. S. T. Coleridge, *Biographia Literaria*, II (London, 1817), pp. 16–17.

3. Price, *loc. cit.*, p. 286.

4. Price, *loc. cit.*, pp. 277–278. One might expect this puritanical view to include *Antony and Cleopatra* as well, but apparently it does not.

5. For sensitive discussion of these and other aspects of *Much Ado*, see John Russell Brown, *Shakespeare and His Comedies*, second edition (London, 1962), pp. 109–123. The antinomies of *A Midsummer Night's Dream* are explored by C. L. Barber, *Shakespeare's Festive Comedy* (New York, 1959), pp. 119–162.

6. In *Not Wisely but Too Well: Shakespeare's Love Tragedies* (San Marino, 1957), particularly Chapter III, "The Divided Nature of Love: Elizabethan Ideals," pp. 19–27, Franklin Dickey admirably surveys the duality in Renaissance notions of love. His view of Venus (pp. 46–53) anticipates mine in its understanding of the limitations of her argument; his reading implies an attitude toward Adonis that might approximate my own if it were developed. Though Professor Dickey does not see the poem as the record of an irreconcilable opposition, his study is closer to mine than that of any other critic whose work I have seen. Geoffrey Bullough, *Narrative and Dramatic Sources of Shakespeare*, I (London, 1957), p. 165, sees *Venus and Adonis* as "an explanation of love's urgencies, perversities, and contrarieties," and therefore as a model for the poet's next plays; he reads the poem, however, as "anything but a Platonic piece; the poet's sympathy is primarily with Venus and the coupling animals, though he also states a point of view which the Spenserians would accept" (p. 164).

7. W. B. C. Watkins, "Shakespeare's Banquet of Sense," in *Shakespeare and Spenser* (Princeton, 1950), sees the poem as an immature and unrealized effort, in which the young poet's intentions are unclear because he is confused. Watkins cites (p. 15) the "sweating palm" as an example of Shakespeare's comic ineptitude, suggesting the "pantomimic portrayal of passion in the silent movie," and unlike Spenser's more mature use of similar details. Watkins recognizes that Shakespeare must be aware of the "humor of his ex-

aggerations," but finds that humor nevertheless "nervous, adolescent, . . . not fully controlled. Partly he seems to be horsing in order to conceal his inability to preserve detachment" (p. 16).

8. Robert P. Miller, "Venus, Adonis, and the Horses," *ELH*, XIX (1952), 261–262.

9. Don Cameron Allen, "On *Venus and Adonis*," *Elizabethan and Jacobean Studies Presented to F. P. Wilson* (Oxford, 1959), p. 102.

10. The difficulties of making a satisfactory generalization about any aspect of Plato's fate in the Renaissance are lucidly discussed by Paul Oskar Kristeller, "Renaissance Platonism," *Renaissance Thought* (New York, 1961), pp. 48–69. It would not be difficult to demonstrate analogues to Shakespeare's problem in such spiritualizing of amorous love as Ficino's. Castiglione's Cardinal Bembo, whose mysticism is less profound than Ficino's, exemplifies perhaps more than his author wants him to the paradox of a love which is of God, yet which originates in the sexual impulse.

11. Denis de Rougemont, *Love in the Western World*, tr. Montgomery Belgion (New York, 1940).

12. G. I. Duthie and J. Dover Wilson, eds., *Romeo and Juliet* (Cambridge, 1955), pp xxxi, xxxii.

13. Alfred Harbage, "Shakespeare and the Myth of Perfection," *SQ*, XV (1964), 1–10.

14. Duthie, *op. cit.*, p. xxx. A suggestive discussion of the problem occupies most of Duthie's Introduction to the New Cambridge edition of the play. Some recent discussions worth consulting are Irving Ribner, "Then I denie you starres: A Reading of *Romeo and Juliet*," *Studies in the English Renaissance Drama*, ed. J. W. Bennett, O. Cargill, and V. Hall, Jr. (1959), pp. 269–286; John Lawlor, "*Romeo and Juliet*," *Early Shakespeare*, Stratford-on-Avon Studies, III (London, 1961), pp. 123–143; Paul N. Siegel, "Christianity and the Religion of Love in *Romeo and Juliet*," *SQ*, XII (1961), 371–392; and Franklin Dickey, *Not Wisely but Too Well*, pp. 63–117.

15. Harley Granville-Barker, *Prefaces to Shakespeare*, II (Princeton, 1947), p. 303.

16. Wolfgang Clemen, *The Development of Shakespeare's Imagery* (London, 1951), p. 73.

17. Granville-Barker, *op. cit.*, p. 301.

18. For valuable discussions of the role of language in two of these plays, see Sigurd Burckhardt, "The King's Language: Shakespeare's Drama as Social Discovery," *Antioch Review*, XXI (1961), 369–387, on *Richard II*, and James L. Calderwood, "*Love's Labour's Lost*: A Wantoning with Words," *SEL*, V (1965), 317–332.

19. Sister Miriam Joseph, *Shakespeare's Use of the Arts of Language* (New York, 1947).

20. Tracing Paris' line to Hieronymo, Harry Levin, "Form and Formality in *Romeo and Juliet*," *SQ*, XI (1960), 6, argues that "the use of antithesis, which is purely decorative with Kyd, is functional with Shakespeare." But in recalling Kyd, Shakespeare allows such lines to reverberate with associations,

some of them comic, that create distance between speaker and auditor. Paris may be more than Hieronymo, but he is less than Romeo. Professor Levin does observe in his article that by comparison with Romeo, Paris always sounds stilted.

21. To cite only two recent examples: J. Leeds Barroll, "Antony and Pleasure," *JEGP*, LVII (1958), 708–720, argues that Shakespeare and his contemporaries viewed Cleopatra as an unfortunate and sinful aberration in Antony's otherwise admirable life and character; Elias Schwartz, "The Shackling of Accidents: *Antony and Cleopatra*," *College English*, XXIII (1962), 550–558, reads the play entirely in terms of the lovers' transcendence of a worthless world.

22. A few essays in particular deserve mention. Perhaps the most succinct and most sensitive statement yet achieved is Maynard Mack's Introduction to his Pelican edition of the play (Baltimore, 1960), which brilliantly discusses the complementary valuations provoked by every event in the play. A pioneering study is the essay on the play in Traversi's *An Approach to Shakespeare*, especially in its discussion of the paradoxical imagery in which the slime of the Nile symbolizes simultaneously both life and death, breeding and corruption; Traversi's study has been expanded in his *Shakespeare: The Roman Plays*. See also John Danby, "The Shakespearean Dialectic: An Aspect of *Antony and Cleopatra*," *Scrutiny*, XVI (1949), 196–213; Kenneth Burke, "Shakespearean Persuasion," *Antioch Review*, XXIV (1964), 19–36; Arnold Stein, "The Image of Antony: Lyric and Tragic Imagination," *Kenyon Review*, XXI (1959), 586–606; Benjamin T. Spencer, "*Antony and Cleopatra* and the Paradoxical Metaphor," *SQ*, IX (1958), 373–378; Thomas McFarland, "Antony and Octavius," *Yale Review*, XLVIII (1958), 204–228; Kenneth Muir, "The Imagery of *Antony and Cleopatra*," *Kwartalnik neofilologiczny*, VIII (1961), 249–264; Lawrence E. Bowling, "Antony's Internal Disunity," *SEL*, IV (1964), 239–246; and Stephen A. Shapiro, "The Varying Shore of the World: Ambivalence in *Antony and Cleopatra*," *MLQ*, XXVII (1966), 18–32.

23. The most recent study of the dates of Shakespeare's last tragedies is J. Leeds Barroll, "The Chronology of Shakespeare's Jacobean Plays and the Dating of *Antony and Cleopatra*," *Essays on Shakespeare*, ed. G. R. Smith (University Park, Pa., 1965), pp. 115–162.

24. See p. 130.

CHAPTER FIVE

The Great Globe Itself

IN HIS LAST PLAYS Shakespeare focuses his complementary vision, with an intensity and self-awareness that grow steadily from one play to the next, on the very art to which he has devoted his career. In the earliest play of the group the theme of art seems almost irrelevant to his purposes; but by the time of *The Tempest*, only three plays and three or four years later, it has become the center of the play's meaning and the vehicle for a summation of what he has had to say in the creations of his entire career.

The new concern appears almost tangentially in *Pericles*,[1] a play generally treated as a failure. Attempts to explain its faults by appeal either to a theory of transcription of its two halves by reporters of different ability or to uncompleted revision on Shakespeare's part run into difficulties, for its virtues and vices are distributed throughout: the naïveté of construction, the imagery of jewels and trees, the role of Gower. The most plausible hypothesis is that, taking over an earlier play, Shakespeare revised the latter half more extensively than the first. Whether or not this is so, and it need not be, the fact is that in *Pericles* we have a play on which Shakespeare has left his mark not only in style but more importantly in "a demonstrable unity of plan which recalls, in its deliberate and sometimes clumsy formality, the similar imposition of a moral pattern in *Timon of Athens*."[2] Yet the play, for all of its attractiveness, is clearly unsuccessful.

Traversi's analogy to *Timon* is fruitful. Both plays seem like studies for or imitations of the successful plays they resemble. Both fail to employ meaningfully forms that Shakespeare uses elsewhere with a great deal of significance. And in both of them the trouble can be localized in the protagonist's relation to the world around him. In considering *Timon* for a moment we may be able to isolate what is wrong with *Pericles*, which itself will help us to identify both what Shakespeare is attempting to do in it and what he will have to learn to do before he can write *The Tempest*.

The trouble with *Timon of Athens* is that it is not complementary. This is not to say that it is without self-contradictions and irony. We recognize the relationship between the hero's early prodigality and his later, equally profligate misanthropy; we judge him for the blindness of his passion while sharing to some extent in the judgment he expresses so passionately on the society that has mistreated him. But at no point do we encounter such tensions as Shakespearean tragedy has elsewhere involved us in. A single standard of human relationship is taken for granted throughout. Athenian society violates it in taking from Timon in his wealth and then refusing to give to him in his need, and again in expelling Alcibiades; Timon violates it throughout, in foolishly casting away his substance and equally foolishly, though often effectively, railing against his betrayal. Because Shakespeare seems to assume a simple moral position, the play is uniquely unable to call into question the nature of being. It never seems, therefore, to get down to the unresolvable conflicts with which, each in its own way, *King Lear*, *Coriolanus*, *Antony and Cleopatra*, and *Othello* are primarily concerned. Even when our response is mixed—as when, for example, Timon delivers a rhetorically powerful misanthropic tirade (IV. iii. 1–47) while all too clearly ignoring the counterevidence surrounding it in the loyal and generous behavior of Flavius and Alcibiades—no basic assumptions are challenged;

we know the single standard by which we can judge both Timon's enemies and his own excesses. The play's universe has the kind of simplicity we find in Jonson's satirical tragedies; whatever passion Shakespeare arouses is directed simply against clearly indicated objects, and no metaphysical or moral questions are asked that are not answered with all the angry self-confidence of the satirist. Thus Timon's invocation of the "blessed breeding sun" and the moon (IV. iii. 1), his curses, his appeal to the "Common mother . . . Whose womb unmeasurable, and infinite breast,/ Teems, and feeds all" (IV. iii. 177–179), and his language of monstrous animals and fertility gone wrong beneath the marbled mansions of heaven ring hollow. Unlike their analogues in *King Lear* they fail to move us from the circumstances of a tragic life to the consideration of the basic question: What is the world all about? We are never forced to be in doubt.[3]

As *Timon* suggests, spiritual growth in Shakespeare's protagonists is always related to their discovery, or our discovery through their sufferings, of the world's complexity. Because Timon's world is simple, a plot that demands of him an inner development like Lear's is an empty shell. Similarly, Pericles moves through the cycle of loss, suffering, penitence, reunion, and reconciliation that we watch in the heroes of the great romances which *Pericles* anticipates, yet is without an inner life. Unlike Leontes and Prospero he does not sin, and so his penitence is meaningless.[4] He is no wiser at the end than he was at the beginning. A passive hero, he is scarcely individualized except in that capacity to suffer which Shakespeare presents repeatedly in the late plays; he is unable to exert any influence over a plot built around his symbolic journey. Leontes, like a reborn Othello, must learn the meaning of his passion and accommodate impulse in an ordered life; Prospero before he can turn for the first time in his life to the competent administration of justice must abandon the craving for retributive justice that has motivated most of his behavior in *The Tempest* and return to Milan instructed in charity and the imperfection of human life. But for Pericles the world, a place of undeserved separations and inexplicable reunions, is so mysteriously simple that there is no lesson his experience can teach him. Thus the apparent rebirth of Thaisa has much less meaning than the analogous resurrection of Hermione, even less than Aemilia's in *The Comedy of Errors*.

Pericles shares *Timon*'s weakness, then, in that the process of the protagonist's education fails to involve the audience in the tension generated by conflicting systems of value. Yet, unlike *Timon*, it is not clearly a failure. An account of its shortcomings does not constitute an adequate description of it; as its frequent success on the stage in the present century and its growing esteem among critics suggest, it is in some respects an achieved play. If the best rhetoric in *Timon* seems inappropriate, wasted on a context which reduces rather than enhances its power, the great poetic passages of *Pericles* bring the whole play to life when they occur. The great moments of *Pericles* indicate that Shakespeare is drawing on a new source of dramatic power, anticipating as he did not do in *Timon of Athens* a particular kind of effect—and a particular kind of significance—characteristic of all the romances.

Such a moment occurs at the beginning of the second act when, washed ashore at Pentapolis, Pericles encounters three fishermen whose broad characterization introduces a comic realism that contrasts as strongly to what has gone before as it does to the melancholy of the hero's opening incantation to the "angry stars of heaven." The effect is more vigorous by virtue of the scene's following on a narrative, self-consciously archaic and tediously inept in style, by the play's presenter Gower:

> All perishen of man, of pelf,
> Ne aught escapen but himself;
> Till fortune, tired with doing bad,
> Threw him ashore, to give him glad:
> And here he comes. What shall be next,
> Pardon old Gower,—this longs the text.
> (II. Prologue 35–40)

Moments like this recur throughout the play, often, as at the beginning of the third act, in juxtaposition with Gower's longwinded narration. All the scenes in which Marina plays a part have this quality of vivid and surprising illusion, particularly the scene in which Pericles and Marina are brought together for their climactic recognition.

Here in fact it is apparent that rather than being hampered, as he was in *Timon of Athens*, by a plot that lends itself only awkwardly to dramatic handling, Shakespeare achieves much of his effectiveness by making the largest contrast possible between unpromising material and the life he invests in it. As father and daughter, improbably reunited by a series of coincidences unparalleled in Shakespeare since *The Comedy of Errors*, make their identities known, the play calls attention to the improbability. Pericles' incredulity increases our wonder that such things can happen:

> O, stop there a little!
> [Aside] This is the rarest dream that e'er dull sleep
> Did mock sad fools withal: this cannot be:
> My daughter's buried. Well: where were you bred?
> I'll hear you more, to the bottom of your story,
> And never interrupt you.
>
> (V. i. 162–167)

And Marina's capsule autobiography calls attention to the make-believe of the entire plot:

> The king my father did in Tarsus leave me;
> Till cruel Cleon, with his wicked wife,
> Did seek to murder me: and having woo'd
> A villain to attempt it, who having drawn to do't,
> A crew of pirates came and rescued me;
> Brought me to Mytilene.
>
> (172–177)

It is not that Shakespeare does not want us to believe his play, for no dramatist in his right mind would throw away his greatest asset, his audience's credulity; rather he plays with our belief. From the beginning he establishes the ambiance as that of romance, where exotic, adventurous, symbolic, and symmetrical plots of coincidence generally amuse and excite but seldom move; like the *Arcadia* and its kin, *Pericles* is closer in its plot to a kind of game than to the mood of tragedy or of high comedy.[5] Into this world, contrived with a naïve artifice that tempts some to say the play is not Shakespeare's, distanced by the pedestrian intrusions of Gower and by a needlessly episodic plot, Shakespeare appeals suddenly to his audience's emotions:

> O Helicanus, strike me, honour'd sir;
> Give me a gash, put me to present pain;
> Lest this great sea of joys rushing upon me
> O'erbear the shores of my mortality,
> And drown me with their sweetness. O, come hither,
> Thou that beget'st him that did thee beget;
> Thou that wast born at sea, buried at Tarsus,
> And found at sea again! O Helicanus,
> Down on thy knees, thank the holy gods as loud
> As thunder threatens us: this is Marina.
> (V. i. 192–201)

The sea imagery works in the fashion of the mature Shakespeare: As a metaphor for the inner action it arises from the literal plot, and so it helps to create the visual world of the play while instructing us in the life within that world. It functions thus like the "music of the spheres" (231) which in releasing Pericles to rest a moment later is more an element of the drama than a detachable symbol.

This sort of power, missing from *Timon of Athens*, is characteristic of *Pericles*. Yet it stands out in each instance against a background that makes it always surprising, as if a black-and-white movie should turn momentarily into technicolor or plainsong into polyphony. Were it not for the role of Gower, one might be willing to accept the paradoxes of *Pericles* as accidental, to believe that in a weak moment Shakespeare was content to leave in the same play such evidence of mastery as the best scenes and such nonsense as the hero's ready wooing of the evil daughter of Antiochus and the extraordinary series of preposterous and unexplained decisions he makes thereafter; such brilliant exposition as the resurrection of Thaisa and such stuff, in Thaliard's "So, this is Tyre, and this the court. Here must I kill King Pericles . . ." (I. iii. 1–2), as we can find mocked in *The Old Wives Tale* and *The Knight of the Burning Pestle*, not to mention A *Midsummer Night's Dream*. But Gower calls attention to the artifice, to the narrative materials not fully transmuted into drama, and to the naïveté of the story, and in so doing he serves, like Time in *The Winter's Tale*, to emphasize the contrast between the illusion the play creates and the incredibility of the materials on which that illusion is erected. Time and again Gower's narrative points up the discrepancy:

> To sing a song that old was sung,
> From ashes ancient Gower is come;
> Assuming man's infirmities,
> To glad your ear, and please your eyes. . . .
> What now ensues, to the judgment of your eye
> I give, my cause who best can justify.
>
> (I. Prologue. 1-4, 41-42)

> But tidings to the contrary
> Are brought to your eyes; what need speak I?
> [DUMB SHOW follows, after which Gower
> resumes his narration, ending]
> And here he comes. What shall be next,
> Pardon old Gower,—this longs the text.
>
> (II. Prologue. 15-16, 39-40)

> Hymen hath brought the bride to bed,
> Where, by the loss of maidenhead,
> A babe is moulded. Be attent,
> And time that is so briefly spent
> With your fine fancies quaintly eche:
> What's dumb in show I'll plain with speech.
> [another DUMB SHOW] . . . .
> And what ensues in this fell storm
> Shall for itself itself perform.
> I nill relate, *action may*
> *Conveniently the rest convey;*
> *Which might not what by me is told.*
> *In your imagination hold*
> *This stage the ship,* upon whose deck
> The sea-tossed Pericles appears to speak.
> (III. Prologue. 9-14, 53-60; italics added)

> The unborn event
> I do commend to your content:
> Only I carry winged time
> Post on the lame feet of my rhyme;

Which never could I so convey,
Unless your thoughts went on my way.
                    (IV. Prologue. 45–50)

Thus time we waste, and longest leagues make short;
Sail seas in cockles, have and wish but for 't;
Making, to take your imagination,
From bourn to bourn, region to region.
By you being pardon'd, we commit no crime
To use one language in each several clime
Where our scenes seem to live. I do beseech you
To learn of me, who stand i' the gaps to teach you,
The stages of our story.
                    (IV. iv. Prologue. 1–9)

In your supposing once more put your sight
Of heavy Pericles; think this his bark;
Where what is done in action, more, if might,
Shall be discover'd. Please you, sit, and hark.
                    (V. Prologue. 21–24)

In Antiochus and his daughter you have heard. . . .
    Here our play has ending.
                    (Epilogue. 85, 102)

To a certain extent, of course, Gower is presenting material
which could not be contained in the dramatic exposition of three
plays; and his appeals to the auditors' imagination are, at least for
a Shakespearean Chorus, conventional. But his bumbling style and
the repeated contrasts between his humble art and the reality of
stagecraft perform a function opposite to that played by the evocative rhetoric of the Chorus in *Henry V*, whose brilliantly imagined
descriptions create illusion even before it appears on the stage. The
Gower speeches establish a tension we have observed within the
dramatic action itself between a naïve and unconvincing art that
makes us uncomfortably aware of awkward conventions and an
art so effective as to make us forget that it is art. Gower himself,
describing the artistic powers of young Marina, provides an emblem for the play at its best: The "absolute Marina" made the
cambric "more sound/ By hurting it," and "when to the lute/
She sung" she "made the night-bird mute,/ That still records with
moan" (IV. Prologue 24–27). Her art, that is, improves while it

competes with nature. Like the mysterious music that lulls Pericles to sleep, it is part of nature itself. This is an idea familiar to us in the late Shakespeare; it is the meaning of the sheep-shearing scene in *The Winter's Tale,* and a good part of the meaning of *The Tempest;* and it stands in such strong contrast to the transparent crudities from which it emerges in *Pericles* that we can recognize in Shakespeare's first romantic tragicomedy the emergence of a new focus of the complementary vision: the paradoxical simultaneity of the convincing illusion created by art and the paltry, often claptrap materials that make that illusion possible.

✑ II ☙

This ambivalence toward art, though it was to become a dominant factor in all Shakespeare's final work, does not appear for the first time in *Pericles.* He suggested it at the beginning of his career, in *Love's Labour's Lost,*[6] by setting up a comic struggle between the ideals of the mastery of life through art and contemplation on the one hand and on the other of the moral education that only growth through time and experience can bring; and in the drama of the Nine Worthies he plays for the first time on the foolishness of what can for some people pass as art. Berowne's "honest plain words" (V. ii. 763) correct the overstylized speech of the King, and the wonderful songs of Spring and Winter at the end implicitly correct the aestheticism of the courtiers. The contrast, as in *Pericles,* is between art and art, and though it is not the play's thematic center it makes us contemplate the art about which we have been thinking since the play's first speech. The same concern is at work in *The Taming of the Shrew,* where the play we watch is a performance put on for the entertainment of Christopher Sly, who remains on stage to watch it with us and who confuses what he sees with his own dreams. The concern with art as art, the reminders that we are watching a play and not "reality," are a recurrent motif in the early and middle plays—in the concern of *As You Like It* with pastoral poetry, the thematic role of music in *The Merchant of Venice,* the players' scenes of *Hamlet,* and the allusions to the stage in *Julius Caesar, Richard II,* and other plays.

Shakespeare's ambivalence toward the art to which he devoted his powers suggests that, like Sidney, he felt himself challenged by the sort of argument against art's mendacity that had found its definitive articulation in Plato's *Republic*. The early play which most reflects this ambivalence, and in so doing most anticipates the last plays, is *A Midsummer Night's Dream*, where triumphantly yet ironically Shakespeare acknowledges the common role of imagination, the intuitive, suprarational element of the mind, in love and art.[7] It is imagination, subjective vision, all that is symbolized by magic potions, and not the reason which Lysander so ludicrously claims as his guide, that enable the lover to perceive the value of his beloved and that in fact create the value he finds. If this fact can have tragic consequences, as Shakespeare was to demonstrate in *Troilus and Cressida*, it nevertheless explains the force and meaning of the most poignant of emotional states; and if Shakespeare never ceases to mock a quartet of lovers sure that they are in respectable control of their own passions when in fact they are the victims of irrational drives, he signals by the marriages to which they commit themselves that, comic though it may be, love must be taken seriously. So it is with art in *A Midsummer Night's Dream*. Because, like love, it is founded on the praiseworthy yet dangerous power of imagination, which makes poets and lovers akin to lunatics, it must be viewed complementarily. In demanding charity toward the players and their silly tragedy, Theseus argues that "the best in this kind are but shadows; and the worst are no worse, if imagination amend them" (V. i. 213–214); as Dent remarks, Theseus is reminding us that "the imagination of the poet commands no more respect than that of the lover."[8] Yet, as he argues further, the entire play constitutes an ironic refutation of its thesis that the imagination is to be despised.

The role played by the moon is as good an index as any of the game that Shakespeare plays in *A Midsummer Night's Dream*. Struggling with the problem of properties for the mechanicals' production, Quince observes that "there is two hard things; that is, to bring the moonlight into a chamber" (III. i. 48–49), and critics have noted with repeated delight that this is a trick that Shakespeare himself brings off with notable success in the "chamber" where the wedding celebration of which *A Midsummer Night's Dream* is part takes place. The illusion of a moonlit night

created by Shakespeare's poetry is in fact more powerful than all
the attempts of theatrical producers to reproduce it through light-
ing. Even the prosaic Bottom's happy assurance to Quince that
the almanac says the moon will shine on the night of Theseus'
wedding celebration helps in conveying an illusion more generally
created by the enchanting language Shakespeare uses elsewhere
in the play: "Why, then may you leave a casement of the great
chamber window, where we play, open, and the moon may shine
in at the casement" (III. i. 57–59).

So successful is the illusion of full moonlight streaming be-
neficently down on the last act that few auditors ever notice a
Mozartean joke at their expense. The authority for our knowledge
of the full moon that shines at the end is unimpeachable: "A
calendar, a calendar! look in the almanac; find out moonshine; find
out moonshine" (III. i. 53–54). Now for Shakespeare's audience
as for us, "moonshine" is nonsense.[9] And the fact is that the
wedding, as we have been solemnly assured in the very first
speeches of the play, is going to take place on the night of a new
moon, when the sky will be dark:

> *Theseus.* Now, fair Hippolyta, our nuptial hour
> Draws on apace; four happy days bring in
> Another moon; but, O, methinks, how slow
> This old moon wanes! she lingers my desires,
> Like to a step-dame or a dowager
> Long withering out a young man's revenue.
>   *Hipp.* Four days will quickly steep themselves in night;
> Four nights will quickly dream away the time;
> And then the moon, like to a silver bow
> New-bent in heaven, shall behold the night
> Of our solemnities.
>   (I. i. 1–11)

What are we to make of this? A slip? Not very likely in a
play in which the moon, in one form or another, is mentioned
more frequently than in any other play in the canon and performs
so important a function. A joke at Quince's pretense at being
able to read an almanac when he can't? A rather obscure joke;
moreover, his performance later shows that Quince's trouble with

reading seems to be localized in the handling of punctuation. No, we are left with a genuine dilemma.

Let me suggest another problem concerning the play's moonlight. If anything in Shakespeare is symbolic, certainly it must be the moon in *A Midsummer Night's Dream*, presented in a shimmering texture of poetic and mythological allusion and claimed time and again as an actual influence on the action. But what does it symbolize? After its initial appearance in the opening speeches as a marker of time and then as a heavenly beholder of the wedding, the angry Egeus proposes another reading: Moonlight is the accomplice of irresponsible lovers who by witchcraft seduce the virtuous daughters of righteous old men (I. i. 30–38). The association of the moon with the ways of lovers is familiar and does not trouble us. But, as perhaps Hippolyta's "silver bow" suggests, the moon has traditional associations with another set of values, and perplexingly Shakespeare reminds us of them only a moment later when Theseus threatens Hermia, unless she decide by the next new moon to marry Demetrius, with either death or a cloistered life in which she will "Live a barren sister all your life,/ Chanting faint hymns to the cold fruitless moon" (72–73). And only a few moments later, within the same scene, Lysander describes the moon to Helena in very different terms:

> Tomorrow night, when Phoebe doth behold
> Her silver visage in the watery glass,
> Decking with liquid pearl the bladed grass . . ."
> (209–211)

We might expect the symbolic value of the moon to settle down as the play progresses; if anything, quite the opposite happens. Thus in II. i alone we hear Puck's fairy friend allude to the "moon's sphere" (7) in a lovely song of dewdrop pearls hung in cowslips' ears that recalls Lysander's description; we learn that

> . . . the moon, the governess of floods,
> Pale in her anger, washes all the air,
> That rheumatic diseases do abound
> (103–105)

and is in fact responsible for the agricultural disaster which Titania accuses Oberon of inciting; we hear Oberon's description of

Cupid "Flying between the cold moon and the earth," of "young Cupid's fiery shaft/ Quench'd in the chaste beams of the watery moon," and even, in his reference to the moon as "the imperial votaress," a possible play on the commonplace emblem of Cynthia as Queen Elizabeth (156–163). Thus by the time the play is in full swing we have evidence that the moon is associated with heaven's celebration of a marriage and with the witchcraft of deceiving love, with fecundity and sterility, nature's riches and her blight. Small wonder that the form of mental derangement Shakespeare names in Theseus' indictment of imagination is lunacy.

One effect of all this is that we do not think of the moon as a consistent symbol. Shakespeare plays on the conventional force of the numerous standard associations with the moon, and we accept each one at its face value. Such associations add to the singular poetic richness of the play; but considered together, as Shakespeare's repetitions of an image always demand to be considered together, do they not cancel each other out? In their ability to suggest meanings while working against each other, to create the illusion of significance in a context in which in fact they cannot signify what they claim to, Shakespeare's allusions to the moon further substantiate Professor Dent's argument that in a large sense *A Midsummer Night's Dream* is a play about the role of imagination in play-making and play-watching. Both more and less than a symbol, the moon finally becomes a token of the poet's power to create illusion and an index of the verisimilitude and the meretriciousness of that illusion. And herein lies the explanation of the curious game Shakespeare plays in confusing us as to whether the moon is in fact full or new on the play's last night: It is whatever the poet wants it to be, so much so that even in the face of our knowledge we will go back to the play and continue to see its shining moon presiding over its imaginary festivities. As Helena muses in response to Lysander's invitation to flee to the moonlit woods, reflecting on Demetrius' defection to Hermia,

> Things base and vile, holding no quantity,
> Love can transpose to form and dignity:
> Love looks not with the eyes, but with the mind.
> (I. i. 232–234)

For the first time Shakespeare has turned his complementary vision in *A Midsummer Night's Dream* to a full examination of art itself, and with his characteristic ambivalence toward the irrational he sees it simultaneously as "base and vile" yet of the highest "form and dignity."[10]

◂§ III §▸

Though scarcely more than a decade was to pass between *A Midsummer Night's Dream* and the late romances, Shakespeare was to change more than most men do in so few years. Yet when he arrived at his last phase his attitude toward art remained very much what it had been in the mid-nineties. It is evident in *Pericles* and may, as we have seen, help to explain the quiddities of the first experiment in a new form. In his next experiment, a play more fully achieved, it is more clearly dominant.

Like *Pericles*, and for many of the same reasons, *Cymbeline* troubles the critic. It is a curious mélange of art and artifice, of convincing drama and preposterous fantasy, of sophisticated technique that represents Shakespeare at the height of his power and naïve dramaturgy that recalls the kind of play *The Old Wives Tale* had mocked a generation earlier. And it poses a problem, as it apparently did for Heminge and Condell when they placed it last among the tragedies in the First Folio, for academic critics who want to classify it by genre.[11] Now the technical question whether *Cymbeline* is a tragicomedy or a tragedy with a happy ending must interest the historian of critical theory more than it does the chronicler of theatrical events, and the play's violation of the Fletcherian stipulation that a tragicomedy must contain no deaths was soon to find numerous analogues in Fletcher's own work. But it is a matter of much greater interest to audiences familiar with Shakespeare's work that like the later romances *Cymbeline* recalls Shakespearean tragedy in an unexpected context. Noting the "critical commonplace" that "the characters in *Cymbeline* are recapitulatory,"[12] J. M. Nosworthy rightly cautions against a critical method which in finding a Shakespearean precedent for every character runs the risk of excessive ingenuity. But his cogent warning against the reduction of a hypothesis should not close our minds to the merits of the hypothesis itself. The story of Posthumus and Imogen and Iachimo unmistakably echoes the story of Othello and Desdemona and Iago, and Iachimo's name, so out of place in a play which moves between legendary Britain and classical Rome, recalls that of his more successful predecessor. And there are echoes of other tragedies. An occasional phrase calls *Hamlet* or *Macbeth* to mind (III. iv. 78–80; I. vi. 38). And Iachimo's description of the decorations of Imogen's bedchamber picks up both the subject of Enobarbus' famous account and its motif of the competition between life and art:

> it was hang'd
> With tapestry of silk and silver; the story
> Proud Cleopatra, when she met her Roman,
> And Cydnus swell'd above the banks, or for
> The press of boats or pride: a piece of work
> So bravely done, so rich, that it did strive
> In workmanship and value; which I wonder'd
> Could be so rarely and exactly wrought . . .
>   (II. iv. 68–75)

These may be insignificant. But there is a series of parallels with another play so striking that one is tempted to see *Cymbeline* as a redaction of it in a new mode, as it is of *Othello*. That play is Shakespeare's first tragedy. Like *Titus Andronicus*, *Cymbeline* employs the myths of Tarquin (II. ii. 12–14) and of Philomela and Tereus (II. ii. 44–46). Its Queen deceives her royal husband as Tamora does Saturninus. Its removal from the court to the rough country of Wales recalls the contrasts effected by the hunt scenes in *Titus Andronicus*. The plotting of the Queen and her son Cloten against Imogen replays the machinations of Tamora and her comically obtuse sons Chiron and Demetrius against Lavinia; Cloten's plan (III. v. 133–150) to destroy her husband before Imogen's eyes, then to rape her, closely resembles Chiron's proposal (*Titus Andronicus*, II. iii. 129–30). And in the last act Cymbeline threatens the captive Lucius with treatment that unmistakably recalls the opening scene of the old tragedy:

> Thou comest not, Caius, for tribute; that
> The Britons have razed out, though with the loss

> Of many a bold one; whose kinsmen have made suit
> That their good souls may be appeased with slaughter
> Of you their captives, which ourself have granted.
>
> (V. v. 69–73)

Only the extraordinary series of revelations that reach Cymbeline in the process of this final scene turn him away from an action that would lead one to expect, if it were perpetrated, a reenactment of the revenges of *Titus Andronicus*.

The naïveté of dramatic design which threatens such disaster only to steer away from it by the most implausible theatrical expedients dominates *Cymbeline*. One wants to agree with Granville-Barker's deprecation of the "cursory criticism that will see in Iachimo a shadow of the master-villain with the 'Italian brain'": Iachimo "and his villainy," he points out, "are nicely suited to the story and its ending; for from the first there is something fantastic about the fellow, and no tragically-potent scoundrel, we should be sure, will ever come out of a trunk."[13] Yet Iachimo *is* "tragically-potent." He causes all kinds of trouble for Posthumus, whose rejection of Imogen is as total as Othello's of Desdemona, but mitigated first by distance and later by better luck than the Moor enjoyed; and if he is "wicked for the pure pleasure of it, for the sake of sport," if "there could hardly be a more hazardous speculation than the adventure . . . into which he incontinently plunges," if "at the bottom of the business is his vanity,"[14]—is not the same true of Iago? And is the handkerchief less intrinsically preposterous than the trunk? Shaw scorned both. By design *Cymbeline* immerses its characters in the destructive element, then pulls them out by miraculous devices that belong more to fairy tale than to tragedy. If such a structure offends readers of certain predilections, Shakespeare has nevertheless expended considerable ingenuity in its construction. It is a brilliant invention, for example, that Imogen, disguised as the young man Fidele, must be driven to apparent death in both of her roles, so that lamentations celebrate the demise of two innocent characters involved in different strands of the plot. And the plot, which may seem episodic and casual, is so tangled up in tragic potentiality almost fulfilled that it requires a fantastic last scene in which at least eighteen surprises[15] must be unfolded, one by one, until peace and harmony are restored.

"The presence [in *Cymbeline*] of diverse and even contradictory artistic purposes seems to point, as in [*Pericles*]," observes Traversi, "to an experimental origin," and suggests "an author feeling his way, with incomplete clarity of purpose, towards a fresh use of the dramatic conventions which lay to his hand."[16] This notion of experimentation is a good deal more helpful than the by now discredited appeals to mixed authorship of earlier critics, and the locating of *Cymbeline* between *Pericles* and the last romances, which Traversi defends by analysis of the developing symbolic technique and the evolving theme of reconciliation in Shakespeare's final phase, is convincing. But Traversi's analysis needs to be supplemented by another which takes account of the ostentatious theatricality we have been noticing.

The beginning of such an analysis has long been ready in Granville-Barker's thesis that much of what strikes us as artless in *Cymbeline* is designed to call attention to its artlessness. We find it difficult to admit, he argues, that we "see Shakespeare, pastmaster in his craft, making such a mess of a job" as the deployment of Posthumus from the moment he orders Imogen's murder until his appearance in the last scene; "nevertheless, Shakespeare's stamp, or an excellent imitation of it, is on much of the actual writing hereabouts."[17] There is "a curious artlessness about nearly all the soliloquies in the play,"[18] which are often merely and superfluously informative, and in such instances as Belarius' revelation of the true identity of his wards and himself, and Cornelius' soliloquizing aside to the effect that he does not trust the Queen and has given her an ineffectual poison, rather "emphasize and advertise" than gloss over the awkwardness of the exposition. This, says Granville-Barker, "is obviously a sophisticated, not a naïve, artlessness, the art that rather displays art than conceals it."[19] So it is with the Vision: "As it stands, the elaborate pantomime really looks not unlike an attempt to turn old-fashioned dumb show to fresh and quaint account,"[20] and with the Jailer and "his stark prose" which we find "cheek by jowl with the jingling twaddle of the apparitions. . . . The elaborate pattern of this, the play upon thought and words, the sententious irony, is as sheer artifice as is the Vision itself, the 'ingenious instrument,' or Iachimo's overhead asides."[21]

But Granville-Barker fails to explain what he so convincingly describes. Having noticed the play's dominant pattern, he accounts for it only in strategic terms: Shakespeare has "an unlikely story to tell," so inexplicable that in order to involve his audience in it he must disarm them by a show of seeming artlessness which as much as says "You see there is no deception."[22] But why, if his material necessitated such sleight-of-hand, did Shakespeare use it? Or why did he not use the alternative procedure Granville-Barker suggests, the method of the earlier romantic comedies, in which the audience is simply handed a plot full of inconsistency and unexplained mystery and asked to swallow the dose? For we do not ask the obvious questions that the plots of *Twelfth Night*, *As You Like It*, *Much Ado*, and *The Two Gentlemen of Verona* awaken in the rational mind. Why in *Cymbeline* does Shakespeare fuse the romance world of pastoral disguise, the world of *As You Like It*, with the jarring worlds of sexual tragedy and quasi-historical politics which, as Eugene Waith has demonstrated, Beaumont and Fletcher carefully removed from their tragicomedy to make room for a romantic form of history that has little resemblance to the real thing?[23] As Nosworthy argues, the moments that remind us of a real historical and political world are at odds with Shakespeare's "method of presentation, with its witch-like Queen, its poisons, its caves, flowers and music,"[24] and his own almost persuasive argument that the real unity of *Cymbeline* is in its quality of romance leads him to assert that the attempt to design a romance which can "carry . . . a Caesar" and "encompass . . . the ordered state of Rome" is no less than an "error in plot selection."[25] One remembers Dr. Johnson's wonderful charge of "unresisting imbecility."

Only one explanation can account for what we have seen as a dominant element in the play: *Cymbeline* is a play as much about plays and play-making and play-going as it is about reconciliation. If it does not succeed as *A Midsummer Night's Dream* had done or *The Winter's Tale* and *The Tempest* would do, it carries further than *Pericles* the experiment that Shakespeare ini-

tiated there. Shakespeare's game is to engage us in the naïve artifice
of the piece, to make us believe in its reality, and then to make us
recognize the game he is playing. If everything comes out happily,
we must be aware in the end that it does so because the playwright has made it do so by tricks which he has made us acknowledge as tricks even while we believe in them. Hence our delight
at seeing *Othello* and *Titus Andronicus* recapitulated, at recognizing the aesthetic jangling of contrasting worlds each of which
is convincing by itself, yet each of which weakens the claim of
the other on our susceptibility to illusion. To an audience in 1609
or so *Cymbeline* must have represented as much of a delight—or
an annoyance—in its playing on the nature of theatrical illusion,
its experimentation with new techniques recognizably related to
old ones, as *Last Year at Marienbad* did to audiences in the 1960's.
The imaginative delight which had ever been a given of Shakespeare's art now becomes its conscious focus: We are delighted to
see fairy-tale characters come to full Shakespearean life; we are
equally delighted to see them elude our grasp and become again
mere pawns in the working out of an elaborately nonsensical plot.
This explains, I submit, the discrepant powers of Posthumus'
theatrically anachronistic Vision and the Jailer's contiguous speech,
equally stylized yet by contrast a model of "realism." It explains
Posthumus' otherwise inexplicable outburst, perhaps the most
striking line in the play, at one of the emotional climaxes of the
final revelations, "Shall's have a play of this?" (V. v. 228), and
the King's awed expression a moment—and three revelations—
later of an attitude he shares with the audience: "New matter
still?" (243). Once we have accepted the play's make-believe as
make-believe and come to expect no more of it we are particularly
susceptible to the poetic power of a line spoken by a suddenly
real and moving Posthumus when Imogen has been restored from
her putative death: "Hang there like fruit, my soul,/ Till the tree
die!" (263–264).

  Finally and not least, it explains the ubiquitous and explicit
occurrence in *Cymbeline* of a motif present in all of Shakespeare
but never so insisted on before, the difference between appearance
and reality. That motif is voiced three times in the first twenty-
five lines of the opening scene. It is the basis of the plot in which

Posthumus is deceived by false report, which ironically uses as its most telling evidence the appearance of the sleeping Imogen and her bedroom. It is the ironic point of the characterization of Cloten, whose role is that of prince while his soul is not, while the truer princes are disguised as crude woodsmen (but look to the disguised Imogen-Fidele like true princes). It underlies the innumerable deceptions which involve every single character in the play in some crucial misunderstanding and which must be unraveled in the last scene, for false appearances unmasked are the point of each revelation. It is explicit throughout the play. And it is so because Shakespeare, while he is creating an illusionary world so successful that no one is willing to take the play from him, is instructing us in the nature of make-believe. The world of tragedy can be redeemed in *Cymbeline* as it could not in earlier Shakespearean tragedy, the play seems to say, simply because the playwright can deny its tragic inevitability by his power over the plot.

This is, to be sure, an odd and perhaps a disappointing theme; yet it seems to be the sum of what Shakespeare has to say in both *Pericles* and *Cymbeline*. It accounts in both plays, as no consistently perceptible pattern of personal growth in character or providential operation of plot will account, for the intrusive figure of the playwright so manifest in the Gower of the one play and the self-consciously naïve dramaturgy of both, for the unmitigatedly outrageous complications of plot and their equally outrageous solutions; for the patterning in *Pericles in* which the adventures of Marina in the second half constitute a symmetrical repetition without discernible meaning of her father's adventures in the first half, which themselves are so altered from the sources as to make the contest Shakespeare invents for Pentapolis a recurrence of the one at Antioch;[26] and for the plotting of *Cymbeline* which juxtaposes jarring illusory worlds and drops its protagonist from the first act until the last. In *A Midsummer Night's Dream* Shakespeare had related the theme of art to a broad thematic concern with the role of imagination in human life, and he had done so in a work which no matter how much it makes us contemplate the anomalies of art never surrenders its power. The joke of the mysterious moon in that first comedy in which the playwright's power over his audience is thematic is that we *don't* notice the discrepancy he has built into the play's illusion, at least until we reflect on it after the fact. In the earliest romances Shakespeare plays a riskier game, provoking our awareness of his art by seeming to mismanage it, creating successful illusion where we have come not to expect it. Even more daringly, he seems to make no effort in *Pericles* and *Cymbeline* to relate the ubiquitous emphasis on the art of his art to the thematic centers of the plays. In *Pericles*, as we have seen, as in *Timon* the materials have not successfully organized themselves about a theme, and in *Cymbeline*, where, as Traversi demonstrates, a plot employing similar materials is shaped so as to suggest a preliminary version of the theme of the last great romances, the concern with art seems irrelevant—one studies it, as Granville-Barker does, or one responds to the play's symbolism, as Traversi does. Only in *The Winter's Tale* and *The Tempest* do Shakespeare's last great concerns coalesce to produce two of his most brilliant plays. The earlier romances are like tentative steps on a path whose end Shakespeare could not yet see, experimental adumbrations of a kind of drama in which he could contemplate art and life as mirrors of each other as at the beginning of his career he had already done but with a new conception of both art and life that the full period of his creative life had brought to him.

◆§ IV §◆

"In the *Odyssey*," Longinus remarked,

narrative predominates, the characteristic of old age. So in the *Odyssey* one may liken Homer to the setting sun; the grandeur remains without the intensity. For no longer does he preserve the sustained energy of the great *Iliad* lays, the consistent sublimity which never sinks into flatness, the flood of moving incidents in quick succession, the versatile rapidity and actuality, brimful of images drawn from real life. It is rather as though the Ocean had shrunk into its lair and lay becalmed within its own confines. Henceforth we see the ebbing tide of Homer's greatness, as he wanders in the incredible regions of romance. In saying this I have

not forgotten the storms in the *Odyssey* and such incidents
as that of the Cyclops—I am describing old age, but the old
age of a Homer—*yet the fact is that in every one of these
passages reality is worsted by romance* [πλὴν ἐν ἅπασι τούτοις
ἑξῆς τοῦ πρακτικοῦ κρατεῖ τὸ μυθικόν]. . . . Homer shows that,
as genius ebbs, *it is the love of romance that characterizes
old age.*[27]

Regardless of the value judgment it makes and of the fact
that it states a law less universal in its application than Longinus
seems to think, this is an arresting observation. It applies with
equal force to Shakespeare in the seventeenth century and in our
own to Thomas Mann, who turned at the end of his long career
to the completion of *Felix Krull* and even more notably to the
sheer romance of *The Holy Sinner*. It points to a phenomenon
that is not—at least after the fact—so hard to understand. For
in a sense romance is the purest form of fictive art. In its direct
confrontations between simplified good and evil, in its freedom
to deal with the marvelous, in the sheer delight of its make-
believe, romance appeals to us with the force of the first stories
we encountered as children. More intensely than other fictions
it betrays the nexus between imaginative literature and dreams
as we have come to understand them: both the wish-fulfillment
in which a Marina can move untouched through the undeniable
evil of the brothel of Mytilene and in so doing make its occu-
pants' "profession as it were to stink afore the face of the gods"
(*Pericles*, IV. vi. 144–145), and the inescapable dread of the evils
life holds in store at every turn. "Your actions are my dreams,"
replies Leontes ironically, possessed by his demon, to Hermione's
"You speak a language that I understand not:/ My life stands
in the level of your dreams,/ Which I'll lay down":

> Your actions are my dreams;
> You had a bastard by Polixenes,
> And I but dream'd it.
> (*Winter's Tale*, III. ii. 81–85)

In a large sense it is superogatory to look for "themes" in the
romances, for the meaning is built into the simple structure of

the plot so thoroughly that to extricate it is to reveal the fundamental simplicity of the hopes and fears implicit in the fable: The
world is full of evil, yet goodness overcomes at the last. The poet
who years before told us that we have "nor youth nor age,/ But,
as it were, an after-dinner's sleep,/ Dreaming on both" now repro-
duces in his art the dreamlike quality, the subjectivity, that art
always mirrors in life: "We are such stuff/ As dreams are made
on, and our little life/ Is rounded with a sleep."

Yet in returning to the romantic origins of narrative art
Shakespeare makes us aware of the art in the mirror itself, the discrepancy between the subjective and aesthetic vision and the reality (τοῦ πρακτικοῦ) of which our objective consciousness keeps us
ever aware. Unlike the naïve artificer of romance, Shakespeare
at the end of his career wants his audience to know that the
romance it so dearly prizes is after all only romance. And in conveying that knowledge he plays endlessly on the question of the
nature of art. The analogy between the late Shakespeare and
the late Mann is as valuable as the comparison often drawn between his final art and Beethoven's,[28] and for the same reason:
All three of these supreme artists, at the end of careers which
in their combination of summation and innovation, experiment
and harvest, stand at the summit of their ages' expression, come
to a kind of art in which the subject is as much art as it is anything. A comment on Beethoven by the music critic Wendell
Kretschmar in Mann's novel about an artist is even more suggestive than Longinus' observation about Homer:

> Untouched, untransformed by the subjective, convention
> often appeared in the late works, in a baldness, one might
> say exhaustiveness, an abandonment of self, with an effect
> more majestic and awful than any reckless plunge into the
> personal. In these forms . . . the subjective and the conven-
> tional assumed a new relationship, conditioned by death.[29]

◆§ V ɜ◆

Now it may be objected that such a grandiose description has
little to do with our experience of two plays so clearly flawed as
Pericles and *Cymbeline,* and the objection is well taken. In these
experiments Shakespeare manifests the new interest in art as

art and in romance that will occupy him for the few remaining years of his career as a playwright; we can see there what will in his last two plays develop into full flower. But for all that is forceful about them, for all the direction they indicate, *Pericles* and *Cymbeline* fail to take us anywhere. What is wrong with them is that—unlike the art that Mann's Kretschmar describes, which because it is written in the new awareness of death "entered the mythical, the collectively great and supernatural" and makes us understand the world in its terms—they say far more about art than they do about life; to put it another way, they show us how art works, but not what it does. They are daringly experimental but finally rather rarefied celebrations of the power of art to involve us passionately in literal nonsense; they are necessary experiments, prologues to the triumphs of the last phase. But they do not lead us back to the world. Only in *The Winter's Tale* and *The Tempest* does Shakespeare manage to join the new technique he has been developing, which calls attention to the artifice of his art, with the power he has been developing throughout the rest of his career to make his plays instruments for the conveyance of a vision of life itself. Unlike the first two romances the last two communicate a moving and profoundly complex moral sense of life, a vision consistent both with the underlying myth of romance and with the comment on art that the plays constitute. In thus fusing his new powers with his old, Shakespeare achieves at the end of his two decades in the theater two works as moving and as ineffably beyond the capacity of the critic to distill in serial discourse as anything he had written before.

Yet he achieves this new power not by soft-pedaling but rather by emphasizing the theatrical self-consciousness of the less successful romances. In *The Winter's Tale*—and, as we shall see presently, this is true as well of *The Tempest*—Shakespeare carries to the extreme his old game of allowing his characters to remind the audience that they are in fact characters in a play:

> Go, play, boy, play: thy mother plays, and I
> Play too, but so disgraced a part, whose issue
> Will hiss me to my grave.
>
> (I. ii. 187–189)

                        You, my lord, best know,
Who least will seem to do so, my past life
Hath been as continent, as chaste, as true,
As I am now unhappy; which is more
Than history can pattern, though devised
And play'd to take spectators.
                              (III. ii. 33–38)

                    I see the play so lies
That I must bear a part
(IV. iv. 668–669; spoken as Florizel and Autolycus change costumes).

Sure the gods do this year connive at us, and we may do
any thing extempore.
                          (IV. iv. 692–693)

                        One worse,
And better used, would make her sainted spirit
Again possess her corpse, and on this stage,
Where we're offenders now, appear soul-vex'd,
And begin, 'Why to me?'
                              (V. i. 56–60)

The dignity of this act was worth the audience of kings and
princes; for by such was it acted.
                              (V. ii. 86–88)

                    Good Paulina,
Lead us from hence, where we may leisurely
Each one demand and answer to his part
Perform'd in this wide gap of time since first
We were dissever'd: hastily lead away.
                    (V. iii. 151–155; the play's last lines)

As before, other devices call attention to illusion. Thus Shakespeare sets the realistic psychological portraits of Leontes and
Paulina and the rest against a plot as implausible as any he has
designed, and structures the play so as to make us recognize its
implausibility. Leontes' sudden plunge into passion presents the
sort of given which we are willing to accept in the pastoral ambiance of the *Arcadia* and *As You Like It* more readily than
in tragedy; set in contrast, as Lear's initial irrationality is not,
with an earlier presentation of apparent normality, unconditioned

by the machinations of an Iago or an Iachimo, it is the kind of
thing that happens in fairy tale; but it happens here in a hitherto
realistic court. The contrasting poetic styles of the play serve
a similar function.[30] The presenter-character Time serves, as Professor Muir notes, to maintain the atmosphere of romance,[31]
but it also disrupts the illusion, particularly because, not present
from the beginning, Time suddenly and arbitrarily appears to
tell us that we must skip sixteen years while he is on stage; and
his language is designed to make us think of his control over the
action:

> Impute it not a crime
> To me or my swift passage, that I slide
> O'er sixteen years and leave the growth untried
> Of that wide gap, since it is in my power
> To o'erthrow law, and in one self-born hour
> To plant and o'erwhelm custom.
>
> (IV. i. 4–9)

Significantly art, so ubiquitous in our consciousness of the action,
is involved in the plot itself. It is the focus of the crucial dialogue
and the three interludes of the sheep-shearing scene; it is Autolycus' stock in trade. And most importantly it is what preserves and
restores Hermione. Like the characters of drama in the imagination of an audience, Hermione is transformed from artifice to
life in the last scene:

> *Paulina.* Indeed, my lord,
> If I had thought the sight of my poor image
> Would thus have wrought you,—for the stone is mine—
> I'ld not have show'd it.
> *Leontes.* Do not draw the curtain.
> *Paulina.* No longer shall you gaze on't, lest your fancy
> May think anon it moves.
> *Leontes.* Let be, let be.
> Would I were dead, but that, methinks, already—
> What was he that did make it? See, my lord,
> Would you not deem it breathed? and that those veins
> Did verily bear blood?
> *Polixenes.* Masterly done:
> The very life seems warm upon her lip.

Leontes. The fixture of her eye has motion in't,
As we are mock'd with art.
 Paulina.   I'll draw the curtain:
My lord's almost so far transported that
He'll think anon it lives.
 Leontes.   O sweet Paulina,
Make me to think so twenty years together!
No settled senses of the world can match
The pleasure of that madness. Let't alone.
 Paulina. I am sorry, sir, I have thus far stirr'd you: but
I could afflict you farther.
 Leontes.   Do, Paulina;
For this affliction has a taste as sweet
As any cordial comfort. Still, methinks,
There is an air comes from her: what fine chisel
Could ever yet cut breath? Let no man mock me,
For I will kiss her.
 Paulina.   Good my lord, forbear:
The ruddiness upon her lip is wet;
You'll mar it if you kiss it, stain your own
With oily painting. Shall I 'draw the curtain?
 Leontes. No, not these twenty years.
 Perdita.   So long could I
Stand by, a looker-on.
 Paulina.   Either forbear
Quit presently the chapel, or resolve you
For more amazement. If you can behold it,
I'll make the statue move indeed, descend
And take you by the hand: but then you'll think—
Which I protest against—I am assisted
By wicked powers.
 Leontes.   What you can make her do,
I am content to look on: what to speak,
I am content to hear; for 'tis as easy
To make her speak as move.
 Paulina.   It is required
You do awake your faith. Then all stand still;
On: those that think it is unlawful business
I am about, let them depart.
 Leontes.   Proceed:
No foot shall stir.

> *Paulina.*   Music, awake her; strike! [*Music.*
> 'Tis time; descend; be stone no more; approach;
> Strike all that look upon with marvel. Come,
> I'll fill your grave up: stir, nay, come away,
> Bequeath to death your numbness, for from him
> Dear life redeems you. You perceive she stirs.
>   [Hermione *comes down.*
>   (V. iii. 56–103)

"We are mock'd with art." One of the most affecting scenes
in Shakespeare, Hermione's rebirth is the index of the advance
The Winter's Tale makes on the previous romances. For, though
more intensely, it leads us—like every other allusion to the artifice
of the play—in two directions. No longer content to make us
aware that the play we take for life is only a play, Shakespeare
makes us understand what I have claimed is implicit in our
assumptions about romance: that life is itself like art. This explains the double force of the ironic references to dramaturgy
cited before. Such lines remind us that what we are watching
is a play; but because they express insights into the characters'
condition as people, the lines point just as forcefully to the ways
in which life must seem to those who live it as a play "devised/
And play'd to take spectators." Like the characters who exist only
in a script, the people of Shakespeare's last imaginary worlds are
at the mercy of forces, both internal and external, which they
think they understand but over which their control, tenuous at
best, works only in ways beyond their comprehension. Time works
in their lives with a freedom and arbitrariness analogous to the
playwright's handling of his materials: It is in the power of both
"To o'erthrow law and in one self-born hour/ To plant and
o'erwhelm custom." The most private events in the characters'
emotional lives are spectactular, experienced not only by them
but also by those around them; seldom before *The Winter's Tale*
had Shakespeare built so many characters into the crucial personal scenes in his protagonists' lives. Polixenes, Camillo, Antigonus, and the Lords seem to exist primarily to respond as an
audience to the mysteries unfolding in the lives of the principals.
Thus the scene in which Hermione is restored to life while Paulina
plays on the difference between art and life is a model of the

entire play. Like lesser devices in *Pericles* and *Cymbeline* it points
to the paradox that we find ourselves believing in imaginary
characters as if they were real. But simultaneously the device
increases the scene's conviction by conveying the illusion of an
imitated life in which miracles occur, as they do in the experience
of art, through the operation of the deepest elements in the
soul's life: emotional purgation, the accepting awareness of one's
history, trusting faith, a love in which the ego surrenders its
claims. Much of the power of *The Winter's Tale* is generated
by our sense of the elusive but compelling analogy between the
art with which it imitates life and the life that it imitates.[32]

The phenomenon I am describing is ubiquitous in Shakespeare's strategy. It is particularly striking in the play's generic
ambiguity. *The Winter's Tale* begins as an apparent tragedy of
jealousy in which, as in *Othello and Cymbeline*, the protagonist
succumbs swiftly and violently to an unjust suspicion, passionate
to the point of murder, of his wife. Especially because it reminds
us of *Othello*, the play gives no hint in its first half that the
second will be comic, and only the palpable sense of immanent
grace in III. i, the romance turn of III. iii, and the environing
of that romance in the ambiance of pastoral comedy in the last
acts create an atmosphere in which we are prepared for the
mitigation of the tragedy we have witnessed. On the other hand,
Paulina insists in III. ii that Hermione is dead—the most famous
of Shakespeare's rare deceptions of his audience—and Leontes'
grief promises to·be unalterable. In fact, the comedy cannot
really be said to begin until the moment when Antigonus exits,
beneath the preternaturally bedimmed midday sky of the tragic
world of *Macbeth*, to be destroyed by the bear that, in chasing
him into the wings, clears the stage of *Othello* to make way for
Mucedorus, of tragedy for pastoral, and is followed on shortly by
the Shepherd who, trading news of the death of Antigonus and
the discovery of the infant Perdita, proclaims "thou mettest with
things dying, I with things new-born" (III. iii. 116–117). This
schematic split in the play's structure is emphasized immediately
by the awkward narrative of sixteen years by the Chorus Time,
beyond which all that occurs is the culmination of Shakespeare's
romantic comedy. The stressed dichotomy between incompatible

genres has all the self-conscious and communicated artifice of the earlier romances.

Yet here, as not there, it calls attention to a world in which miracles occur, in which what promises to be tragic may not be so, in which evil is not always final. Because for the first time in the romances Shakespeare has managed to create a protagonist whose spiritual life is mimetic and significant, *The Winter's Tale* conveys more persuasively than any previous work the sustained illusion that the world of dramatic romance is directly related to the world in which we live. Thus in Leontes Shakespeare embodies a new Everyman figure, the tragic king who can be redeemed in this life through penitence and love and the renewal that time brings. Without an Iago or Iachimo to share the blame with him, self-tempted, his own worst enemy, allowing a fatuous and suicidal passion to destroy a life that seemed charmed, Leontes is as bitter a comment on human psychology as Shakespeare has ever made. The imagery of blood and disease suggests the psychological determinism of the late tragedies, and the language of fortune, ill planets, and the stars suggests a universe unfavorable to the continuation of human happiness. The reformation of Leontes in the second half demonstrates, however, that the immutable laws implied by the tragedies may here be abrogated. Yet in opting to dramatize the two major turns in Leontes' spiritual life by transparently theatrical devices, Shakespeare makes him a more ostensible creature of artifice than any previous hero. If Leontes' sudden plunge into passion constitutes a statement about the dangerous potentialities of apparently healthy character, it also lets us know that we are in the fairy-tale world of *As You Like It*, not the world of tragedy. Similarly Hermione is preserved from Leontes' passion by a device which is both self-consciously artificial and successfully illusionary. Her miraculous salvation paradoxically underlines the more general probability of other conclusions to so dangerous a business; in so doing it calls attention at the same time to the naïveté of the plot and to the comic reversal of the tragic assumption that, in Paulina's echo of Lady Macbeth's "Things without all remedy/ Should be without regard" (*Macbeth*, III. ii. 11–12), "What's gone and what's past help/ Should be past grief" (III. ii. 223–224). When we recognize in the com-

edy that emerges in the play's second half the familiar environ-
ment of heavy fathers and lurking passions that threaten to engulf
young lovers, we find ourselves again qualifying our startled recognition that what we are seeing is stage comedy with the equally
compelling realization that Leontes' sin and its tragic consequences
have not purged the darker elements of the self. Thus what is fantastic in the action of *The Winter's Tale* serves simultaneously to
make us aware of its fantasy and to make us see that the real
world it imitates is a proper subject for fantasy.

The Winter's Tale communicates a joy new in Shakespeare
by suggesting the possibility of grace and innocence in a world
which presents every appearance of being able to overthrow them.
Its comedy is therefore more poignant, achieved at greater expense
than in the earlier comedies in which benevolent providence had
less to strive against. Focusing on the spiritual regeneration which
makes Leontes worthy of his restored wife, suggesting that Perdita expresses an enduring aspect of the natural order as Marina
and Imogen scarcely can be said to do, it affects us as the greatest
of the earlier plays have done. But it does so, as we have seen,
with an added force, for it plays on our knowledge that the play
is a work of art as well as a window to reality; and like *A Midsummer Night's Dream* it provokes us to a fruitful awareness of
the analogy between art and the world that it represents. Yet
some readers may agree with me that though in *The Winter's
Tale* Shakespeare has moved far beyond *Cymbeline* in weaving
together the warp of theatrical self-consciousness and the woof
of a theme of rebirth and reconciliation, he has still not succeeded so well as he will in his last play.[33] Only the triumph of
The Tempest can make us understand the full potentiality of the
implicit theme with which Shakespeare has been concerned since
his last tragedy. In contemplating the final romance, we shall
discover how fully the attitude toward art embodied and made
part of the theme of a play can correspond with the moral understanding of its illusionary world. In his greatest play on the theme
of art and life Shakespeare fully expresses that complementary
vision of the value of art which we have watched growing more
explicit in his last works.

❧ VI ❧

The Tempest succeeds most strongly in both the areas in which the first romances tended to fail: It makes explicit and functional the insistence that a play is a play, and it creates a world, complete with a growing protagonist, in which we are compelled to believe. What I have been calling theatrical self-consciousness is, as everyone knows, even more dominant in *The Tempest* than in *The Winter's Tale*. It takes the form as before of language that alludes to plays:

> She that—from whom?
> We all were sea-swallow'd, though some *cast* again,
> And by that destiny to *perform* an *act*
> Whereof what's past is *prologue*, what to come
> In yours and my *discharge*.[34]
> > (II. i. 250–254; italics added)

It is involved in the masque, which calls to mind the similar performances given at the sheep-shearing and in Posthumus Leonatus' prison cell. It is an implication of the way in which the bare stage takes whatever shape a character perceives in it (II. i), of the allusions to Shakespeare's theater and even to his earlier plays, of the role that Prospero plays in stage-managing the events that transpire on his island, and, almost at the outset, in his expository narrative which, like Aegeon's in *The Comedy of Errors*, recounts the years that molded the present action. Shakespeare makes Prospero's exposition even more a reminder that the play is a play through the fiction that it is tedious as well as long: Prospero must continually break into it to recall Miranda's interest.[35] Never before has Shakespeare kept us so conscious of his artifice.

Yet at the same time the illusion he seems at such pains to dispel is the most convincing he had created in years. One explanation of his success in this respect is the fact that he has finally written a romance in which he has solved the problem of the hero. He had come close to doing so in *The Winter's Tale*, but the sixteen years' break and the emergence of Florizel and

Perdita in the second half take the play away from Leontes for much of its action. His primacy unchallenged by the lovers, Prospero is unmistakably the central figure throughout *The Tempest*. Like Leontes and Cymbeline, he too must be transformed by the magical events of the action. This time, however, there are no years in which he can develop. His movement to the benign and charitable renunciation of the last act is a spiritual revolution that we watch on stage, and it has a curiously double effect. On the one hand it makes him seem more plausible; his growth is not a given but a witnessed (and moving) event, and we believe it as much as we do Lear's. On the other hand, occurring in a context in which such growth in character does not normally take place in Shakespearean drama,[36] it makes him also a clear instance of authorial manipulation, an example of the make-believe of a charming fantasy.

A more striking manifestation of Prospero's dual function is his role as stage manager, which is itself of two sorts. In the end he becomes a literal Master of the Revels in arranging and presenting the divine masque. But, as he realizes with some alarm, his theatrical entrepreneurship puts him in danger of abandoning another kind of play that he has been staging, in which life and death are at stake; and this play he has been directing from the outset as he sets up the storm, coaches Ariel in the manipulation of dialogue between the participants, nurtures the romance between Ferdinand and Miranda (by assuming the theatrically familiar role of heavy father), provides sound effects, and distributes rewards and punishments.

So much is his role that of surrogate playwright, in fact, that numerous critics have seen in Prospero a symbolic representation of Shakespeare himself. One piece of evidence often cited is the speech he makes at the end of his masque, commenting on the fact that the play is over, drawing an analogy between its ephemerality and that of life itself, creating an image that looks simultaneously like the backdrop for a fairy tale and a picture of a romanticized London, and punning at the climax of a rhetorical sequence on a word which indicates both the whole world and Shakespeare's chief theater:

> You do look, my son, in a moved sort,
> As if you were dismay'd: be cheerful, sir.
> Our revels now are ended. These our actors,
> As I foretold you, were all spirits and
> Are melted into air, into thin air:
> And, like the baseless fabric of this vision,
> The cloud-capp'd towers, the gorgeous palaces,
> The solemn temples, the great globe itself,
> Yea, all which it inherit, shall dissolve
> And, like this insubstantial pageant faded,
> Leave not a rack behind. We are such stuff
> As dreams are made on, and our little life
> Is rounded with a sleep.
>
> (IV. i. 146–158)

Equally evocative of Shakespeare himself is the speech in which Prospero renounces his magic arts, which begins with an account that sounds more like an allegory of Shakespeare's own history as dramatist than a description of what we know Prospero to have done:

> I have bedimm'd
> The noontide sun, call'd forth the mutinous winds,
> And 'twixt the green sea and the azured vault
> Set roaring war: to the dread rattling thunder
> Have I given fire and rifted Jove's stout oak
> With his own bolt; the strong-based promontory
> Have I made shake and by the spurs pluck'd up
> The pine and cedar: graves at my command
> Have waked their sleepers, oped, and let 'em forth
> By my so potent art. But this rough magic
> I here abjure, and when I have required
> Some heavenly music, which even now I do,
> To work mine end upon their senses that
> This airy charm is for, I'll break my staff,
> Bury it certain fathoms in the earth,
> And deeper than did ever plummet sound
> I'll drown my book.
>
> (V. i. 41–57)

Here as in *The Winter's Tale* but with the new clarity provided by Prospero's role Shakespeare establishes an analogy between the imaginary world of his play and the art which creates that world: Life is like a dream, and so is art; works of art dissolve and leave not a rack behind, life fades into a sleep which will overtake all who inherit the earth. Art and life—the life which in *The Tempest* we take as a mirror of our own—are equally involved in magic; events have a logic—for the deceived actors in the play Prospero stages on his island, for Prospero as Shakespeare creates him, for us who live in a world we have not shaped —not of our knowing. Evanescent, dreamlike as are all the events of art and life, they are nevertheless potent, bound up in what for the players are undeniable realities, and beautiful.

Only a line-by-line commentary on this pellucid yet most complex play could do justice to the richness and subtlety with which Shakespeare has created his profoundly touching, mysterious analogy between life and art. I shall point at only one more instance. Recall the last words of Prospero's farewell to his art:

> I'll break my staff,
> Bury it certain fathoms in the earth,
> *And deeper than did ever plummet sound*
> *I'll drown my book.*   [*Solemn music.*

The image calls us back to another moment, in which Prospero summoned music to the stage and only Alonso heard it:

> O, it is monstrous, monstrous!
> Methought the billows spoke and told me of it;
> The winds did sing it to me, and the thunder,
> That deep and dreadful organ-pipe, pronounced
> The name of Prosper: it did bass my trespass.
> Therefore my son i' the ooze is bedded, and
> *I'll seek him deeper than e'er plummet sounded*
> And with him there lie mudded.
>   (III. iii. 95–102; italics added)

Alonso's son is buried, he thinks, in the ooze at the sea's bottom. In fact, he is not: Ferdinand's sea-burial is imaginary, the depths beneath which he lies as much a creation of fancy as the ocean in which, on another level of imagination, Prospero promises to drown his book. Once more Shakespeare will recall the image, in the moment when Alonso learns the truth about his son.

> *Alonso.*   I wish
> Myself were mudded in that oozy bed
> Where my son lies. When did you lose your daughter?
>   *Prospero.* In this last tempest.
>
> (V. i. 150–153)

Never in all his miraculous career has Shakespeare worked more powerfully on our minds, or to more profound effect. It is impossible to make a prose statement of the effect these linked passages achieve as they identify the sphere of the creative imagination with the image of experience that imagination creates. Involved as they are in the dominant image of the sea, both setting and symbol of what happens in *The Tempest*, pointing simultaneously to the reality and the illusion of the action, they are the play in little.

If such effects cannot be paraphrased, nevertheless they contribute to a coherence which can be understood and articulated. As Shakespeare's last image of the natural world, *The Tempest* says as much about nature as it does about art. At one irreducible extreme, which in certain moods and times may seem its realest aspect, nature is brutal, earthy, fleshbound, treacherous; such it is in Caliban ("thou earth"), consigned by predilection and language to the life of elemental earth, and in different ways in Stephano and Trinculo and Antonio. At the other end of the scale, as embodied in the fleshless Ariel whose realm is fire and air, whose worst memory is having been imprisoned for a dozen years in a cloven pine, nature is freedom of movement, the play of invisible and gracious forces. As a man Prospero is a compound of the elements of which nature is composed; as a man of imagination and the power to harness Ariel, he is able to play with these forces, all of which are involved in the tempest. But despite the role that subjectivity plays in the action (the island's landscape is lush and green to Gonzalo and burned out to Antonio, the air sweet to Adrian and fetid to Antonio and Sebastian), certain facts are absolute and finally beyond the distorting vision of a single mind—such facts as the evil of Antonio, the stupid brutality of Stephano and Trinculo, the irremediable bestiality of Caliban. Innocence does not seem so absolute: Ferdinand must be restrained from dalliance and Miranda saved from rape. There is yet another limitation of the subjective control of experience, for Prospero, though he can exercise considerable influence on those who come into his sphere, is not responsible for the providential voyage that brings the royal party to his island. The island is thus an image of life, and in its differences from the real world it is at the same time an image of the powerful yet limited art which imitates life.

The play between the reality and the unreality of each character's experience on the island is the key to its meaning. The island provides a stage for the dream vision of its inhabitants: Gonzalo constructs a Floriesque vision of a commonwealth; Stephano would be king of the island as Prospero in fact is; Antonio and Sebastian play Macbeth to Alonso's Duncan though as far as they know there is no hope of returning to Milan and receiving the benefits for which they have contemplated murder. Finally the island provides a corrective to their misapprehensions, a test of their ability to learn from and be regenerated by their experience. It is not a place to live. Like Odysseus renouncing the immortality of Phaeacia for the rocky humanity of Ithaca, Prospero willingly leaves his island to return to Milan and death. In Milan justice—administered by a Prospero who has learned the responsibilities he failed to acknowledge in his earlier reign—rules alongside charity, the boatswain may reach the gallows rope that Gonzalo prophesied for him at the beginning, and Antonio, included in the final pardons of a comic resolution, may earn such punishment as he has escaped here.

But not in the world of Prospero's art, the island we have inhabited in our imaginations—or in a play whose form is comic. For this, Shakespeare implies, is the difference between life and art; and it is the reason for leaving art, as we do at the end of every encounter with it and as he does at the end of his career, to return to life. In life events have consequences, and we must deal with the immutable realities suggested in *The Tempest*. Prospero's island is the perfect symbol of Shakespeare's art. In it crime and punishment, sin and redemption, envy and love, and all the capacities of human nature are displayed, acted out as spectacle, conditioned as the final contrast between Milan and the island suggests by the demands of aesthetic decorum. We succumb to art because it plays on the peculiar vulnerability of our imaginations; we learn from it because it is the greatest of teachers. And what it teaches us, we know from *The Tempest* as from all of Shakespeare's work, is charity, a charity akin to that required of us if we are to believe it, for as Shakespeare has repeatedly told us, imagination and faith and love are one great complex. At the last we leave it for the world it mirrors but only partially resembles, in which events have consequences and men are agents rather than spectators.[37]

In suggesting such an attitude in *The Tempest* Shakespeare has come at the end of his career, in a play whose resemblance in texture as in theme to *A Midsummer Night's Dream* seems scarcely accidental, to an understanding of the role of art in life that goes beyond what he suggested in *A Midsummer Night's Dream*. In this last play as in the earlier one the attitude is complementary, and *The Tempest* again sets against each other the magnificent and the ludicrous aspects of the power of illusion. But in *The Tempest* something new is present: the idea that art is simultaneously an end in itself and, as a gateway back to the life it imitates, an element of moral education. We enjoy art as if it were life, and Shakespeare devoted his life to it; yet after the spell has passed we remember that life is its subject and its goal. Thus Prospero's renunciation is at once the artist's farewell to his creations, the credo of an Olympian spectator who has spent his life commenting on the scene that passes below, and a reminder that apart from our loving spectatorship of a world whose powers for good and evil hold our imaginations bound we are also actors in what we see. The last of Shakespeare's complementary visions is not new; in fact, it is a personally experienced version of the assertion about art most often repeated in the Renaissance, Horace's dictum that it both delights and instructs. But in the final work of Europe's greatest artist it is as if that understanding of art is being felt for the very first time.

VII

Whether or not *The Tempest* is literally intended as Shakespeare's farewell to the theater, we can understand why a poet who had reached the attitude toward art it embodies should feel no compulsion to write more. *The Tempest* is a complete fulfillment of Shakespeare's career as no other play is. It carries to the point of final clarity his complementary vision, his ethical commitments, his interest in art and its meaning, and what he has been saying in his tragedies and his comedies. Having entwined all the strands of his interests in a play in which he seems to understand, and is able to make us understand, their essential unity, having done so through the vehicle of a beautiful and moving play as successful in its illusion as anything he had ever created, and having suggested in its final triumph the unconquerable limitations of his art, Shakespeare may well have felt like Prospero that his job was done; the converging lines of his life's work had reached the point to which *The Tempest* makes one feel that they had been moving.

It is as close to confirmation of this hypothesis as one can get that when Shakespeare returns to his art, as he does at least once in his remaining years, he does so with a strange new detachment. We strain fruitlessly to find any evidence in *The Two Noble Kinsmen* of the Shakespeare of the last phase, yet can scarcely doubt that he wrote it.[38] The redaction of Chaucer's *Knight's Tale* is nothing less than frivolous; ironically, like the Dryden-Davenant version of *The Tempest*, *The Two Noble Kinsmen* sacrifices verisimilitude and depth for the empty symmetry of Fletcherian tragicomedy—introducing a romance between Palamon and his jailor's daughter to match the pairing off of Emilia and Arcite. Shakespeare seems to have chosen simply to submerge his own personality in the efficient manufacture of a play which evidently means nothing to him, in the newly popular mode in which Fletcher was filling the coffers of the King's men.

Henry VIII, in which Shakespeare's hand is more certain, is a more poignant example of the same phenomenon.[39] In many respects it is a fine play, unmistakably Shakespearean; yet its structure is almost cynically arbitrary. *Henry VIII* is built on a cyclical form: the rhythmic failures of Buckingham, Katherine, and Wolsey. Each of these characters seems a threat, each must be put out of the way for the common good. As in the earlier history plays, we find our attitudes being changed as each character meets the death that the plot makes us wish for him, and their elegiac laments, which may well be the authentic work of a poet who like Prospero has retired to his Milan, "where/ Every third thought shall be my grave," move us with their implicit reminder of the familiar logic of history that demands for the sake of the common good the sacrifice of the ego. So far, this is no less than what we would expect of Shakespeare. But a sudden and surprising turn constitutes the climax and the denial of the play: As Cranmer, structurally a repetition of the earlier victims of the King, seems on the verge of sharing their fate, Henry puts an end to the series by affirming his faith in him; Elizabeth is born, and the closing speeches prophesy the glorious future of England under the new order.

If Shakespeare had taken it seriously, *Henry VIII* could have been another great chronicle play. But it is instead a half-hearted and unconvincing piece. Like his victims, Henry is half-good, half-evil, without embodying any sense of a functioning dialectic; the author seems hardly aware of the two halves of each or of his play. By 1613, of course, the birth of Elizabeth could have seemed to very few sentient Englishmen the harbinger of the second coming, and all knew that Cranmer himself was approaching a notorious destiny not encompassed in the play. The marriage with Ann looked forward, moreover, to the most vicious of Henry's tricks. Thus the end, whether regarded from the point of view of common knowledge or of the apparent structure of the play, seems unconsciously ironic, and the whole shares with Fletcher's characteristic work a delectable lack of conviction, a hedonistic nostalgia, and the substitution of spectacle and pageant for meaning.[40] As to the reasons for this failure by the most anonymous of artists one can only guess. But it is a guess with perhaps some force that having harkened to his Prospero, Shakespeare is no longer interested in the art which, by his removal to Stratford, he has formally abjured.

⋖§ VIII §⋗

"Now, to let matters of state sleep," Sir Henry Wotton wrote to his nephew on July 2, 1613,

> I will entertain you at the present with what has happened this week at the Bank's side. The King's players had a new play, called *All is True*, representing some principal pieces of the reign of Henry VIII, which was set forth with many extraordinary circumstances of pomp and majesty, even to the matting of the stage; the Knights of the Order with their Georges and garters, the Guards with their embroidered coats, and the like: sufficient in truth within a while to make greatness very familiar, if not ridiculous. Now, King Henry making a masque at the Cardinal Wolsey's house, and certain chambers being shot off at his entry, some of the paper, or other stuff, wherewith one of them was stopped, did light on the thatch, where being thought at first but an idle smoke, and their eyes more attentive to the show, it kindled inwardly, and ran round like a train, consuming within less than an hour the whole house to the very grounds. This was the fatal period of that virtuous fabric, wherein nothing did perish but wood and straw, and a few forsaken cloaks; only one man had his breeches set on fire, that would perhaps have broiled him, if he had not by the benefit of a provident wit put it out with bottle ale.[41]

Ben Jonson was there that day. For him the event had another significance, for though he did not miss the occasion to mock Puritan moralizing on the demise of the theater, he could suggest another attitude as, punning on the theater's name, he lamented "the worlds ruines."[42] The great Globe itself, as Prospero had prophesied, had dissolved and left not a rack behind—destroyed by its own sound effects and by the failure of an audience too engrossed in the illusions being created on the stage to notice the smoking thatch until, in the words of another account, "in a very short space the whole building was quite consumed."[43] "One fire drives out one fire," observed Aufidius in another context. Shakespeare's colleague Heminge, we are told, looked on with swollen eyes.[44] But Shakespeare himself, if he was present, may well have been amused by the ease with which the image of the world in which he had conjured his mighty illusions was reduced to tinder and smoke. The tragicomic burning of the Globe is as authentic a living emblem as he might have designed himself for what at the end he had come to know about art. And the contrast between the "wood and straw, and a few forsaken cloaks" and the imaginary universes Shakespeare built of them provides a final, ironic emblem of the complementary vision.

NOTES

1. Most likely written about 1607–8, *Pericles* is inscrutable with respect to authorship, relation to sources, and text. It has been traditional to credit Shakespeare only with the last acts, assuming either dual authorship or an incomplete revision by Shakespeare of someone else's play. A good summary of the problem is F. D. Hoeniger's Introduction to the New Arden Shakespeare edition (1963).

2. Derek Traversi, *Shakespeare: The Last Phase* (London, 1954), p. 19.

3. Despite a good deal of enthusiastic criticism of the whole and of parts, the majority of writers on *Timon of Athens* continue to be reluctant to regard it as one of Shakespeare's finished plays. Numerous hypotheses have been advanced: The play we have is a partially revised version of another writer's work; it is a Shakespeare play revised by another writer; it is a rough draft Shakespeare abandoned before he had achieved a successful play. The best general discussions of the problem are the Introductions to the New Arden edition by H. J. Oliver (1959) and the New Cambridge by J. C. Maxwell (1957). For a view which disagrees with mine see E. A. J. Honigman, "*Timon of Athens*," *SQ*, XII (1961), 3–20.

4. Traversi, who sees the pattern of the romances more successfully worked out in *Pericles* than do most critics (including myself), argues convincingly that "the play represents an early approach to the conception of drama which later produced *The Winter's Tale* and *The Tempest*" (p. 19).

5. For the best discussion of Shakespeare's use of romance material in his plays, see E. C. Pettet, *Shakespeare and the Romance Tradition* (London, 1949). Pettet is suggestive in his discussion of what he calls "Shakespeare's detachment from romance" and in his analysis of the structure of the last plays as conventionally romantic.

6. On *Love's Labour's Lost* as perhaps Shakespeare's first play see Alfred Harbage, "*Love's Labour's Lost* and the Early Shakespeare," *PQ*, XLI (1962), 18–36. For a splendidly detailed study of the thematic role of language in the play see James L. Calderwood, "*Love's Labour's Lost*: A Wantoning with Words," *SEL*, V (1965), 317–332.

7. On this aspect of A *Midsummer Night's Dream* see Paul N. Siegel, "A *Midsummer Night's Dream* and the Wedding Guests," *SQ*, IV (1953), 139–144; C. L. Barber, *Shakespeare's Festive Comedy* (Princeton, 1959); J. R. Brown, *Shakespeare and His Comedies* (London, 1957); and particularly R. W. Dent, "Imagination in A *Midsummer Night's Dream*," *SQ*, XV (1964), 115–129, and James L. Calderwood, "A *Midsummer Night's Dream*: The Illusion of Drama," *MLQ*, XXVI (1965), 506–552.

8. Dent, *loc. cit.*, p. 124.

9. See for example *Love's Labour's Lost*, V. ii. 208.

10. At the conclusion of his indispensable article on the play, Professor Dent argues that, albeit indirectly and implicitly, A *Midsummer Night's Dream* suggests a distinction between the imagination as it functions in art and as it does in love, since in the latter it operates indiscriminately, while in the former it is allied with reason in order to fulfill a purpose which "combines *utile* with *dulci*." I do not find this discrimination suggested in the play, even by the implicit contrast between the artistry of the play itself and the absurdity of Bottom's presentation. For Theseus' point as he instructs Hippolyta in the way of charity is that the best in art is unconvincing if we do not suspend disbelief, while imagination can make of the worst—as it does for Bottom and his confrères—a believable vehicle. Though for a moment he may suggest the tragic potentialities of the imagination in misdirected love, Shakespeare does not raise in this nuptial comedy the question of the dangers of subjective valuation; and similarly in dealing with the question of poetry he implies that the differences among works of art of varying merit matter less than the perceiver's willingness to extend his sympathy and allow them to work on his imagination. This is an important point, for it indicates that while in A *Midsummer Night's Dream* Shakespeare celebrates the power of the imagination surrendered to art, he enables us to recognize the corollary fact, Theseus' whole view of things, that art is entirely a technique for allowing the imagination to deceive us.

11. For a useful survey of the kinds of problems raised by *Cymbeline* and the other romances in the present century, see Philip Edwards, "Shakespeare's Romances: 1900–1957," *Shakespeare Survey*, XI (1958), 1–18. For a discussion of tragicomedy as an evolving genre to which *Cymbeline* does not quite conform see Marvin T. Herrick, *Tragicomedy: Its Origin and Development in Italy, France, and England* (Urbana, 1955), p. 258. For discussions of the relation of *Cymbeline* and the romances as a group to Beaumont and Fletcher, see H. S. Wilson, "*Philaster* and *Cymbeline*," *English Institute Essays* (New York, 1951), pp. 146–167, and the New Arden edition of *Cymbeline*, ed. J. M. Nosworthy (1955), pp. xxxviii–xli.

12. *Cymbeline*, The New Arden Shakespeare, p. lxxxi.

13. Harley Granville-Barker, *Prefaces to Shakespeare*, I, p. 512.

14. *Ibid.*

15. Granville-Barker's conservative count (*Ibid.*, p. 490); it is possible to count a good many more.

16. *Shakespeare: The Last Phase*, p. 43.

17. Granville-Barker, *op. cit.*, p. 462.

18. *Ibid.*, p. 463.

19. *Ibid.*, pp. 465–466. It is curious, given this understanding, that Granville-Barker should begin his next paragraph with the non sequitur, "A fair amount of the play—both of its design and execution—is pretty certainly not Shakespeare's," particularly in view of his own persuasive arguments against disintegrationist assumptions about the play.

20. *Ibid.*, p. 477.

21. *Ibid.*, pp. 478–479.

22. *Ibid.*, pp. 466–467. The theatricality of *Cymbeline* is discussed by Pettet, *op. cit.*, pp. 176ff., who develops Ellis-Fermor's idea of "theatrical romance" but does not argue that it is of any thematic significance, and by J. P. Brockbank, "History and Histrionics in *Cymbeline*," *Shakespeare Survey*, XI (1958), 42–49, whose opinion is that the play is less unified than Knight, Traversi, Nosworthy, and others have thought and that the motif we have been observing is just part of the fun.

23. Eugene M. Waith, *The Pattern of Tragicomedy in Beaumont and Fletcher* (New Haven, 1952).

24. Nosworthy, *op. cit.*, p. xlvii.

25. *Ibid.*, p. li.

26. I am indebted to Mrs. Coppelia Kahn for this insight.

27. *On the Sublime*, IX, 13–14, 12, tr. W. Hamilton Frye, Loeb Classical Library (London, 1932).

28. See Nosworthy, *op. cit.*, p. lxxx, for an interesting discussion of melodies "often so artless as to seem childish," of the use of "archaic elements," and of works that "appear so dispersed, so spasmodic, that Beethoven's early critics were pleased to dismiss them as 'unresisting imbecility,' or, rather, raving lunacy."

29. *Doctor Faustus*, tr. H. T. Lowe-Porter (New York, 1948), p. 53.

30. See Wolfgang Clemen, *The Development of Shakespeare's Imagery* (London, 1951), pp. 195–204; Clemen admits his indebtedness to S. L. Bethell, *The Winter's Tale: A Study* (London, 1948).

31. Kenneth Muir, *Shakespeare as Collaborator* (London, 1960), pp. 84–86.

32. In answering the question of why Shakespeare's "dramatic technique" is "crude and apparently incoherent" in *The Winter's Tale*, Bethell proposes "a quite conscious return to naïve and outmoded technique, a deliberate creaking of the dramatic machinery" (pp. 47, 50). Like me he argues that Shakespeare deliberately calls attention to his play as a play, but he argues (pp. 51ff.) that Shakespeare does so for the sake of distancing—here his argument resembles Pettet's—and of manipulating "planes of reality." Bethell sees that Shakespeare has invented in *The Winter's Tale* a device for playing on the "nature of reality" (p. 67), but not that he is equally concerned with the nature of art. Thus in its aims and assumptions his reading of the play anticipates that of Traversi, who though he notes "the repeated stress laid on the fact that we are following a fable, a 'tale' not subject to the normal laws of probability," is concerned only with Shakespeare's "consistent desire to make this action,

this fable, the instrument for a harmonious reading of human experience" (*Shakespeare: The Last Phase*, p. 105). J. H. P. Pafford, in his New Arden edition (1963), argues, against the mainstream, that only a criticism divorced from theatrical realities has become—wrongly, he feels—concerned with the questions raised by Shakespeare's handling of conventions; the audience is "engaged with what is happening, what is coming, not with searching for reasons to account for what has happened" (p. lii). But this view necessarily ignores too much in the play that should not be ignored.

33. There is no positive evidence that *The Tempest* was written after *The Winter's Tale*, though most critics assume it was. The two plays were written most probably within a short time of each other, and it is not necessary as far as my argument is concerned that the one precede the other, though for a good many reasons I agree with the consensus that *The Tempest* is the last play.

34. The word "cast" first occurs in its theatrical sense in 1631 ("Whinzies: or a new Cast of Characters"). "Discharge" is a technical term referring to the actor's performance of his part.

35. Bethell notes this device: *The Winter's Tale*, pp. 51–52.

36. See Appendix.

37. In the finest essay yet written on *The Tempest*, the Introduction to the New Arden edition (1954), Frank Kermode argues that the theme of the play is nature and art. Though his reading parallels mine in some respects—its interpretation of Caliban, for example—he approaches the play from a radically different point of view.

38. In a study which may very well prove definitive in matters of authorship, *Shakespeare and "The Two Noble Kinsmen"* (New Brunswick, 1965), Paul Bertram demolishes traditional claims of dual authorship; there remains no reason to believe that the play is the product of a collaboration with Fletcher, or by anyone but Shakespeare himself. Bertram's critical evaluation, however, which occupies only a relatively small part of his book, fails to establish a case that the play is successful or significantly resembles Shakespeare's previous work. For another view of the play, see Philip Edwards, "On the Design of the *The Two Noble Kinsmen*," *REL*, V. (1964), 89–105.

39. Like R. A. Foakes, editor of the New Arden edition of *King Henry VIII* (1957), Bertram agrees with Peter Alexander, "Conjectural History, or Shakespeare's *Henry VIII*," *Essays and Studies*, XVI (1930), 85–120, that the play is entirely Shakespeare's.

40. Professor Waith's observations on *Henry VIII* are pertinent: "Among Shakespeare's history plays *Henry VIII* is conspicuous for its disunity. . . . No theme unites [the] successive stories except that most general of tragic themes: How are the mighty fallen! And even this unifying principle does not apply to Cranmer" (*Pattern of Tragicomedy in Beaumont and Fletcher*, p. 119). He notes that pageantry substitutes for the missing continuity and perspicaciously comments on the shallowness of the pathetic if affecting dying speeches of Wolsey. In response to this attack, Professor Bertram argues that the play is unified: "The action of the play shows us a King who reigns becoming a King

who rules, and the principal episodes are made to serve this development" (p. 163). The argument is valiant but not convincing. The change in the King is sudden, and I do not find Henry as convincingly a great king at the end as Bertram does; moreover, the final ironies vitiate Bertram's claim, in support of G. W. Knight's reading, that "King Henry is the one king in Shakespeare in whom you cannot dissociate man from office" (p. 176). The proof that *Henry VIII* and *The Two Noble Kinsmen* are Shakespeare's does not disprove that they are Fletcherian in technique.

41. E. K. Chambers, *The Elizabethan Stage*, II (Oxford, 1951), pp. 419–420.

42. "Execration upon Vulcan," *Underwoods*, xliii, in *Ben Jonson*, ed. C. H. Herford, P. and E. Simpson, VIII (Oxford, 1947), p. 209.

43. Chambers, *op. cit.*, p. 419.

44. MS "sonnett upon the pittiful burning of the Globe playhouse in London," *ibid.*, p. 421.

Shakespearean Mimesis, English Drama, and the Unity of Time

*

A NOTABLE FACT ABOUT SHAKESPEARE'S DRAMA IS ITS ALMOST CON-
stant failure to heed the rule of unity of time stipulated by
Sidney and his prestigious Italian counterparts. However we
choose to explain the playwright's unconcern with neoclassical
principle, we cannot blame it on ignorance. The more one thinks
about the problem, in fact, the clearer it becomes that Shakespeare's violation of the unity of time is a conscious decision
made in deference to the exigencies of the kind of play he wanted
to write. By exploring the differences between the kind of drama
to which unity of time is appropriate and the characteristic Shakespeare play, and by watching his treatment of time in the years in
which he developed as a dramatist, we may learn a good deal about
the meaning of the conventions Shakespeare chose.

Significantly the Renaissance convention of unified time,
linked in Sidney's great *Apology* with a deeply felt and carefully
reasoned advocacy of poetry for its mimetic power, originates in
a similar context in Aristotle's *Poetics*. Bound by no inherited critical rules, Aristotle complacently observes that the drama on

which his theory of mimesis is founded tends to confine itself to a single revolution of the sun. Most of Shakespeare's plays would have been impossible had he followed Aristotle, and yet Aristotle believes that an effective mimetic drama presents actions at most a day long. If Shakespeare's drama demands conventions that differ from those on which the original theory of mimesis was founded while constituting the most mimetic drama since the Greek, we must conclude that he found the classical conventions irrelevant to the authenticity of his own imitation. I would argue that two dramas so similarly mimetic yet so dissimilar in their conventions must differ from one another not because the artist's drive to imitate has changed, but because the worlds that the classical dramatists and Shakespeare saw and imitated are themselves radically different from one another.

I am merely reiterating something that we all know: Conventions are not lucky accidents which happen to make great art possible. They serve artists as they do because they manage to embody the assumptions on which a significant art form is built. Like other artists, the classical dramatists made so much of the conventions they inherited because those conventions constituted adequate vehicles for the imitation of the world they saw.

What assumption, then, underlies the unity of time which Aristotle observes as a convention of the drama of his day? We might do best to explore it in terms of contrasts. Given the myth on which Aeschylus bases the *Agamemnon*, Shakespeare would not allow his whole play to take place on the day of Agamemnon's return. Fundamental in his conception and his dramaturgy would be the fascinating and richly significant fact of Clytemnestra's development, which he could exploit as he does that of Macbeth. Yet Aeschylus entirely ignores any changes in Clytemnestra's character in time, presenting that character, in a magnificent complexity I do not want to derogate, as a *fait accompli*.[1] If he were interested in Clytemnestra's growth, or in that of any other character, the setting of his play within a few hours' span would make the presentation of such development almost impossible. The entire *Oresteia* is concerned with characters of certain sorts in predicaments of certain sorts: Orestes can no more change than can the conflicting demands made upon him by his allegiances.[2] The point is, as Auden suggests,[3] that Aeschylus' drama is built on the assumption that character does not change, and therefore that what a play does is to explore in depth the potentialities of a character already fully formed. Although the Greeks were the first to develop a theory of the development of the human personality—of virtue and vice as manifested and developed in action over a period of time—and although there are some conspicuous examples of the treatment of human growth in Greek literature (perhaps Telemachus in the *Odyssey* is the most important), nevertheless the overwhelmingly dominant view of character in Greek literature is that it is static; and, paradoxically enough, Aristotle himself furnished a theory of dramatic character which insisted that it must be consistent—which, in the light of Greek dramatic practice, essentially means static.

Radical as it may seem, the point is not difficult to substantiate. It is true, after all, of Greek epic as well as drama even though the epic is hardly concerned with the unity of time. In fact, as we all know, the *Iliad*, though it suggests the entire Trojan war, actually deals with only a few days in the tenth year of that war; and though we follow Achilles through the crucial experiences of his life we do not perceive much in the way of development. In his final encounter with Priam he is enabled to feel for perhaps the first time an apparently transforming compassion; but, as both men recognize, the transformation is no more than a full expression of the self already there, of the egotism which is Achilles' vital principle: For one brilliant moment Achilles can recognize Priam as a mortal caught like himself in the tides of the generations. Even here, of course, Achilles must warn Priam that his anger is likely to return in a moment. And much of what we find most charming in the *Odyssey*, which unlike the *Iliad* spans ten years, is our sense of its hero moving unchanged and unchangeable through the most potentially transforming of experiences. If this is so of epic, we should not be surprised to find it so of tragedy.[4] We should not make too much of the fact, perhaps, that the persons of Greek tragedy wear masks, but it would be difficult to imagine an appropriate mask for Richard III or Macbeth.

For comedy the case scarcely has to be proved. Menander's

genre and its Plautine and Terentian offspring are concerned not
with process but with the possibilities of one moment for revealing what time and chance have already wrought. The fixed scene
and the short time in which the action occurs put the emphasis
rather on the playwright's virtuosity in revealing what is already
inevitable and ordained at the beginning, or extricating characters
from a situation already fully established, than on the growth of
character; and character, we cannot forget, consists of stock types,
fixed forever in the possibilities defined by their roles. In taking
over the structure of the new comedy, the *commedia erudita* of
the Italian Renaissance inherits both its primary emphasis on the
intricate plot and the concomitant use of stock characters. The
very notion of the character type—the senex, the adulescens, the
servus callidus—of course implies a belief in the fixity of character.
And given such a belief there would be little to be gained and
much to be risked in allowing dramatic action to sprawl over long
periods of time. Thus for dramatists and critics whose orientation
is to a classical notion of character the observance of the unities
is decorous, both appropriate and efficient.[5] It is worth noting
that Ben Jonson, the one dramatist of the high Renaissance in
England to believe in the propriety of the unities and the comedy
of stock types, is also the only dramatist of the period who sees
character as fixed, determined either by imprisoning humours or
by equally imprisoning dispositions to ape them. For Jonson only
the character who lives by a rational principle—young Knowell
and Brainworm, Lovewit, Horace—is free, and his rationality is
itself a permanent and defining quality. Thus Jonson's profound
harmony with the classical art on which he bases his own is the
result of something much deeper than superficial imitation of
superannuated forms.

That such an orientation could have been Sidney's is implicit in the fact of the *commedia erudita* and, more particularly,
in the fact that the learned drama of his own childhood in England was based on it. To an audience no doubt rather contemptuous of the plebeian and apparently formless drama dominating
banquet halls as well as public theaters, the experiments in stock
characters such as Roister Doister and Matthew Merrygreek, in
the unity of time and place of the school comedies, and in Gas-

coigne's superb Englishing of Ariosto's utterly Plautine *Suppositi* must have been an exciting experience. This, they may well have felt, is what theater is all about. Given his classical education and aristocratic allegiances, we might indeed be surprised to find Sidney breaking with critical tradition on the question of the unities.[6]

But Sidney's allegiance to the unities is notoriously out of touch with much Elizabethan dramatic practice. As a matter of fact, he could hardly have noticed that even in the works which he presumably admired there are strong tendencies toward a kind of mimesis quite different from that of the neoclassical models they imitate. To see the difference one need only contrast *Gammer Gurton's Needle* and *Supposes*. In the latter, plot is everything, the play is an ingeniously designed engine to confound confusion, to produce every embarrassing encounter possible between individuals and their conniving imitators, and to bring about the almost unimaginable untangling of the play's snarled world. But in *Gammer Gurton's Needle*, whose neoclassical pretensions are its ostensible *raison d'être* and which is similarly built on a plot dependent upon discovery, the plot devices are not an end in themselves. The needle that occasions the search is almost unnecessary, because the complications in the play's world are primarily the doing of Diccon the Bedlam, and the vigor of the play resides not in the process of discovery but in the revelation of characters who are not stock types—Dame Chat, Dr. Rat, Hodge. Though character no more develops in *Gammer Gurton's Needle* than it does in *The Supposes*, the center of the play is character as it is not in Ariosto-Gascoigne.

And if we look at the neoclassical tragedy which but for its failure to keep time Sidney would thoroughly have approved, we make an interesting discovery. There is no intrinsic reason why, in a play designed to demonstrate the evils attendant upon improper succession, Sackville and Norton needed to violate the unity of time; as a matter of fact, their play might well have been more effective had they dealt only with the consequences. But the structure of *Gorboduc* reveals that its authors are interested at least as much in the process of decision in the protagonist, and the effects on him of that decision, as they are in the outcome of the decision.[7] So much is suggested even by the dual title: As *Ferrex and Porrex* the tragedy is centered on the inevitable conflict resulting from the decision, while as *Gorboduc* it presents a story that in its feeble way anticipates *King Lear*. The authors seem scarcely aware of what they are really about: A drama based on neoclassic models has not yet learned how to present character in process, and no reader fails to note the fatal weakness in a drama that stages the central conflict in its protagonist's mind through the medium of formal debates on the issues of which Gorboduc has made up his mind before each debate begins. From the vantage point we have achieved by knowing the drama of decades to follow, however, we can easily see how Sackville and Norton, like Mr. S. in *Gammer Gurton's Needle*, are faced with the problem of using to advantage conventions that do not fully embody their purposes. The fundamental difference between these two plays and the tradition from which they spring is that they are built on forward motion.

Even in some of the first neoclassical plays in England, then, one finds a tendency to move away from the kind of mimesis with which that kind of drama found itself at home elsewhere. Interestingly enough, the two devices in *Gammer Gurton's Needle* and *Gorboduc* which work against neoclassical tradition derive from the native theater: the Vice in the comedy, the debate in the tragedy; and these devices carry us back to a theater whose aims are different from those of plays we have so far considered. Both of them elements in the morality tradition, the Vice and the debate alike play vital roles in the transformation of character. The Vice tempts and corrupts, or, seen more radically and accurately as a projection of an element of personality, he represents tendencies toward particular and general vice which can become dominant only as time passes. The debate similarly forces a character to make choices, or to choose between elements of his personality, so that in time he may change. Until the experiments of the humanists, English drama, both mystery cycle and morality play, is eschatological. In its Christian context it has no choice but to see character entirely in terms of change in time, whether through gradual development or through sudden conversion.

Nor did even Christianity invent the concepts implicit in the conventions of medieval English plays. Auerbach points out in his great "Odysseus' Scar" the "road" and the "fate" which "lie between Jacob who cheated his father out of his blessing and the old man whose favorite son has been torn to pieces by a wild beast!—between David the harp player, persecuted by his lord's jealousy, and the old king, surrounded by violent intrigues, whom Abishag the Shunnamite warmed in his bed, and he knew her not!" As he observes, Old Testament narrative is always interested above all in the differentiation "into full individuality" which makes the passage of time so significant in and to our culture.[8] To imagine Achilles at any moment in his life is to imagine his whole life; to imagine Joseph at *any* one point—boasting to his brothers, fleeing Potiphar's wife, languishing in prison, interpreting Pharaoh's dreams, managing Egypt's economy, confronting and tricking his brothers, weeping at the sight of Benjamin, attending Jacob at the old man's death, becoming himself the patriarch—to imagine Joseph at any one of these points without being aware of its context in the parabola of his entire life is to deprive the moment of that dimension which gives it its meaning. If in its treatment of characters like Saul or Joab, or in the generational repetitions of patterns in the lives of the patriarchs of Genesis, the Old Testament is capable of implying that character can in some ways be seen as fixed, the emphasis could only be underlined as Pauline Christianity, with its particular concern with conversion, put a Hebrew sense of the movement of the soul in time at the base of European culture.

Hence, designed to imitate the movement toward salvation, the Christian morality play is crucially focused on time, so much that in *The Castle of Perseverance* the character named "Mankind" must violate every canon of dramatic illusion in order to be presented in his full dimensions: Though his language remains the same, Mankind appears first as an infant who cannot stand unsupported, and ends as an old man departing life. To a neoclassical critic such a barbarity would be unthinkable. But whatever impetus the sixteenth century's interest in fashionable neoclassicism gave to the formation of a new kind of English drama, and that impetus is immeasurably important, the primary source of the idea of character and therefore of what drama attempts to imitate is to be found, like the vigor of the new theater, in the eschatologically oriented native theatrical tradition.

Our consideration of the problems raised in measuring Elizabethan drama by Sidney's standards leads us thus to realize that the hybrid nature of that drama, its fusion of conventions derived from divergent mimetic traditions, builds into it a kind of internal conflict between notions of character; it builds in as well a source of versatility unprecedented in theatrical history, and may help explain why the theater of Shakespeare and his contemporaries is able to present, with the aid of a finite number of conventions, such a varied set of personal visions of the human condition. By founding a play on conventions derived from the classical or the medieval tradition, a playwright is enabled to embody a view of character as fixed or in process, of life as determined or free. By combining conventions, he is able to ascribe theatrically fruitful ambiguity to the human condition, and to find a vehicle most admirably suited to his own view.

The theater into which Shakespeare comes is not of course the halting one of neoclassical experimentation, or even the still primitive one that Sidney describes. In the near decade between the *Apology for Poetry* and Shakespeare's emergence as a major dramatist comes that sudden and crucial eruption of genius among Shakespeare's exact contemporaries, the University Wits. Because their work explores the possibilities only implicit in what we have considered thus far, and develops the conventions with which Shakespeare begins, I must say something, all too briefly, about them.

It may be that the most promising fact about the use of time in University Wit plays for those that follow theirs is that one can make no simple generalization about it; on the whole, however, one sees in the work of the eighties and early nineties a tendency toward the presentation of fluid character in extended time. Lyly seems an immediate exception. Asked whether his plays observe the unity of time, the scholar in the street is as likely as not to guess that they do, though as a matter of fact they do not. The reason may be the classical ambiance of the majority of them; or it may be that Lyly is generally not concerned to show the kind of character development that can take place only in a play that violates the rule of twenty-four hours. Only in *Campaspe* does the subject require time; the hero must learn the decorum of a ruler's life, and Lyly conveys the illusion that considerable time passes by stringing together a series of only loosely connected episodes. But, more characteristically, in *Endymion* Lyly presents fixed characters—the constant hero, the constantly treacherous Tellus—against a background of passing years. One reason for the play's air of frivolous make-believe may be the fact that characters arise from decades of magically induced sleep to find themselves unchanged from what they were. At any rate, when in *A Midsummer Night's Dream* Shakespeare borrows Lyly's device, he will use it to reflect an inner transformation with which Lyly is not concerned, thus making the convention do what his play allows no time for, and what Lyly with decades of stage time has no interest in doing.

Writing for Lyly's theater and dealing with classical material, Peele structures *The Arraignment of Paris* on the confrontation of fixed characters, but for the popular theater he writes plays that strike us as more characteristically Elizabethan. His best play, *David and Bethsabe*, owes much to Peele's ability to translate into dramatic terms David's moral growth in the narrative of II Samuel; and in *The Old Wives Tale* Peele parallels the magical transformation of character through enchantment with a redemptive transformation achieved by inner growth.[9] Kyd, in evolving the revenge play, is, as recent criticism has been showing, deeply interested in the changes that occur within the hero-villain, and he therefore represents a sweep of time which would have been irrelevant in his Senecan models. Greene, the only University Wit whose work is entirely popular in nature, is the most clearly committed to the notion that time is a dimension of character (even in *James IV*, whose argument is the irredeemable evil of the times, the protagonist reforms). In his two best plays, against characters whose principle is their ability to grow and reform Greene sets other characters whose unwillingness and inability to grow exclude them from the world of normal life. Thus the clown in *A Looking Glass for London and England*,[10] who willfully violates the ordinances established for the city's repentance, is hanged unregenerate; and like him Miles leaves the charmed circle at the end of *Friar Bacon and Friar Bungay* to ride to hell on a devil's back rather than participate in the process of growth, education, and conversion shared by all the other major characters. Note that both of these characters are unmistakably Vices: that is, they are allegorical embodiments of intransigent spiritual inadequacy which derive from a drama whose central assumption is the ability to change.

And finally Marlowe. Unlike his lesser contemporaries he is too complex to sum up on any issue. What makes him so hard to categorize is doubtless the complexity that keeps us interested in his work. But I wonder if part of our trouble in agreeing about the meaning of his plays is not the ambiguity that stems from his characterization. In no instance, with the possible exception of Barrabas' daughter Abigail, does Marlowe establish a character in whom growth is a principle. Yet he moves each of his extraordinary protagonists through a plot that inherits its system of time and such other crucial conventions as the morality devices of *Faustus* and the biography of *Tamburlaine* from Christian traditions. Questions about the ability of Tamburlaine and Edward and Faustus to change force themselves to our attention; and in answering them each critic determines not only his reading of a particular play, but even his interpretation of the Marlovian universe.[11]

Shakespeare inherits a set of materials ambiguous in their potentialities, then, and I shall want to demonstrate shortly that his first responses to them shov him feeling his way, not yet fully aware of the implications of the choice he makes. What justifies the investigation, of course, is the work of his maturity, in which the underlying concept of character necessitates the theatrical imitation of extended time. What groped inarticulately for expression in *Gorboduc* becomes in Shakespeare the central fact of drama. Whether politics or revenge or love is the subject, that subject is stageworthy for Shakespeare because it can be presented in terms of character moving in time. Not the least evidence of Brutus' error in attempting naïvely to purge history by criminal means is the toll his action takes on his own character; like Hamlet and Macbeth he is irrevocably changed by his

own actions, and the changes point to the meaning as well as
the pathos of the political tragedy. The plays of love focus on
the process of spiritual education. Romeo, as we have seen, must
grow from jejune Petrarchism to maturity so that his love for
Juliet may become the transcendent and consuming principle his
love for Rosaline pretended to be. Moral growth, awakening, re-
fining define the progress of Bassanio, Orlando and Oliver and
Phebe, Olivia and Orsino, Beatrice and Benedick and Claudio,
while against such characters Shakespeare sets others whose inability and unwillingness to change make necessary their rejection of and from his redeemed comic worlds: Shylock, Don John,
Malvolio, Jaques, and even Mercutio, whose animated but essentially fixed way of seeing becomes one element in a more complex
and growing Romeo. Even so the view of character in the second
cycle of histories is bound up with time. Of Richard's growth I
have already spoken. I shall not here contribute to the debate about
the virtue of Hal's rejection of Falstaff, or about whether his
first soliloquy shows him already what he will be by the time he
turns away the fat knight. The precise nature of Hal's development and the moral evaluation Shakespeare puts on it are not at
issue. What matters is that by the time he rejects Falstaff Hal
has put away the festal side of himself; and that by the comic
end of *Henry V* he has, or Shakespeare wants us to believe that
he has, learned to reintegrate that side of his nature into the
fabric of his political life. If Hal's development is moot, Bolingbroke's is not. His progress from self-confident and self-righteous
youth to guilt-ridden age is a clearly marked journey. And as in
the comedies the spiritual movements of characters in transition
are set off by those significantly incapable of change: As embodiments of fixed principles Hotspur and Falstaff suggest both the
poles between which Hal moves and the dangers of subjection
to fixity.

Now it is obvious that, for all of two centuries of talk about
"character," literary criticism has not yet developed an adequate
vocabulary for the analysis of techniques of characterization, and
that when it comes to the discussion of change in character our
limitations are particularly poignant. To say as I have done that
Oedipus' character does not change is certainly to oversimplify,

and I shall gladly stop saying so when a finer mode of analysis becomes available. On the other hand one need only think of the ways in which Hamlet, Lear, and Macbeth—to cite only three of the characters of Shakespeare's maturity—change over the course of their plays' actions in language, characteristic response to crisis, Weltanschauung, and bearing to realize the central manner in which Shakespeare's concept of character differs from Sophocles'.

In his mature work, then, Shakespeare portrays extended time because he sees character as changing. But at the beginning of his career no such principle seems to link characterization to the treatment of time. In fact his first plays, the Henry VI plays, dramatize some forty years of historical material in which the development of character is never an issue. Characters like Talbot and the King himself grow older but remain the same in all respects; Shakespeare denies La Pucelle's claims that she has been transformed by her vision. Perhaps the most characteristic touch is the scene (III Henry VI, II. v) in which the weary King yearns for the static life of the shepherd while exemplifying the rigidity of his own inept unkingliness; and his monologue is followed revealingly by the stagy and formalistic episode in which a son kills his father and a father his son. The implication is of a world populated by types,[12] a politics generated by the clash of men irrevocably what they are. If characters change, their changeability is of allegiance and constitutes a fidelity to the principle of commodity that the Bastard will mock in King John. It is characteristic of these plays that as the suddenly emergent Richard murders Henry VI, both men affirm the myth that Richard was born with all his teeth, ready to "snarl and bite and play the dog"; Heaven has shaped Richard what he is, and he mechanically allows his "mind to answer it." In another ideologically determined and stagy scene Henry sees the young Richmond fully developed as a kingly fellow in every way. Both present villain and future savior are what they are by nature.

Richard III represents the climax of Shakespeare's shaping of material in which character is essentially a given. But as the play in which he creates great drama for the first time, it also represents a turn in a new direction. The Richard adumbrated

in the last Henry VI play comes fully to life here as the first in
the line of Shakespearean villains whose villainy consists in their
Vice-like inability to change. We hear reiterations of Richard's
dental precocity, and we watch with alternating amusement and
horror his unswerving fidelity to the life of nihilistic wit. But at
Bosworth, as the procession of dreams which Shakespeare em-
broiders on his sources appears to the hounded monarch, we observe a sudden and unprecedented change in Richard's character
as for a moment conscience overwhelms him. To deny him that
change would be to make him a Vice, a devil, a figure for metaphysical evil such as Iago is, and it no longer serves Shakespeare's
purposes to do this. At this moment, crucial both in the play
and in Shakespeare's career, the play turns to tragedy.

Richard's recognition of the worthlessness of the principle
on which he has operated is only a momentary lapse; he denies
conscience and braves out the battle. But in his moment of re-
morse *Macbeth* is adumbrated, and the play becomes something
radically different from its predecessors. For Richard comes for a
moment, through the power his past experience has stored in him,
to recognize the emptiness of his ambition and the self-destruction
he has made inevitable—that is, the futility of the very principle
of his energy. This is growth, a leap forward in consciousness, a
change from what we have assumed possible; it is unlike anything before it in Shakespeare; and in the shape it takes it is
more like tragedy than history.[13]

Interestingly Shakespeare thus seems to come to the dramatic
portrayal of development in character not because of his historical material—it had been there to be used in the earlier plays;
not because of a Christian view of life which suddenly puts him
in accord with a view of character that I have postulated as Christian—the world view of the whole tetralogy is Christian, with its
punished sinners and its providential reading of English history;
but because he has at last reached a moment when his notion
of what a play is seems to have coalesced. When next he writes
a history, its meaning will be centered, as Professor Calderwood
has beautifully demonstrated,[14] in the degeneration of King John
on the one hand, and on the other the maturing of the Bastard
from the recognition of commodity's hegemony through his en-

suing cynicism to the profound understanding of the nature of honor that lies at the heart of the action.

Like the later histories, *King John* belongs to a genre that contemporary criticism did not know and to which I suspect we all subscribe: the Shakespearean play. Regardless of its formal genre—comedy, history, tragedy—the mature Shakespearean play satisfies certain expectations in its audience; it sees with a characteristic vision; and, perhaps most important for my purposes, it finds itself in an understanding harmony with the conventions it employs, so that we never feel as we do with other plays that Shakespeare is using a convention for its own sake. How many Elizabethan dramatic conventions do we fully understand only because Shakespeare saw so clearly what was implicit in them. And when in his maturity Shakespeare allows to the action of a play a certain period of time, that time is like everything else entirely significant. The weakness universally recognized in the Henry VI plays is their structural flaccidity; and it seems to me that this flaw arises from the fact that Shakespeare allows them to cover years only because his material demands them. Not until *Richard III* does the time dramatized in the play become itself significant in terms of its relation to character; and when this happens the Shakespearean play springs to recognizable life. In the later histories one watches Shakespeare develop what he seems to have realized in conceiving the fifth act of *Richard III*. Thus in *King John* the play's historical time is necessary to a theme which can be dramatized only by the movement in time of two spiritual histories. And in the second cycle of histories Shakespeare goes even further in making the time in which his actions occur part of their dramatic fabric: From *Richard II* to *Henry V* it might be said that the idea of time actually underlies, almost comprises, the theme of the tetralogy.

That idea of time is a far cry from the one on which Sophocles builds *Oedipus Rex*, though it shares with it a powerful sense of ineluctable destiny. The difference, as we have seen in examining a number of plays—most notably *Troilus and Cressida*, where the role of time in human affairs is most explicit—is that in the work of Shakespeare's maturity the meaning of the mysteriously organic process of time lies in what it does within character. Troilus, Cressida, and Pandarus, Brutus, Coriolanus, and Mark Antony all come to know in their various ways that the significance of the time in which their lives transpire is not simply the events it brings about, but far more crucially what it creates within the centers of their being; not what it does to them, but what it makes of them. Not only the English chronicles but in fact all the great plays that use historical material set fixed attitudes and dispositions against a life that is in constant flux and demands constant adaptability of the character who wants to survive and prosper. Given a predisposition to cherish unchanging ideals, yet always aware of the fluid medium in which life moves, Shakespeare finds himself inevitably committed, I have been arguing, to complementary ideas of what is most desirable in human character. The same commitment impels him as well to a mode of drama in which he can explore the relation between character and time which is increasingly at the center of his concern. And basic to that mode is the treatment of stage time which we can see developing in the history plays.

When he turns for the first time to formal tragedy, Shakespeare anticipates his later plays in the genre. *Titus Andronicus* has its gallery of types both Senecan and medieval. But in his central figure Shakespeare creates, though primitively, his characteristic tragic hero, one who gives meaning to his play by describing a trajectory. Titus' growth is what makes him tragic. Like Lear he moves from the irksome fatuousness of the opening scene through anguish and madness to self-knowledge and to a final competence simultaneous with his destruction. The similarity ends there, of course, for unlike Lear Titus takes the road of revenge; but the growth is marked throughout. Its significance is the ethos of the revenge play: Turning his back explicitly on the tears whose imagery has dominated much of the play (III. i. 267ff.), Titus transforms himself into something new, a revenger, a hero-villain, a man as much sinning as sinned against. This is not yet the philosophical transformation of Hamlet. But Titus' movement from his initial to his final state is an element in revenge tragedy with which neither Aeschylus nor Seneca was concerned. And it justifies Shakespeare's imitation of the Senecan milieu in a form which cannot abide the non-Senecan restriction on the flow of time that Cinthio imposed on his tragedies. Time will always be crucial in Shakespearean tragedy, as Professor Driver argues in his fine study of the difference between the Greek and the Shakespearean senses of history. To be schooled in the transcendence of the world and time Antony and Cleopatra will have to move through years of commitment and change; Coriolanus like Macbeth will not become tragic until time has taught him the implications of his own commitments, and written the lesson on his character and thus his freedom. And note: In the two tragedies where time is short because Shakespeare wants to dramatize the lightning dart of character toward its self-destructive goal, in *Romeo and Juliet* and *Othello*, he notoriously fools the audience through the use of "double time" into the simultaneous illusion that time is moving with awful swiftness while character has time to grow and change.

Only in comedy does Shakespeare ever attempt the unity of time, and his practice here is most revealing. In the development of his comedy, in fact, we can watch him learning the meaning of his conventions. In *The Comedy of Errors* he carries off with the utmost virtuosity a stunt which, except in its brilliance, has little to do with his later work. Combining two already fiendishly complicated plays, he beats Plautus at his own game. The characters are the traditional types—courtesan, merchant, witty servant. Aegeon's long exposition of the dark backward and abysm of time at the beginning puts behind the play's represented day decades of separation, adventure, and chronological growth in which what we have been talking about as growth plays no part (thus the two boys grow into manhood without changing enough in facial expression or speech or manners to be distinguishable from each other). The supreme decorum of the piece suggests that Shakespeare realizes the implications of the unity of time.

I need hardly say that *The Comedy of Errors* is conceived in a mode not characteristic of Shakespeare. But it is not entirely adventitious that he should start out in comedy this way. Professor Harbage has argued persuasively that *Love's Labour's Lost* may be a revision of Shakespeare's earliest comedy, and that the original may have been composed under the influence and for the company of Lyly.[15] Like the witty subject and its equally witty treatment, like the emphasis on clever rhetoric and pretty songs, like the learned allusions and the rather hermetic world of the play, the treatment of time—the action covers two days—suggests the ambiance of Lylyan comedy. But Shakespeare is attempting in *Love's Labour's Lost* something more ambitious than he did in *The Comedy of Errors*, and the play's unusual ending suggests that he has already found reasons why a neoclassical handling of dramatic time will not serve his purposes in comedy.

The trouble could have been avoided. There is obvious irony in the opening dialogue as the young men plan to war on their own affections, to remain still and contemplative in living art for three passionless years. But the irony that undercuts their speeches could consist of an idea consistent with the values underlying neoclassical time: It might simply be that the young scholars are wrong because they are denying not their capacity to grow, but the fixed reality of what exists in them as *adulescentes*. In fact, a Benedick like Berowne will argue in IV. iii that love is in the nature of young blood and that "we cannot cross the cause why we were born." One notices also the high incidence in the play of traditional comic types: Armado, Costard, Holofernes.

But Shakespeare takes a different tack, and in so doing anticipates his future comedies. For though the theme of the play might easily have been that young men are by nature lovers, Shakespeare chooses rather to demonstrate that love and engagement in the world educate better than cloistered virtuosity. Therefore Berowne's awed, "And I, forsooth, in love! I, that have been love's whip" (III. i. 176), signals a comic conversion. True, it acknowledges what has been potential in him, but as in Benedick later, it is growth, and more importantly it entails further growth. It may take us back to Berowne's own witty objection at the outset to academic study, that it tries to do through intellect what can only come through normal growth, and that life must be taken in its own seasons. In his great argument, "O, we have made a vow to study, lords," Berowne presents love explicitly, and virtually in the terms of Castiglione's Bembo, as nature's educating agent; and he argues that the young men will have to lose their oaths to find themselves. Already for Shakespeare love is not the simple and sensual egoism that makes the Plautine comedy go 'round; it is a transforming force.

But the education that Shakespearean love brings is not

simply the conversion of nonlovers to lovers, and nothing demonstrates this more clearly than the last acts of *Love's Labour's Lost*. Berowne and friends have decided to love. But their mistreatment of the Nine Worthies reveals that much remains to occur within them. Still only a redirection of ego, their love is not yet charity, and Marcade's arrival at the comic height of their witty assault on Armado's group suggests, with its powerful reminder of the real world, that life is more than wit and playful pleasure. But here we are at the end of the comedy, expecting marriages to signal that all is well in its world when Shakespeare has taken pains to show us that all is far from well. The convention of the unity of time is irrelevant; it belies the theme of the play. Shakespeare gets out of his impasse by declaring in effect that the comedy will not end for a twelvemonth and a day. During that time the young men will have to go out into the world and get the education that in later comedies Shakespeare will build into the time of the plays themselves.

It seems that we can see the direction of his work more clearly now than Shakespeare could in the early 1590's. For in *The Two Gentlemen of Verona*, his first attempt at a romantic comedy essentially freed from Plautine love games, he finds himself in a predicament quite like that of the Henry VI plays: He needs time for the playing out of his plot, but the time has little to do with the realities of the action. As the play gets under way we become aware of a freedom in the handling of time we have not seen before in Shakespearean comedy. Months pass in the action.[16] But during those months character cannot be said to change: Proteus simply justifies his name in abandoning Julia for Silvia. The weakness of the play, in fact, is that all of Proteus' moral education occurs in the last scene, when he is confronted by those he has wronged and shamed into recognizing his culpability. The point of the closing action is his transformation and therefore the happy sorting out of the plot, and the comedy ends consistently with Valentine's successful petition to the Duke that the outlaws, regenerated in the same forest in which Proteus has awakened to reality, may return forgiven from their exile. Thus the first Shakespearean play to resemble his mature romantic comedy is also the first comedy in which Shakespeare abandons the unity of time.

But the long time is all in the wrong place. Shakespeare needs it, yet seems not to know quite what to do with it. Nevertheless, this flawed comedy shows him on the road to the fruitful marriage of convention and the world-view which will mark his best work.

The last early play I want to discuss is *The Taming of the Shrew*. Here as in *King John* Shakespeare has fully learned the meaning of time in his dramaturgy—so fully, in fact, that he is able to play off against each other two plots each conceived according to a convention radically opposed to that of the other. The main plot concerns Petrucchio's education of Kate to a recognition of what she is and what a wife is, until, schooled in sovereignty she is ready to live in comic harmony with her husband. This action transpires in weeks of stage time. But the subplot is a reworking of the *commedia erudita* par excellence, the Ariosto-Gascoigne *Supposes*. It is similarly focused on the question of identity, but that question is presented not through the education of characters, but rather through the symbolic stripping away of masks. Its comedy-of-errors confusions are cleared up in a single day of stage action. The motif of deceived sight which operates the subplot is transformed in the main plot to the inward image of dreams.[17] In terms of the comic resolution they reach, the plots are versions of each other; in terms of the conventions they employ and the assumptions about character on which they are based, they reflect the brilliant fusion of two long traditions which Shakespeare has come fully to understand.

In *The Taming of the Shrew* Shakespeare first evinces that freedom to use his conventions as vehicles for the mimesis of what he sees that is his mark. In it he seems to reach, if he has not done so before, a conscious awareness of the significance of the conventions employed in the two plots. Henceforth, concerned with character in time, he will write plays in which more time must pass than the neoclassical rule could accommodate. But once more in his career, Shakespeare returns to the unities which he has ignored virtually since its beginning; and in his last play he does an extraordinary thing.

Though theatrical self-consciousness is a familiar motif in Shakespeare's work, it is more insistent, as we have seen, in *The Tempest* than elsewhere. One result is that we are directed to look at the play as an artifact, and when we do we make a startling discovery. Responding to Prospero's narrative and to the constant signals of the schedule on which the action hinges, no audience with the slightest sophistication could fail to realize that Shakespeare has abandoned the chronological sweep of his characteristic drama to write a neoclassically unified play. Yet it is one of the stunning facets of *The Tempest* that Shakespeare builds on its formal conventions a presentation of character that has nothing to do with neoclassical drama and everything to do with what I have helplessly called the Shakespearean play.[18] Ferdinand and Miranda learn not only to love, but under Prospero's tutelage to love decorously, and their love explicitly brings them a second life. The education deferred for a twelvemonth and a day in *Love's Labour's Lost* takes place here in an afternoon. There are those—Caliban, Antonio—on whose nature nurture can never stick; but set against them as in another kind of Shakespearean play are those who lose and find themselves. And above all is Prospero, who in the four hours represented moves through twelve years of growth, from calculating subscription to the ethos of revenge to a resigned and responsible commitment to the justice and charity afforded by normal society, and to an understanding of his own limitations and of the providence above him. This is to say that Shakespeare has returned to the convention of the unity of time in order to subvert it, to use it for such slow growth and rapid conversion as he has shown us he knows it cannot be used for. In the course of doing so he shows us what he thinks drama is all about; and he makes us ponder the magic he has learned to perform through the understanding of the conventions he has inherited.

NOTES

1. Material that Shakespeare might have stressed included Clytemnestra's ten years of brooding on the wrong to Iphigenia and to the feminine principle in the family, and the changes in her relationship with her surviving children and with her subjects. The moment at which she joins the worthless Aegisthus and his motives to herself is perhaps the event most revealing of a degenerative

change in her, but that moment does not exist in the time of Aeschylus' play, and the Greek dramatist reduces Aegisthus to the point where his sudden and surprising emergence *after* the killing of Agamemnon serves rather as a grotesque parody of Clytemnestra's righteous but nonetheless self-seeking and criminal murder in the name of justice than as an element in that action.

2. It might be argued that the climax of the trilogy is the change of the supernatural avengers into the Eumenides; but the point of what Aeschylus is doing is the fact that the transformation is miraculous. Moreover, as Athene's imploring speeches to the Chorus reveal, the transformation is not a basic change: The furies must maintain, though veiled, their bitter avenging spirit in order that the benediction they bring to Athens may have meaning.

3. *The Portable Greek Reader* (New York, 1948), p. 25.

4. Thus Sophocles in each of the Oedipus plays focuses on a crucial moment of revelation and self-realization rather than on the process of growth. In *Antigone* he presents the sisters fixed in complex political stances which fully express their psychologies and Creon floundering, like the Richard II of Shakespeare's first scenes, between the poles which define the well-meaning but weak and authoritarian tyrant. So it is also that Euripides concentrates on the passion already waiting in Medea and emergent in Phaedra, and makes a ghastly joke of a Menelaus never fully able to free himself, even after the war, from his subjection to Helen.

5. Commenting on Aristotle's stipulation of consistency (τό ὁμαλόν) as the fourth quality of character (*Poetics*, 1454a), Renaissance critics unanimously reflect the assumption that character is essentially stable. *Cf.* Bernard Weinberg, *A History of Literary Criticism in the Italian Renaissance* (Chicago, 1961), I, p. 419 *et passim*. Consistently with this assumption Giason Denores argues in the year of Sidney's death that the moral value of the unity of time lies in its capacity to teach us what fortune can do to us (not what happens within us), and the concept of plot he bases on Aristotle is entirely a matter of changes in the fortunes of characters (Weinberg, p. 318). Regardless of their critical sophistication, Italian Renaissance critics generally link the unity of time with credibility.

6. Though Sidney is not the center of my present concern, it is worth observing that his own literary practice reveals a mode of perception surprisingly amenable to the classical. Like the *commedia erudita*, the *Arcadia* is based, for all that its action occurs in the time appropriate to works of epic proportion, on the plot devices of the comedy of supposes and concomitantly on the assumption of essentially static character. The genius of the *Arcadia*, like the genius of *The Supposes*, is plot which calls attention to itself as plot. Sidney's masterpiece does not begin the English novel because it is not concerned with the development of character in time. The implication of the disguises so important to the plot of the *Arcadia* is that beneath the disguise lies a fixed identity which will be revealed in time. And, as in the learned comedy, the names of characters suggest sometimes their generic, always their fixed natures: Musidorus, Pyrocles, Basilius, Gynecia, Euarchus, Mopsa. The principals are educated in the course of the romance, but Musidorus, born a

coward and grown an aesthete, and Pyrocles, the man of passion, remain essentially the same. Thus like Plautus and the Ariosto of *I Suppositi* Sidney locates the genius of his work in its ingenious plotting. Pyrocles disguises himself as the ravishing Zelmane, causing both the king and the queen to be catastrophically in love with the same character; Amphialus woos the captive Philoclea in prison through Petrarchan clichés—I am your prisoner, you have the power of life and death over me—which, as Philoclea wittily observes, are in fact literally true of *his* power over her. For an interesting study of Sidneian characterization which, though conceived along different lines from mine, sees it as essentially static, see Virgil B. Heltzel, "The Arcadian Hero," *PQ*, XLI (1962), 173–180.

7. In a play designed to persuade Queen Elizabeth perhaps they had no other choice.

8. Erich Auerbach, *Mimesis: The Representation of Reality in Western Literature*, pp. 17–18. The importance of Auerbach's essay can hardly be overstated. Similarly attempting to differentiate Judeo-Christian from classical conceptions of character in "The Idea of the Person and Shakespearian Tragedy," *SQ* XVI (1965), 39–47, Elias Schwartz, like Auerbach, discusses the "existential uniqueness" of the "person" as conceptualized in the Christian tradition (p. 41). Interesting as his account of the individuation of Christian character is, Schwartz fails to recognize what Auerbach sees, that in Judeo-Christian eschatology what makes men fully individual is "the course of an eventful life." Time is thus an integral part of character for the modern western tradition as it was not for the classical world. Auerbach's thesis has been explored with brilliant success by Tom F. Driver, *The Sense of History in Greek and Shakespearean Drama* (New York, 1960). Except for Professor Driver's book, the most useful study of the handling of time in Shakespeare remains Mable Buland, *The Presentation of Time in the Elizabethan Drama*. Though restricted largely to an account of the phenomenon of "double time," this study contains a number of acute observations. Rather oddly, while Miss Buland recognized that the illusion of long time was more necessary in Elizabethan drama than in Greek because of the modern interest in character, she failed to see that change in time is the significant factor in Elizabethan characterization.

9. Thus to Eumenides' "Tell me, just Time, when shall I Delia see?"—a request that calls to mind the plots of the *commedia erudita* and might lead us to expect a resolution by discovery—Erestus, the old man at the Cross, responds that he must "Dream of no rest,/ Till thou repent that thou didst best" (504–519; text in C. F. T. Brooke and N. B. Paradise, *English Drama 1580–1642* [Boston, 1933]).

10. Written in collaboration with Lodge.

11. Questions of the sort that trouble Marlowe's critics are: Does Tamburlaine's career end as it does because he has degenerated and must be punished, or is the character apparently punished at the end the same man who seemed to earn only rewards at the outset? Does the loss of Zenocrate reveal a change in his state, or signal a downward turn in his character? Does Edward

seem so much more admirable in the depths than in his glory because schooled by errors he has become a better man or because Marlowe like Shakespeare wants us at the moment of regicide to react against the crime? And, most perplexing of all, does Faustus have it in his power to repent and achieve salvation, or is the machinery provided to urge him to repentance a bitter sham devised to make more awful the spectacle of predetermined damnation?

12. Robert Y. Turner, "Characterization in Shakespeare's Early History Plays," *ELH*, XXXI (1964), 241–258, argues that the "characters in the Henry VI plays are static because their behavior illustrates moral qualities" (p. 253). His article is helpful, but though he discusses the heritage of the morality plays he does not see the notion of character in transition as a central fact of Christian tradition, and therefore finds the static characterization of the early histories less divergent from the mainstream of English drama than I do. As my discussion of the University Wits should indicate, I must disagree with Turner's contention that the dramatists of the eighties "felt uneasy about motives, that is internal causes, in dramatizing change" (p. 253).

13. Both Turner and Driver see something new in Shakespeare's characterization of Richard III; Turner argues that the new dimension is present to considerable extent in other characters in the play.

14. James L. Calderwood, "Commodity and Honour in *King John*," *UTQ*, XXIX (1960), 341–356.

15. Alfred Harbage, "*Love's Labour's Lost* and the Early Shakespeare," *PQ*, XLI (1962), 18–36.

16. Though not necessarily the sixteen months Valentine claims in the tale he tells the bandits (IV. i. 18–22).

17. Both motifs are included in the Sly Induction-frame, which is likewise centered on the comic problem of identity.

18. Driver argues, on the contrary, that by observing the unity of time Shakespeare makes *The Tempest* incapable of reflecting "that orientation of man to a genuine temporal world which Western man understands and which elsewhere Shakespeare has used as the basis and accompaniment of his imaginative creations" (p. 191). Derek Traversi, *Shakespeare: The Last Phase* (London, 1954) discusses Shakespeare's fusion of a plot about "reconcilement" with "dramatic Unity of Time" (p. 171).

Index